Mining and Intelligent Analytics - Methods, Interpretability, and Cross-Domain

rg/10.5772/intechopen.1008100
a Sultana, Md Delowar Hossain and Ashis Kumar Mandal

, Babangida Ibrahim Babura, Eden Emuna, Eyal Brill, Fawagreh Khaled, Hannington Odido
th Barner, Lenah Muema, Manuela Larissa Schreyer, Md. Abid Hasan Rafi, Md. Delowar
Bakri Adam, Pankaj Bhowmik, Pijush Kanti Roy Partho, Ron Elkayam, Samet Bayram,
a

published in London, United Kingdom, 2026 by IntechOpen
hOpen is the global imprint of INTECHOPEN LIMITED, registered in England and Wales,
tration number: 11086078, 167-169 Great Portland Street, London, W1W 5PF, United Kingdom

U product safety concerns: IN TECH d.o.o., Prolaz Marije Krucifikse Kozulić 3, 51000 Rijeka,
tia, info@intechopen.com or visit our website at intechopen.com.

ish Library Cataloguing-in-Publication Data
atalogue record for this book is available from the British Library

vances in Data Mining and Intelligent Analytics - Methods, Interpretability, and Cross-Domain
plications
ited by Tangina Sultana, Md Delowar Hossain and Ashis Kumar Mandal
. cm.

his title is part of the Artificial Intelligence Book Series, Volume 45
opic: Machine Learning and Data Mining
eries Editor: Andries Engelbrecht
opic Editor: Marco Antonio Aceves-Fernández

Print ISBN 978-1-83634-269-4
Online ISBN 978-1-83634-268-7
eBook (PDF) ISBN 978-1-83634-270-0
ISSN 2633-1403

If disposing of this product, please recycle the paper responsibly.

Advances in Data M
and Intelligent Anal
- Methods, Interpretal
and Cross-Domain
Applications

Edited by Tangina Sultana,
Md Delowar Hossain and Ashis Kumar M

Published in London, United Kingdom

Advances in Data
Applications
http://dx.doi.o
Edited by Tangin

Contributors
Anwar Fitrianto
Ochieng, Kenn
Hossain, Mohd
Tangina Sultan

First
Inte
regis

For
Cro

Bri
A c

Ad
Ap
Ed
p

IntechOpen Book Series

Artificial Intelligence

Volume 45

Aims and Scope of the Series

Artificial Intelligence (AI) is a rapidly developing multidisciplinary research area that aims to solve increasingly complex problems. In today's highly integrated world, AI promises to become a robust and powerful means for obtaining solutions to previously unsolvable problems. This Series is intended for researchers and students alike interested in this fascinating field and its many applications.

Meet the Series Editor

Andries Engelbrecht received the Masters and Ph.D. degrees in Computer Science from the University of Stellenbosch, South Africa, in 1994 and 1999 respectively. He is currently appointed as the Voigt Chair in Data Science in the Department of Industrial Engineering, with a joint appointment as Professor in the Computer Science Division, Stellenbosch University. Prior to his appointment at Stellenbosch University, he has been at the University of Pretoria, Department of Computer Science (1998-2018), where he was appointed as South Africa Research Chair in Artifical Intelligence (2007-2018), the head of the Department of Computer Science (2008-2017), and Director of the Institute for Big Data and Data Science (2017-2018). In addition to a number of research articles, he has written two books, Computational Intelligence: An Introduction and Fundamentals of Computational Swarm Intelligence.

Meet the Volume Editors

Dr. Tangina Sultana, SMIEE, is an Associate Professor in Electronics and Communication Engineering at Hajee Mohammad Danesh Science and Technology University. She earned her Ph.D. in Computer Engineering from Kyung Hee University in South Korea, where she also conducted postdoctoral research. Her expertise includes artificial intelligence, IoT, edge computing, big data analytics, and machine learning. She has published widely in SCIE-indexed journals, contributed to patents in RDF data compression, and serves in leadership roles within the IEEE Computer Society Bangladesh Chapter. She is actively engaged in research, mentoring, and international academic collaboration.

Prof. Dr. Md. Delowar Hossain, SMIEE, is a Professor of Computer Science and Engineering at Hajee Mohammad Danesh Science and Technology University and has served as Dean of the Faculty of CSE. He obtained his Ph.D. and postdoctoral training from Kyung Hee University, South Korea. His research focuses on edge computing, IoT, big data, networking, and machine learning. He has led multiple projects funded nationally and internationally and has received several best paper awards. With extensive administrative and project management experience, he contributes to academic leadership, research development, and digital capacity-building initiatives.

Prof. Dr. Ashis Kumar Mandal is a Professor of Computer Science and Engineering at Hajee Mohammad Danesh Science and Technology University. He completed his Ph.D. in Software and Information Science in Japan and pursued postdoctoral research in Canada. His research interests include artificial intelligence, machine learning, quantum computing, metaheuristics, and software engineering. He has authored numerous publications in SCIE- and Scopus-indexed journals, particularly in the areas of feature selection and optimization. He has held academic positions from lecturer to professor and actively participates in professional training, research supervision, and international scholarly activities.

Contents

Preface

The expanding scale and complexity of data in today's digital world continue to reshape how knowledge is discovered and how decisions are made across science, industry, healthcare, and agriculture. Data mining stands at the center of this transformation, offering theories, methods, and tools to extract meaningful patterns from data and convert them into actionable insights. As the field matures, it increasingly integrates statistics, machine learning, visualization, and intelligent systems, creating a rich and evolving research landscape.

Advances in Data Mining and Intelligent Analytics - Methods, Interpretability, and Cross-Domain Applications is conceived as a focused volume that captures both the essential foundations and selected cutting-edge directions of data mining. The book brings together contributions from researchers working on visualization, industrial analytics, machine learning optimization, deep learning, AI creativity evaluation, and scalable data management. The goal of this volume is not to be encyclopedic, but to provide readers with a coherent snapshot of important themes that reflect how data mining is practiced and advanced today.

The volume is organized into four thematic sections, each highlighting a key dimension of the field.

Section 1: Foundations of Data Mining Methods and Visualization addresses core techniques and conceptual understanding. The chapter *A Stairboxplot Construction Methods and Applications* revisits exploratory data analysis through enhanced visualization, showing how graphical summaries can deepen statistical insight and support robust interpretation. This is followed by *Key Concepts and Challenges in Industrial Processes with a Focus on Defining Target Variables in Multi-Stage Production and Batch Data*, which examines how careful problem formulation and target definition are essential for successful data mining in complex industrial environments.

Section 2: Advanced Machine Learning and Model Optimization focuses on algorithmic improvements for predictive performance and efficiency. *Perspective Chapter - Optimized Random Forests for Effective and Efficient Healthcare Data Analytics* discusses how ensemble learning methods can be refined for demanding healthcare applications, where both accuracy and computational efficiency are critical. The chapter, *Data Augmentation and Graph Regularization for Adversarial Training*, explores strategies that enhance model robustness and generalization, addressing challenges in adversarial and data-scarce scenarios.

Section 3: Deep Learning and Intelligent Systems Applications presents AI-driven approaches in domain contexts. *Discriminative-Encoder GAN and Lightweight CNN for Interpretable Plant Disease Detection and Deployable Diagnosis* demonstrates how deep learning can support agriculture through interpretable and deployable diagnostic systems. Next, *Perspective Chapter - Toward a Quantitative Framework for*

Evaluating AI-Generated Creativity – A Linguistic and Computational Analysis of Language Model Outputs extends data mining into the evaluation of generative AI, proposing quantitative viewpoints on creativity and language model behavior.

Section 4: Data Infrastructure, Collection, and Management emphasizes that effective analytics depend on reliable data ecosystems. *Scalable Data Collection and Management for Agricultural Research: Foundations and Advancements in Data Mining Applications* highlights frameworks for collecting, managing, and scaling agricultural data, reinforcing that data quality and accessibility are foundational to successful mining and analysis.

Across these sections, a common message emerges: progress in data mining is driven not only by new algorithms but also by a deeper understanding of data, stronger infrastructure, and thoughtful application design. The chapters collectively illustrate how foundational ideas remain relevant while new techniques open additional possibilities. Readers will find perspectives that are methodological, applied, and forward-looking, reflecting the interdisciplinary nature of the field.

The editors sincerely thank all contributing authors for sharing their expertise and for their commitment to clarity and quality. We also appreciate the reviewers for their careful evaluations and constructive suggestions, which helped strengthen the chapters. The support and guidance of the publishing team throughout the editorial process are gratefully acknowledged.

We hope this volume will serve as a useful reference for students, researchers, and practitioners, and encourage further exploration and responsible innovation in data mining. As data continues to shape modern society, the ability to analyze it rigorously and ethically becomes ever more important. This book is offered as a contribution to that ongoing journey.

Dr. Tangina Sultana
Department of Electronics and Communication Engineering,
Hajee Mohammad Danesh Science and Technology University,
Dinajpur, Bangladesh

Section 1

Foundations of Data Mining Methods and Visualization

Chapter 1

A Stairboxplot Construction Methods and Applications

Babangida Ibrahim Babura, Mohd Bakri Adam and Anwar Fitrianto

Abstract

Data visualization techniques have increasingly become the subject of interest in both scientific and technical reporting processes. There exists a significant dependence on exploratory data analysis (EDA) tools to achieve a custom presentation and examination of results in statistical techniques and data science research. Consequently, exploring data through an understanding of its structure and finding new insights is significantly supported by data visualization. Boxplots are recently becoming more popular than ever in terms of their powerful and simple glimpse into the most important robust data summaries. A newly boxplot-inspired plot called a stairboxplot was introduced in this chapter through a step-by-step construction method. Stairboxplot was robustly designed and constructed to implement multi-functionalities of classical boxplot, histogram, and dot plot in a single call to a plotting function. The chapter highlighted some justifications behind the selection of most of the important construction tools in the method, such as fence estimates, outlyingness, and quardbins. Applications of the stairboxplot were explored using real-life data and simulation. We hope this work will serve as a fundamental guide and inspire others toward the construction of visual EDA tools in general.

Keywords: boxplot, quartiles, fences, stairboxplot, outlyingness

1. Introduction

Data Visualization techniques have increasingly become popular exploratory data analysis (EDA) tools for data analytics and a common research and application tool in data science. The early version of EDA tools can be traced back to the sixteenth-century work of Michael Florent van Langren [1]. EDA techniques were generally regarded as graphical or numerical detective work for data insight. An excellent graphical EDA tool shall communicate ideas with clarity, precision, and consistency [2]. The boxplot display attribute maintains such excellent features and became popular among researchers of this century since its introduction by Tukey [3]. The boxplot's primary characteristics are defined using a robust algorithm for spotting outliers in a univariate dataset. The first quartile Q_1 and third quartile Q_3 are approximate estimates of the dataset's lower and upper fourths, respectively, where Q_2 is the dataset's median. The resistance rule classifies observations as "outside" if they fall outside of $Q_1 - 1.5IQR$ or above $Q_3 + 1.5IQR$, where $IQR = Q_1 - Q_3$, the Tukey's traditional boxplot rule [3]. The literature contains further studies on the classical boxplot creation methods that redefine the resistance rule [3–11].

Similar variants of boxplot construction were proposed with additional display requirements and information, among which are: the notch boxplot with the incorporation of the notch to represent a confidence interval around the median [12], the circular boxplot for circular (angular) data [13], and the K-boxplot specifically constructed for mixture data [14].

As against the initial construction philosophy of the classical boxplot of simplicity (with paper and pencil) [3], the development in computational power and accessibility has consequently brought in new contributions that have no regard for the initial philosophy. Such literature advances made a considerable transformation to the entire boxplot display characters to enable the capture of additional distributional attributes of interest in the data. To name a few, a violin plot [15], a vase plot [16], the raindrop plot [17], a beanplot [18], and other plots [19–21] are regarded as boxplot-inspired EDA tools. The general observation among the recent visualization enhancements and transformation of boxplots is the non-incorporation of the resistance rule to visually identify outliers. Additional literature for boxplot-inspired EDA visualization tools are indeed readily available [19–21].

In this chapter, a more computationally advanced boxplotting method called stairboxplot [22] is proposed. The advanced features were embedded along with the classical boxplot features including the robust display summaries with additional features of the histogram and dotplot [1]. A robust outlier rule estimation method [11] was clearly outlined in a step-by-step description. The robust fence estimate (outlier rule) incorporates a Bowley skewness [23] measure of a skewed distribution called the generalized extreme value (GEV) distribution. The plot depicts each observation in a dataset based on outlyingness estimates within the quadbin levels [1]. Connected stairs of four boxes were drawn to represent quadbins, with width proportional to the density of observations and height equaling one-fourth of the data range. Definitions of some conventional and new terms used in the construction of stairboxplot were given. The terms include: statistical estimators of range, quadbin, Bowley skewness measure, outlyingness, scale outlyingness, and a description of how to incorporate them in the construction of the proposed enhancement to stairboxplot. Implementation of stairboxplot was later given with a demonstration of its application to both real and simulated datasets. The stairboxplot was used to illustrate real-world data on monthly maximum rainfall data, 46-year monthly maximum precipitation data, and annual maximum river flow discharge data.

2. Stairboxplot components descriptions

2.1 Definition of terms

Definition 2.1. Let X be an ordered univariate dataset of order n given by $\boldsymbol{X} = \{x_{(1)}, x_{(2)}, \dots, x_{(n)}\}$, then *the range* of X is the difference between the minimum and maximum observation and is given by $r = x_{(n)} - x_{(1)}$ where $x_{(i)}$ and $x_{(n)}$ are the minimum and maximum observations in $\boldsymbol{X}$, respectively.

Definition 2.2.: For a univariate sample X, Let

$$\begin{cases} q_1 = \{x \in \mathbf{X} : x \leq r_1\}, \\ q_2 = \{x \in \mathbf{X} : r_1 < x \leq r_2\}, \\ q_3 = \{x \in \mathbf{X} : r_2 < x \leq r_3\}, \\ q_4 = \{x \in \mathbf{X} : x > r_3\}, \end{cases} \tag{1}$$

and define $r_1 = x_{(1)} + \frac{1}{4}r$, $r_2 = x_{(1)} + \frac{1}{2}r$, $r_3 = x_{(1)} + \frac{3}{4}r$, then q_i for $(i = 1,2,3,4)$, is to be *the quadbin level i* of $\mathbf{X}$ for $i = 1,2,3,4$ respectively.

Definition 2.2 simply illustrates the term quadbin as a synonymous term to histogram bins with a specific restriction in the number of bins, which happens to be exactly four.

Definition 2.3. [24] The Bowley skewness measure, sometimes called the *Bowley coefficient*, is defined as

$$\delta = \frac{Q_3 + Q_1 - 2Q_2}{Q_3 - Q_1} \tag{2}$$

where Q_i's are the three quartiles of a data.

δ meat the required benchmark metrics for any reasonable skewness measure [24].

Definition 2.4. [8] The *outlyingness* is a distance metric of an observation $x_{(i)} \in X$ which measures the extent of a data point $x_{(i)}$ is away from an estimate of a central point of the dataset, usually standardized by means of a robust scale (e.g., the median).

However, Hubert [8] has redefined Definition 2.4 by observing that it is irrelevant if a data point is smaller or bigger than the center point (median). But for a skewed distribution, a scale to each side of the median was introduced [8], such that the term *adjusted outlyingness AO* is compactly given by

$$AO_i = \begin{cases} \dfrac{Q_2 - x_i}{Q_2 - w_l} & \text{if } x_i < Q_2, \\ \dfrac{x_i - Q_2}{w_u - Q2} & \text{if } x_i > Q_2. \end{cases} \tag{3}$$

where w_l and w_u are referred to as the lower and upper whiskers of an adjusted boxplot method [8] as applied to the dataset X.

2.2 Outlyingness and asymmetric fence estimate

As demonstrated in Subsection 2.1, outlyingness can simply be related to the classical boxplot fence estimation in describing the outlier fence rules. Tukey's fence rule was generally described as $Q_2 - kIQR$ for the lower fence and $Q_2 + kIQR$ for the upper fence [25]. We incorporate δ in the new definition of boxplot fences by replacing the constant multiple of IQR with a lower fence function $f_l(\delta)$ and upper fence function $f_u(\delta)$ which are functions of δ into the outliers cut off value.

So, the proposed fences will be given by

$$\begin{array}{ll} Q_1 - f_l(\delta)IQR & \text{for the lower fence,} \\ Q_3 + f_u(\delta)IQR & \text{for the upper fence.} \end{array} \tag{4}$$

We require our definition to correspond with Tukey's definition of fence with the functions $f_l(\delta)$ and $f_u(\delta)$ equating to 1.5 when $\delta = 0$ (symmetric data) in which the GEV distribution assume symmetry.

We assume to consider two models and choose the best one that characterizes the fences in terms of the coefficient δ, namely:

1. A linear model is described as

$$\begin{aligned} f_l(\delta) &= 1.5 + h\delta, \\ f_u(\delta) &= 1.5 + k\delta, \end{aligned} \tag{5}$$

where δ is the skewness estimate of a dataset, $h, k \in \mathbb{R}$ are to be determined as the model coefficients using resistance fit procedure [2] and the value 1.5 is the known intercept when the skewness $\delta = 0$.

2. An exponential model given by

$$\begin{aligned} f_l(\delta) &= 1.5e^{m\delta} \\ f_u(\delta) &= 1.5e^{n\delta} \end{aligned} \tag{6}$$

where δ is the skewness estimate, $m, n \in \mathbb{R}$ are to be determined constants after a transformation to a linear form and applying a resistance fit scheme. The value 1.5 is a pre-defined model intercept when the $m\delta = n\delta = 0$.

2.2.1 Determination of the models parameters

Now, by assuming the values of f_l and f_u to be according to Tukey's fences markup expected percentage outliers of 0.7% all regular sample observations as investigated by Beaumont et al. [26]. We simulate extreme data from GEV distribution to have a proper estimate of the parameters of f_l and f_u.

We substitute Eq. (5) in Eq. (4) to obtain

$$\begin{aligned} &Q_1 - (1.5 + h\delta)IQR \quad \text{for the lower fence,} \\ &Q_3 + (1.5 + k\delta)IQR \quad \text{for the upper fence.} \end{aligned} \tag{7}$$

Let Q_α and Q_β denote the αth and βth quantiles, respectively, such that $\alpha = (0.7\%)/2 = 0.0035$ and $\beta = 1 - \alpha = 0.9965$, are the expected quantile positions recommended by Beaumont et al. [26] for the lower and upper fence estimates, respectively. Then, we require that the constants h, k in Eq. (7) should satisfy;

$$\begin{aligned} Q_1 - (1.5 + h\delta)IQR &\approx Q_\alpha, \\ Q_3 + (1.5 + k\delta)IQR &\approx Q_\beta, \end{aligned} \tag{8}$$

So that the system in Eq. (8) can be rewritten as;

$$\begin{aligned} Q_1 - Q_\alpha &\approx (1.5 + h\delta)IQR, \\ Q_\beta - Q_3 &\approx (1.5 + k\delta)IQR, \end{aligned}$$

$$\Rightarrow \begin{array}{l} \dfrac{Q_1 - Q_\alpha}{IQR} \approx 1.5 + h\delta, \\ \dfrac{Q_\beta - Q_3}{IQR} \approx 1.5 + k\delta, \end{array}$$
$$\Rightarrow \begin{array}{l} \dfrac{Q_1 - Q_\alpha}{IQR} - 1.5 \approx h\delta, \\ \dfrac{Q_\beta - Q_3}{IQR} - 1.5 \approx k\delta, \end{array} \tag{9}$$

We can also substitute Eq. (6) in Eq. (4) to obtain

$$\begin{array}{ll} Q_1 - 1.5e^{m\delta} IQR & \text{for lower fence}, \\ Q_3 + 1.5e^{n\delta} IQR & \text{for upper fence}. \end{array} \tag{10}$$

using similar assumptions on Q_α and Q_β for the linear model, Eq. (10) should satisfy the relation

$$\begin{array}{l} Q_1 - 1.5e^{m\delta} IQR \approx Q_\alpha, \\ Q_3 + 1.5e^{n\delta} IQR \approx Q_\beta, \end{array}$$
$$\Rightarrow \begin{array}{l} Q_1 - Q_\alpha \approx \dfrac{3}{2} e^{m\delta} IQR, \\ Q_\beta - Q_3 \approx \dfrac{3}{2} e^{n\delta} IQR, \end{array}$$
$$\Rightarrow \begin{array}{l} \dfrac{2}{3}\dfrac{Q_1 - Q_\alpha}{IQR} \approx e^{m\delta}, \\ \dfrac{2}{3}\dfrac{Q_\beta - Q_3}{IQR} \approx e^{n\delta}. \end{array} \tag{11}$$

We finally arrived at the linear form of the exponential model in Eqs. (6) by taking log of Eq. (11) to obtain;

$$\begin{array}{l} \ln\left(\dfrac{2}{3}\dfrac{Q_1 - Q_\alpha}{IQR}\right) \approx m\delta, \\ \ln\left(\dfrac{2}{3}\dfrac{Q_\beta - Q_3}{IQR}\right) \approx n\delta. \end{array} \tag{12}$$

For both two systems in Eqs. (9) and (12), we employ the resistance fit, an EDA procedure to estimate the parameters h and k for Eqs. (9), m and n for Eq. (12). In the two linear resistance fit, we require the intercept to be zero. Having this will enable both the linear and exponential models to be exactly 1.5 when $\delta = 0$.

The required quantities on the left-hand side (LHS) and right-hand side (RHS) of Eqs. (9) and (12) were generated through a well-structured simulation process. Initially, a sample size of 100 was generated from a GEV distribution. The location and scale parameters were fixed to $\mu = 0$ and $\sigma = 1$, respectively. This is simply because the simulated quantities in both Eqs. (9) and (12) are structured to be location scale-invariant. In the case of the GEV shape parameter, it was varied within the interval $(-0.8 \le \xi \le 10)$ with a step size increment of $\frac{1}{100}$. Hames [27] develops a method that determines an acceptable minimum sample size to be implemented for a GEV distribution for the modeling of extremal events, in which a minimum sample size of 40 is recommended, and consequently, our choice of $n = 100$ to be a sufficient sample size for this simulation process. Also, the defined choice of parameter values of ξ was based on the EVT practical recommendation in the literature by Coles [28]. Coles [28] gave a detailed explanation of the non-regular cases for the MLE estimation of the parameters of the GEV distribution. When $\xi \leq -0.5$ we have a scenario where the GEV distribution will have a short bounded upper tail, which is a situation difficult t encounter in practice [28]. Consequently, we can run the simulation process without regard to a non-regular case. As such, we consider choosing a value of -0.8 as a lower limit for ξ for the simulation experiment. However, the Bowley coefficient of skewness (δ) converges to 1.0 when $\xi \geq 10$, thus $\xi = 10$ was set to be the upper limit for ξ in the simulation band.

A replicated process of 5000 in the simulation was conducted with a fixed choice of location, scale, and shape parameter for every generated sample. From each process, an estimate of δ and corresponding quantities in the LHSs of Eqs. (9) and (12) were recorded. As a Markov chain Monte Carlo (MCMC) process, an average δ and an average of the corresponding quantities in the LHSs of Eq. (9) and (12) were obtained from the replicated process to achieve a finite sample estimate of the quantities. The retrieved simulated quantities were sorted while excluding those with skewness values greater than ($\delta \geq 0$). The underlying assumption was that we could transform the estimated parameters for each model into a reverse coefficient for a model with negative skewness $(delta0)(\delta < 0)$. To obtain the lower fence models, the estimated quantities were further sorted for $\delta \leq 0.9$, whereas for the upper fence models, the estimated quantities were sorted for $0 \leq \delta \leq 0.6$. The choices made are intended to allow for a more robust linear fit, as both models explode exponentially when $delta > 0.9$ for the lower fence and $\delta > 0.6$ for the upper fence.

The plots in **Figures 1** and **2** represent the linear and exponential fits for the lower and upper fences, respectively. By examining the residuals and clustered points around the resistance line, it is clear that the exponential is the best model.

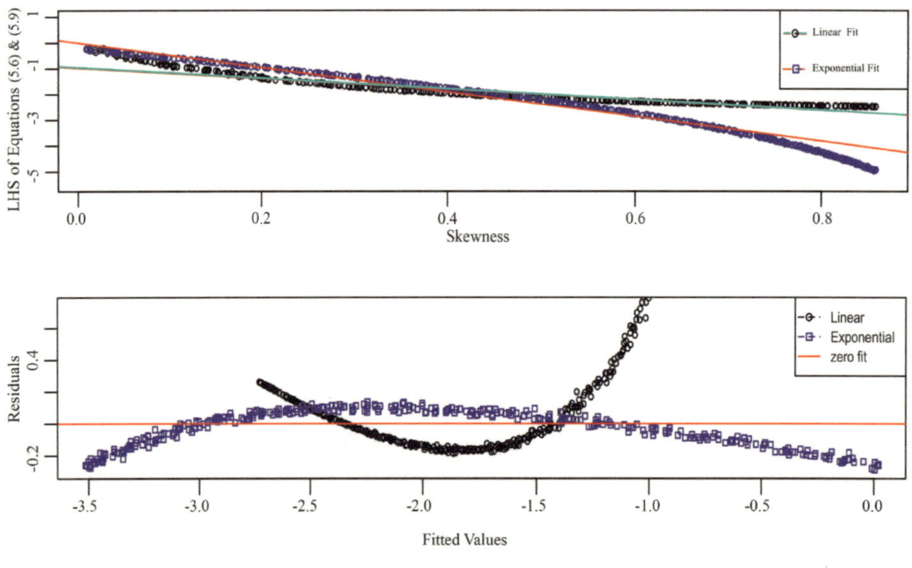

Figure 1.
Median resistance line fit implementation for Eqs. (9) and (12) (lower fence).

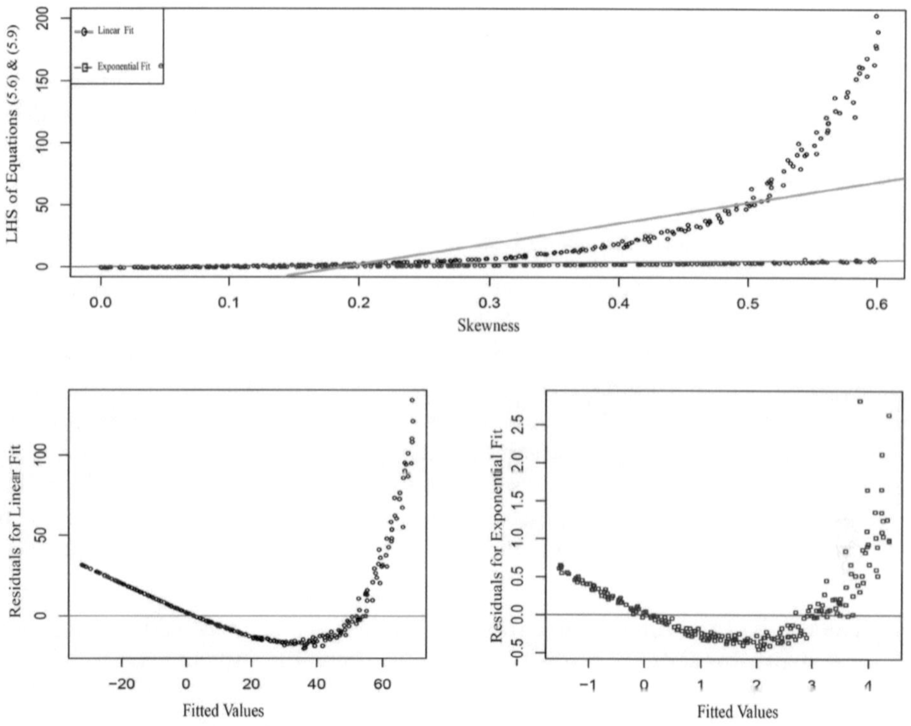

Figure 2.
Median resistance line fit implementation for Eqs. (9) and (12) (upper fence).

2.2.2 Implementing the fence modification

The simulation result shows that the half slope ratio of both lower and upper fences in the linear fit of **Figure 1** was 0.87 and 3.74 respectively. As such, the linear fit model is relatively non-linear and can fail to accurately estimate the fences. However, the exponential fit gives a better half slope ratios of 0.78 and 0.69 for the lower and upper fences, respectively. Thus, we have acceptable half-slope values, which are required to be one for an absolute linear relationship.

To finally implement the fence modification using the estimates in the most acceptable exponential model of Eq. (12) with $m = -3.06$ and $n = 5.52$ obtained from the simulation process. For a robust estimate, we truncate the estimated values to $m = -3$ and $n = 5$, a recommendation by Hubert and Vandervieren [8]. However, our consideration of selecting simulated population values with non-negative skewness will let us consider a swap of values between m and n for negative skewness.

Below is the summarized implementation of the proposed fence markup by replacing $f_l(\delta)$ and $f_u(\delta)$ in Eq. (4) with the new fence rule.

$$\begin{array}{ll} \left[Q_1 - 1.5e^{-3\delta}IQR; Q_3 + 1.5e^{5\delta}IQR\right] & \text{if } \delta \geq 0 \\ \left[Q_1 - 1.5e^{5\delta}IQR; Q_3 + 1.5e^{-3\delta}IQR\right] & \text{if } \delta < 0 \end{array} \quad (13)$$

2.2.3 Evaluation of the fence modification

The proposed modification of the boxplot fence was evaluated alongside two existing boxplot fence definitions of Hoaglin et al. [2] classical boxplot fence and [8] adjusted boxplot fence in this section. The evaluation is done with simulation data and a rainfall dataset for the application.

I. Performance Evaluation Using Data Simulation

Let the location and scale parameter of a GEV distribution be fixed as $\mu = 10$ and $\sigma = 2$. Let us also vary the shape parameter within the interval $(-0.1 \leq \xi \leq 2.0)$ with an increment of $\frac{1}{100}$ to generate a zero or positive skewed extreme sample from the GEV distribution with a fixed choice of parameters (μ, σ, ξ). For each sample generated, we record the Bowley skewness estimate and percentage outlier of the sample according to the three fence rules; Tukey's classical fence rule, the Hubert's adjusted fence rule, and the proposed modified fence rule. The simulation process is replicated 10,000 times so that we record the average skewness, δ along with the corresponding average percentage of outliers.

The result of the simulation is shown in **Figure 3**. The modified boxplot fence rule maintains stability across the increased skewness with an expected percentage of outliers close to the benchmark requirement [26] of not more than 5% as against the classical and adjusted fence rules. To illustrate the simulated performance of the lower and upper fences of the proposed modified fence rule, with its benchmark peers of Tukey's classical fence rule and Hubert's adjusted fence rule in contaminated samples. We consider 5% and 10% contaminations of the extreme dataset. We adapt the contamination algorithm as proposed by [29]. The contamination steps of the algorithm are given as follows.

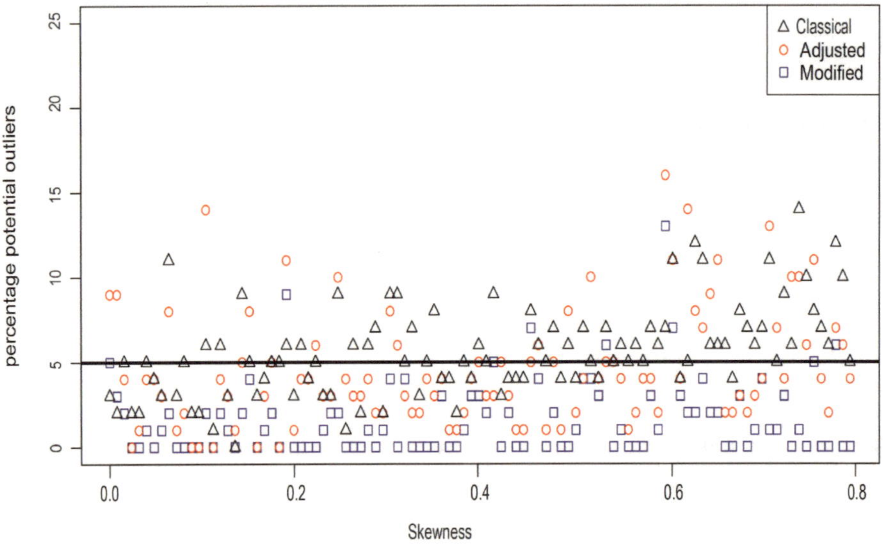

Figure 3.
Performance of the modified fence estimate in an uncontaminated data.

Step 1 Generate the regular observations $x_1, x_2, \cdots, x_n$ from the hypothesized distribution F with pre-specified parameters. That is, in our framework, we generate a finite sample X_n from the GEV distribution at a standardized combination of fixed parameter values of $\{\mu = 0, \sigma = 1, \text{ and } (-0.1 \leq \xi \leq 2.0)\}$ and a sample size of $n = 100$.

Step 2 Estimate the lower and upper fences for the sample X_n according to classical, adjusted, or modified boxplot fence rules as the case may be and then calculate the skewness $\delta(X_n)$.

Step 3 Generate a value z from an arbitrarily chosen distribution H with parameters different from F, at a fixed location and scale parameters. Make a large deviation of parameters of H from that of F to have a large outliers that are easier to detect. In this case, we choose z to be from the GEV distribution with parameters $\mu = 1, \sigma = 10$ but we choose ξ to be the same value as in Step 1.

Step 4 Repeat Step 3 to generate an $n_o = \alpha \times n$ number of outlying observations where α is the contamination level (e.g $\alpha = 0.05$ at 5% contamination), such that for each z generated it must satisfy the outlier criteria in Step 2.

Step 5 A set of n_o observations selected randomly from the regular observations X_n as generated in Step 1 is then replaced by the n_o outliers generated in Step 4.

We replicate the above algorithm 10,000 times for fixed values of $\mu, \sigma,$ and ξ by setting the values of the GEV shape parameter ξ to be a sequence of values between 0 and 2.0 with an increment of $\frac{1}{100}$ to allow generation of samples with zero or positive skewness. For each replicated sample, we record the percentage of outliers detected and the sample skewness, δ. An average percentage of outliers to the lower and upper fences, along with a corresponding average skewness, was obtained for each resampling process and recorded. **Figure 4** shows a plot of skewness versus percentage outliers as an illustration of the performance of three boxplot rules with contaminated samples.

We expect a capture of around 2.5% outliers below the lower or above the upper fence positions in order to have good performance at $\alpha = 5\%$ contamination level. **Figure 4(a)** and **(c)** illustrates the lower fence and upper fence performance, respectively, at $\alpha = 5\%$ contamination for all three boxplot methods. The figure indicates that the proposed fence modification in the modified boxplot has performed better than the classical and adjusted boxplot methods. In **Figure 4(a)**, the classical method overestimates the lower fence position, leading to non-detection of the outliers, especially when the skewness is higher, while the adjusted method deviates to capture regular observation as outliers, an indication of underestimation of the fence position. Also in **Figure 4(c)**, the classical and adjusted methods show percentage outliers significantly above the expected value of 2.5% especially when the skewness value increases, a clear sign of under estimation of the fence position.

The performance of the modified boxplot was similarly maintained in comparison with the classical and adjusted boxplots with contamination at

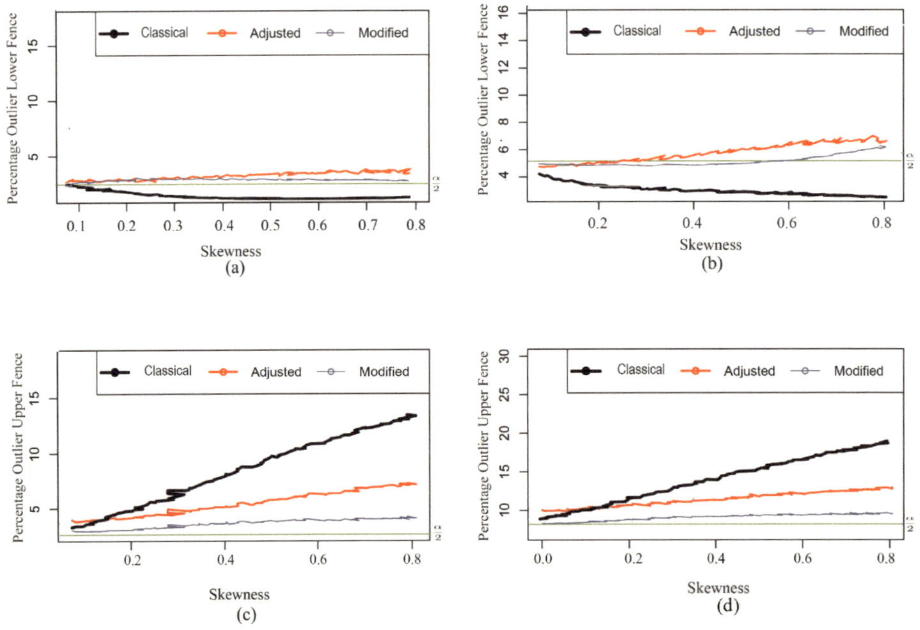

Figure 4.
Performance of the modified boxplot fence with a contaminated data.

$\alpha = 10\%$. **Figure 4(c)** and **(d)** indicates that the modified boxplot demonstrates a similar performance as in **Figure 4(a)** and **(b)** at both lower and upper fence contamination, with expected percentage outliers of around 5% at each of the two fence estimates.

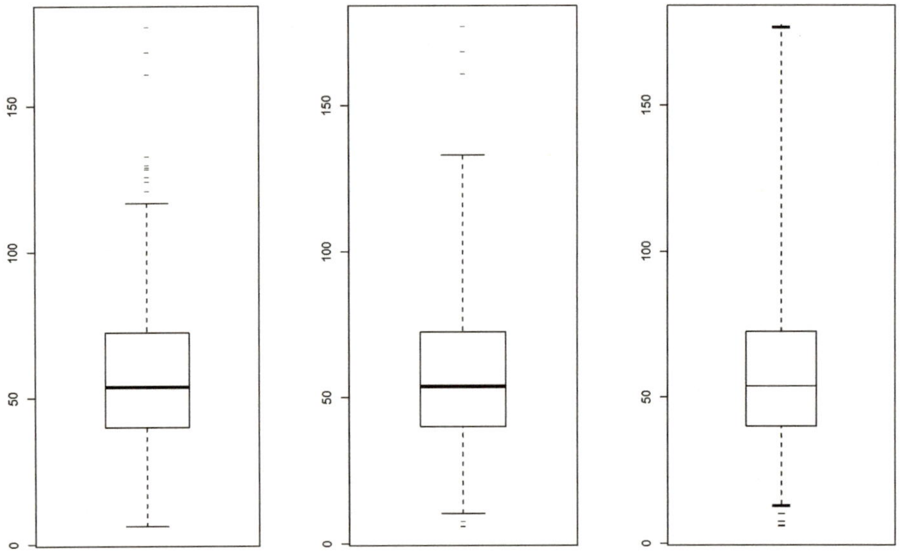

Figure 5.
Maximum monthly rainfall data Tukey's classical (Left), Hubert's adjusted (Middle), and proposed modified (Right).

II. Performance Evaluation Using Real Data[1] **Figure 5** illustrates three distinct boxplot displays for the 30-year data (1974–2003) of maximum monthly rainfall at Subang Station, Malaysia. Tukey's standard boxplot is on the left, Hubert's adjusted boxplot is in the middle, and the proposed modified boxplot with asymmetric fence estimate is on the right. The display demonstrates a slight improvement in data capture when compared to the adjusted boxplot and a significant improvement when compared to the modified boxplot. While the modified boxplot captured all of the extreme data, it also indicated that some values near the bottom of the data set may be outliers and require additional attention. The highest value is a record set in 2001, during what is considered Malaysia's worst flood in over a century.

3. Implementation of stairboxplot construction

This section presents some components specifically defined for the implementation of the new visualization method of stairboxlot. A step-by-step implementation of the construction of the stairboxplot was given. The advantages and applications of stairboxplot were explored with simulated and real-life datasets.

Definition 3.1. [1] The *stairboxplot outlyingness* SO_i of a data point $x_i \in X$ is define as an absolute difference between an observation x_i and median (Q_2) of the data set X scaled with the distance between a corresponding fence estimate value m_j, $(j = 1, 2)$ to the median Q_2, given by

$$SO_i = \begin{cases} \dfrac{Q_2 - x_i}{Q2 - m_2} & \text{if } x_i < Q_2, \\ \dfrac{x_i - Q_2}{m_1 - Q2} & \text{if } x_i > Q_2. \end{cases} \tag{14}$$

Definition 3.2. The *scale-adjusted stairboxplot outlyingness* is given by

$$SO_\alpha = \alpha SO_i \quad (0 < \alpha \leq 1) \tag{15}$$

The essence of Definition 3.2 is to control the display width of SO_i. In some instances, according to data visualization of SO_i, especially for a skewed dataset, the line representing SO_i might explode to overlap during batch comparison. Hence, the α control on the stairboxplot outlyingness. For a symmetric dataset $\alpha = 1$ while we play along $0 < \alpha \leq 1$ for a skewed dataset depending on the extent of skewness.

The essence of Definition 3.2 is to control the display width of SO_i. In some instances, according to data visualization of SO_i, especially for a skewed dataset, the line representing SO_i might explode to overlap during batch comparison. Hence, the α control on the stairboxplot outlyingness. For a symmetric dataset, $\alpha = 1$ while we play along, $0 < \alpha \leq 1$ for a skewed dataset, depending on the extent of skewness.

3.1 Display and application of stairboxplot

The construction methodology of the stairboxplot is synonymous with the histogram in the first instance. Initially, the dataset was subdivided according to quadbin levels. Unlike the histogram bins, which are usually side (left, right, up, or down)

[1] A 30 years (1974–2003) annual maximum rainfall record at Subang station, Malaysia. Source: Earth Observation Center(EOC), Institute of Climate Change, UKM.

aligned, the stairboxplot quadbins are center-aligned with either horizontal or vertical orientation. The default setting for this implementation is chosen to be vertical orientation. In this case, connected stairs of four boxes are drawn according to the quadbins levels of equal height of $\frac{1}{4}r$ and width that is proportional to the number of data points within. Where the individual point $x_i \in X$ is displayed as a horizontal line and placed (plotted) with a width proportional to the value of its corresponding outlyingness SO_α. **Figure 6** gave an illustration of how to measure SO_α from a boxplot. For this implementation, $\alpha = 1/4$ to account for skewness in the GEV distribution. However, regular observations are displayed as a full line, while potential outlying observations will be displayed with a dashed line.

In order to maintain other boxplot display properties such as the quartiles Q_1, Q_2, and Q_3 of X. The quartiles as data points were represented with a vertical full line thicker than a regular observation, with a length equal to the width of the quadbin level for which the quartile falls within. For additional visual enhancement, each observation that lies below the median line is plotted in blue, and those above the median are plotted in black, while outlying observations are inked in red. Furthermore, for the positively skewed dataset, the median is plotted in blue color while for negatively skewed data the median is plotted in black line.

Figure 7 depicts a visual comparison of the regular boxplot display method to the left and the proposed stairboxplot display method. The figure illustrates the center, spread, and outliers in the two plots for the same dataset. The stairboxplot displays each individual observation relative to its outlyingness SO_α, which is a noticeable difference between the two plot methods. As a result, the identification of skewness in data is better illustrated with the stairboxplot than with the classical boxplot, in which the skewness can be seen regardless of how small it is in the stairboxplot method.

Figure 8 illustrates another advantage of the stairboxplot in terms of displaying the shape of a distribution. The two figures represent two batches of datasets created from distinct distributions. The first batch (on the left) is generated using a normal distribution, while the second batch (on the right) uses a uniform distribution. The traditional boxplot simply shows a difference in data spread in the middleboxes, but it does not reveal much about the distributional difference. However, the distribution of the two batches of data is different, as seen by the stairboxplot approach. The uniformly distributed data reveals nearly symmetric boxes at each quadbin level, whereas the Gaussian sample exhibits larger but symmetrical boxes for the second and third quadbin levels, as opposed to smaller symmetrical boxes for the first and fourth quadbin levels.

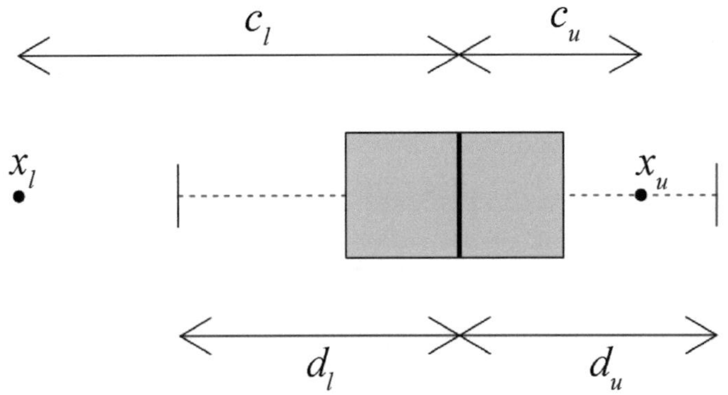

Figure 6.
A boxplot illustration of measurements of c_l, c_u, d_l and d_u required to estimate the outlyingness of a data point.

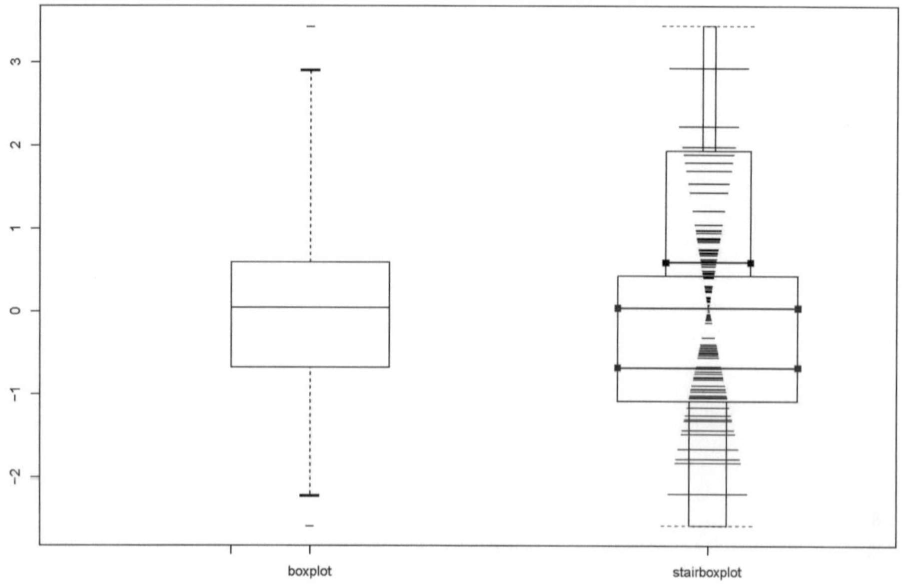

Figure 7.
A regular boxplot display method on the left versus a stairboxplot display method on the right for the same univariate dataset.

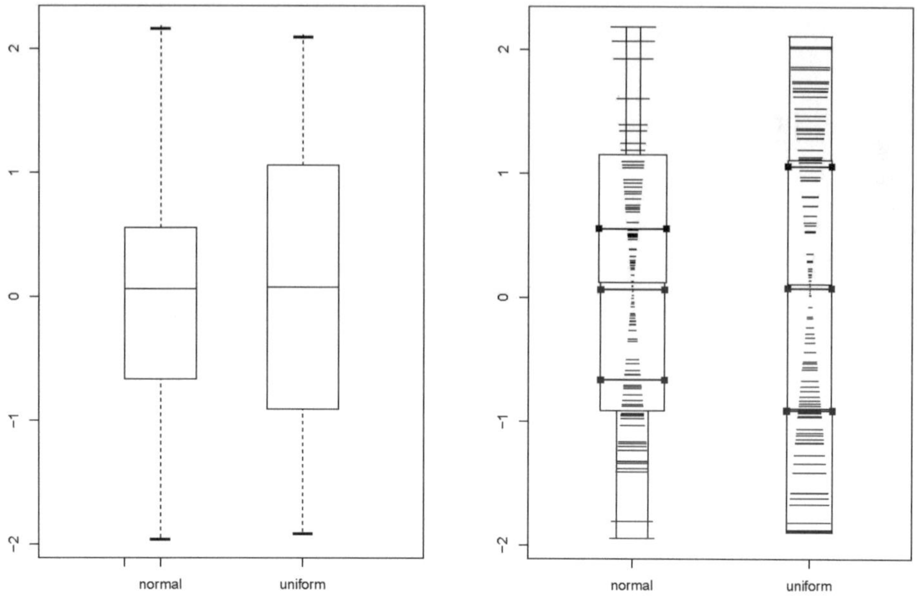

Figure 8.
Comparison of regular boxplot with stairboxplot display shape of distribution.

3.2 Exploratory analysis of real-life dataset

Observing trends in batches of datasets is one of the most fascinating functions of a boxplot. **Figures 9-11** show how stairboxplot keeps these qualities while also providing additional information to the traditional boxplot display, as explained below.

3.2.1 The rainfall intensity dataset

Figures 9 and **10** show stairboxplot trend visualizations of 31 years of maximum monthly rainfall data from the Petaling Jaya record station, obtained from the UKM Earth Observatory Center. Each batch is a collection of annual monthly maxima. The most

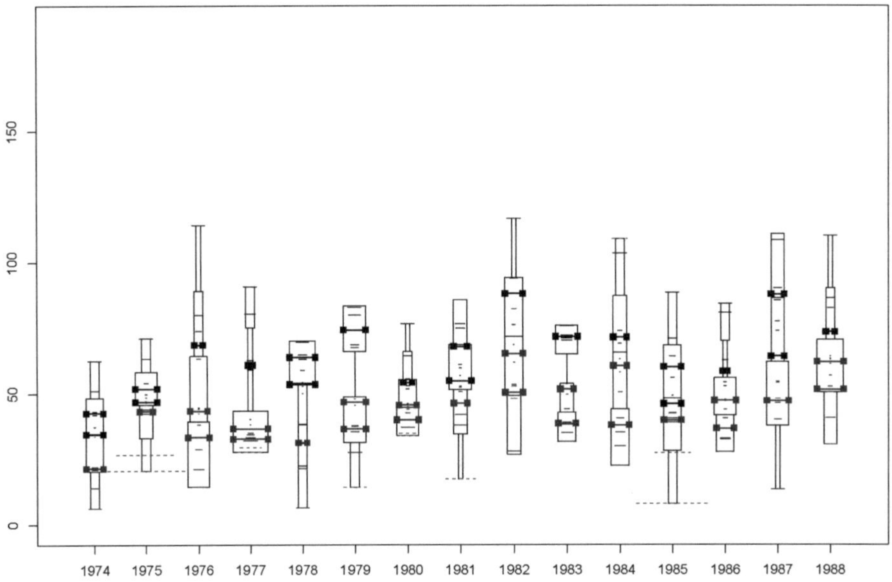

Figure 9.
Trend in rainfall data for 31-year monthly maximum rainfall data (1974–1988) at Patalin Jaya.

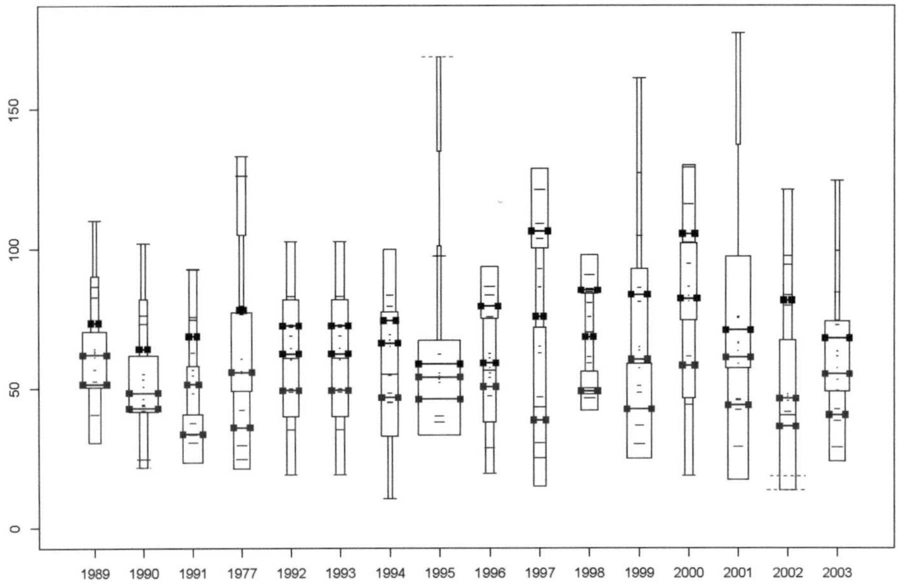

Figure 10.
Trend in rainfall data for 31-year monthly maximum rainfall data (1989–2003) at Patalin Jaya.

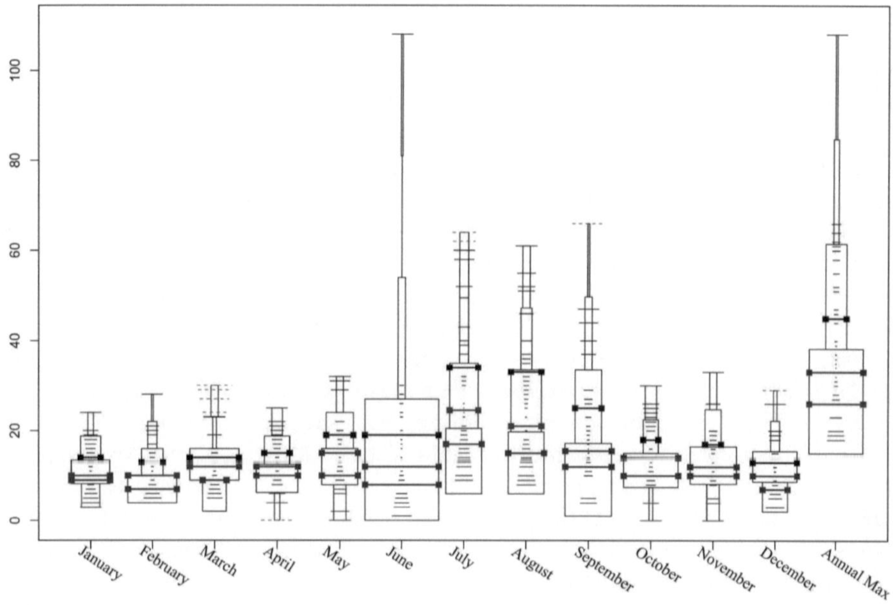

Figure 11.
Trend in monthly maximum precipitation for 46 years (1947–1993) for Colorado (US) precipitation data [30]

immediately visible feature in this trend is that rainfall statistics show an uneven pattern over 31 years. According to the given sequence, both the center and spread deviate. For the first 8 years (1974–1981), the median records were typically below 50 mm, but after that, they were mostly above 50 mm (1982–2003). The greatest temperature was recorded in 2001, a year that was marked by disastrous floods in Malaysia.

One of the most common assumptions used to describe a display of similar data using a regular boxplot is that the data is Gaussian [31]. It is fascinating to note that the stairboxplot provides additional details to avoid such misunderstandings. The trends in 1977, 1978, 1979, 1980, 1995, 1997, and 2001, for example, show a different distributional pattern than the usual distribution. Consider the skewed data from 1999, which shows a symmetric pattern inside the interquartile range. When shown with the conventional boxplot approach, this would appear to follow a Gaussian distribution. However, the stairboxplot provides additional information about the shape of the distribution that may fit a Gumbel-type GEV distribution.

Many batches of the dataset, such as 1977, 1980, 1995, 1996, and 1999, show the shape of extreme data and can be linked to the GEV distribution family [31]. Multi-modality in some batches, such as 1977, 1979, 1983, 1992, and 2001, is another piece of information that can go overlooked with a standard boxplot display method.

3.2.2 The maximum precipitation dataset

Precipitation is any form of water particle, regardless of state, that forms in the atmosphere and falls to the ground under the influence of gravity [30]. Meteorologists observe and study various types of precipitation, including drizzle, rain, sleet, snow, graupel, and hail.

Since the late 1800s, the technical report [24] has identified over 300 storms that have produced very heavy precipitation over large areas in and near Colorado's mountains. Thomas and Nolan [24] contains 36 heavy precipitation events from more severe extreme storms that stand out for some selected geographical regions of Colorado State for analysis on safety policy considerations. Using stairboxplot, we examine the trend of the dataset for over 46 years, that is, from 1947 to 1993. Throughout the 46 years of maximum precipitation events, the trend was specifically compared between months of the year. The trend between batches of monthly maximum precipitation events in Colorado (US) precipitation data records for 46 years (1947–1993) [24] is depicted in **Figure 11**. We compare the trend over 46 years in monthly intervals rather than yearly intervals since the data contains recurring tie values, rendering an annual event batch less informative. The monthly maximum, as opposed to the annual maximum batch, can provide a seasonal pattern of maximum precipitation events. The trend continues by examining how the monthly maximum events compare to the total annual maximum events. The monthly maximum spread pattern, as shown in the figure, can be divided into two categories: a narrow spread observed in January, May, October, and December, and a widespread observed in June and September, when the most extreme events occurred. When we compare the batches of monthly maximum events to the 46 years of annual maximum events, we can see that almost all of the batches in the narrow spread monthly maximum events fall below the median annual maximum events, whereas the widespread maximum events have approximately 25% of the records above the median annual maximum events, indicating that the events come from a severely extreme storm occur between June and September.

3.2.3 The annual maximum river flow discharge dataset

The maximum annual flood discharges for the preceding 60 years, in cubic meters per second, at an unknown river site are available at [32]. Castillo [32] employs extreme value statistical analysis to analyze and construct a flood protection mechanism for that specific area. Since the data are presented in a single batch and contains less information than the other datasets in Sections 7.6.1 and 7.6.2, we will concentrate on analyzing the data using a single batch stairboxplot presentation.

The stairboxplot representation of the annual maximum flood discharge dataset records using the modified boxplot outlyingness method is shown in **Figure 12**. The stairboxplot identified the two observations as probable outliers, indicating that the dataset can be fitted to a Fréchet-type GEV distribution for modeling purposes. The stairboxplot enables us to observe the dataset's asymmetric behavior in essentially two ways:

- Non-symmetry of boxes at the first and fourth quadbin levels, as well as boxes at the second and third quadbin levels, the outlyingness display for about 75% of the data points falls within the first and second quardbins.

4. Conclusion

This chapter gives comprehensive details of a novel EDA procedure for the visualization of a univariate data set. The boxplot-inspired method was structured to incorporate the functionalities of boxplot with other visualization techniques

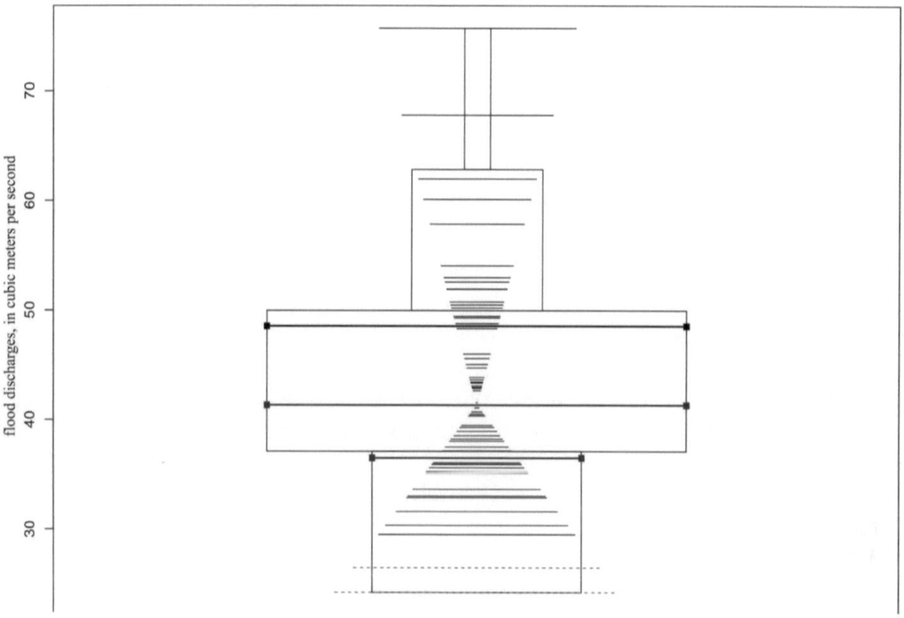

Figure 12.
Annual maximum river flow discharge data for Colorado, displayed using a stairboxplot [24].

such as dotplot and histogram. We introduce and define some new concepts of quadbin, stairboxplot outlyingnes, and scale-adjusted outlyingness that are principal components utilized in the new visualization method called stairboxplot. The main functionality of a boxplot, and, of course, a stairboxplot, was the identification of outliers in data. As such, we describe a detailed procedure to estimate a fence markup according to an underlying distribution of extremal events. The new fence markup was utilized and incorporated in the construction of the stairboxplot.

Stairboxplot is synonymous with the histogram in terms of dividing a dataset into bins (or quardbins). Histogram bins are often aligned to the left, right, up, or down, whereas stairboxplot quadbins are aligned to the center in either horizontal or vertical orientation. This is an ascending joint box constructed with quadbins levels of equal height ($\frac{1}{4}r$) and breadth proportional to the number of observations contained. Each point $xi \in X$ is represented by a horizontal line with a width proportionate to its outlyingness value $SO\alpha$. In this situation, typical observations were denoted by solid lines, whereas possible outliers were denoted by dashed lines. The data quartiles Q_1, Q_2, and Q_3 were indicated by a vertical thicker complete line with a length proportional to the width of the quadbin in which the quartile lies.

The novelty of the stairboxplot visualization method was proved extensively through the use of simulated and real-world data sets. Additionally, stairboxplot retains key boxplot features such as batch comparison and the presentation of probable outliers while adding the following enhancements:

- better enhancement in the display of distributional shape with a display of density of a dataset at range levels,
- display of individual points according to stairboxplot outlyingness (SO),

- display of multi-modality,
- strong advantage in identifying trends in batches/components of a dataset,
- can be constructed with at least two data points,
- design according to Tukey's EDA philosophy of exploratory, not confirmatory data analysis.

Acknowledgements

This research was conducted under the Federal University Dutse (FUD) TETFUND2013 Fellowship Intervention and University Putra Malaysia (UPM) Research Grant No. FRGS5524846.

Conflict of interest

No conflict of interest.

Nomenclature

Quadbins	stairboxplot bins
SO	stairboxplot oulyingness
SO_α	scale-adjusted stairboxplot outlyingness

Abbreviations

EDA	exploratory data analysis
GEV	generalized extreme value

Author details

Babangida Ibrahim Babura[1,2*†], Mohd Bakri Adam[2†] and Anwar Fitrianto[3]

1 Department of Mathematics, Federal University Dutse, Jigawa State, Nigeria

2 Institute for Mathematical Research, Universiti Putra Malaysia, Selango, Malaysia

3 Department of Statistics, IPB University, Bogor, Indonesia

*Address all correspondence to: bibabura@gmail.com

† These authors contributed equally.

References

[1] Babura BI, Adam MB, Sani M, Waziri U, Eguda FY. Construction and applications of Stairboxplot for exploratory data analysis. Journal of Physics Conference Series. 2021;**1863**(1): 1-10

[2] Hoaglin DC, Mosteller F, Tukey JW, Wiley J. Understanding robust and exploratory data analysis. Technometrics. 2001;**43**(3):384-384

[3] Frigge M, Hoaglin DC, Iglewicz B. Some implementations of the boxplot. The American Statistician [Internet]. 1989;**43**(1):50-54. DOI: 10.1080/00031305.1989.10475612

[4] Kimber AC. Exploratory data analysis for possibly censored data from skewed distributions. Journal of the Royal Statistical Society Series C: Applied Statistics. 1990;**39**(1):21-30

[5] Carling K. Resistant outlier rules and the non-Gaussian case. Computational Statistics and Data Analysis. 2000;**33**(3): 249-258

[6] Schwertman NC, Owens MA, Adnan R. A simple more general boxplot method for identifying outliers. Computational Statistics and Data Analysis. 2004;**47**(1):165-174

[7] Schwertman NC, de Silva R. Identifying outliers with sequential fences. Computational Statistics and Data Analysis. 2007;**51**(8):3800-3810

[8] Hubert M, Vandervieren E. An adjusted boxplot for skewed distributions. Computational Statistics and Data Analysis. 2008;**52**(12):5186-5201

[9] Bruffaerts C, Verardi V, Vermandele C. A generalized boxplot for skewed and heavy-tailed distributions. Statistics & Probability Letters. 2014;**95**:110-117

[10] Adil IH, Irshad AR. A modified approach for detection of outliers. Pakistan Journal of Statistics and Operation Research. 2015;**11**(1):91-102. DOI: 10.18187/pjsor.v11i1.500

[11] Babura BI, Adam MB, Fitrianto A, Rahim ASA. Modified boxplot for extreme data. In: AIP Conference Proceedings. American Institute of Physics Inc. NY USA; 2017

[12] McGill R, Tukey JW, Larsen WA. Variations of box plots. The American Statistician. 1978;**32**(1):12-16

[13] Abuzaid AH, Mohamed IB, Hussin AG. Boxplot for circular variables. Computational Statistics. 2012;**27**(3):1-12

[14] Qarmalah NM, Einbeck J, Coolen FPA. k-boxplots for mixture data. Statistical Papers. 2016;**59**(2):1-16

[15] Hintze JL, Nelson RD. Violin plots: A box plot-density trace synergism. The American Statistician. 1998;**52**(2): 181-184

[16] Benjamini Y. Opening the box of a boxplot. The American Statistician. 1988;**42**(4):257-262

[17] Barrowman NJ, Myers RA. Raindrop plots: A new way to display collections of likelihoods and distributions. The American Statistician. 2003;**57**(4): 268-274

[18] Kampstra P et al. Beanplot: A boxplot alternative for visual comparison of distributions. Journal of Statistical Software. 2008;**28**(1):1-9

[19] Zani S, Riani M, Corbellini A. Robust bivariate boxplots and multiple outlier detection. Computational Statistics and Data Analysis. 1998;**28**(3):257-270

[20] Hyndman RJ, Shang HL. Rainbow plots, Bagplots, and boxplots for functional data. Journal of Computational and Graphical Statistics [Internet]. 2010;**19**(1):29-45. DOI: 10.1198/jcgs.2009.08158

[21] Adam MB, Babura BI, Gopal K. Range-box plotting relating to discrete distribution. MATEMATIKA. 2018;**34** (2):187-204

[22] Babura BI, Adam MB, Fitrianto A, Mohammad AT. Stairboxplot and Visual Analysis of Univariate Dataset2019. p. 050041. DOI: 10.1063/1.5136429 [Accessed: December 11, 2019]

[23] Bowley AL. Elements of Statistics. Vol. 2. Michigan USA: PS King; 1920

[24] Thomas BM, Nolan JD. Colorado Extreme Storm Precipitation Data Study [Internet]. Colorado Climate Center; 1997

[25] Tufte ER, Graves-Morris PR. The Visual Display of Quantitative Information. Vol. 2, No. 9. Cheshire, CT: Graphics Press; 1983

[26] Beaumont C, Hoaglin DC, Mosteller F, Tukey JW. Exploring data tables, trends and shapes. Stat. 1986;**35**(3)

[27] Cai Y, Hames D. Minimum sample size determination for generalized extreme value distribution. Communication in Statistics- Simulation and Computation Ohio (USA). 2010;**40**(1)

[28] Coles S. An introduction to statistical Modeling of extreme values [Internet]. In: Lecture Notes in Control and Information Sciences. Springer; 2001. Available from: https://books.google.com.my/books?id=2nugUEaKqFEC

[29] Sim CH, Gan FF, Chang TC. Outlier labeling with boxplot procedures. Journal of the American Statistical Association Ohio (USA). 2005;**100**(470): 642-652

[30] Potter TD, Colman BR. Handbook of Weather, Climate, and Water: Atmospheric Chemistry, Hydrology, and Societal Impacts [Internet]. Hoboken N. J: Wiley-Interscience; 2003. 1020 p. Available from: http://www.worldcat.org/title/handbook-of-weather-climate-and-water-atmospheric-chemistry-hydrology-and-societal-impacts/oclc/123158897 [Accessed: January 6, 2018]

[31] Brillinger DR. Time Series: Data Analysis and Theory. Soc Ind Appl Math, 2001 [Internet]; 2001. pp. 392-540. Available from: https://epubs.siam.org/page/terms [Accessed: February 15, 2022]

[32] Castillo E. Extreme Value Theory in Engineering. London: Academic Press; 1988

Chapter 2

Key Concepts and Challenges in Industrial Processes with a Focus on Defining Target Variables in Multi-Stage Production and Batch Data

Manuela Larissa Schreyer

Abstract

In addition to topics such as data heterogeneity and missing values, there are numerous other issues that arise in the industrial context when optimizing processes using data-derived methods. A key issue is often the determination of an appropriate target variable that is comparable across all samples in the database, which is critical to the success of any analysis. A particular challenge arises when defects occur at the beginning of the process chain but are only detected at the end, given that products undergo 10 to 20 different systems in the meantime, undergoing several forming steps that influence defect detectability. A further challenge that is present in many industries is process data that describes entire batches. The challenge arises from the fact that all products in a batch often have the same process data, while the product quality within batches often varies considerably. This necessitates a comprehensive analysis to calculate a target variable for a batch. The chapter provides a detailed discussion of these challenges associated with the analysis of industrial process data. Additionally, it offers a perspective on the utilization of data analysis for the purpose of process optimization.

Keywords: industrial processes, target variable definition, multi-stage production, batch data, process data analysis, process optimization

1. Introduction

In the context of the ongoing digitalization of industry, the field of data science has emerged as a central element in numerous industrial domains, with the purpose of improving, monitoring, and analyzing production processes. This development can be attributed to the growing demand for increased product quality and sustainability [1–3].

In the industrial context, when processes are optimized using data-driven methods, a number of challenges must be addressed:

In order to ensure efficient data processing, there is, for example, a need for cloud storage as a scalable storage option (e.g., AWS, Azure) and highly developed ETL processes (Extract-Transform-Load). These enable data to be extracted from various sources, transformed, and converted into a standardized schema [4–6]. The utilization of high-performance computing devices or cloud-based platforms is imperative for the establishment of an AI infrastructure. In addition, AI tools and analysis platforms are required, such as BI tools, machine learning platforms, and AI services [7, 8].

In addition to the challenges that arise in relation to the infrastructure, there are other aspects that need to be considered. For instance, data is sometimes incomplete or incorrect, for example, due to sensor errors or failures.

Furthermore, the allocation of process data to a final product and to a specific position on the product (time-length transformation) poses a significant challenge.

A further characteristic of many industrial companies is the very broad product range. This characteristic is further compounded by the tendency of specialty products to be produced in limited quantities. Consequently, the establishment of a comparable target variable for multiple products is imperative for their use in data analysis.

In numerous companies, a significant aspect pertains to the batch-based production of numerous products, wherein the quality of the products within a batch can exhibit considerable variability, despite the process data of the individual elements of the batch often being the same.

Furthermore, the tracking of defects over the entire process chain is of paramount importance, particularly in instances where a defect is caused at the beginning of the process and can only be detected at the end of the entire process chain. The interpretation of such data typically necessitates a deep understanding of the process, which requires close collaboration with the engineers.

It is acknowledged that there are numerous other significant aspects in this context. The subsequent discussion will describe key concepts for some of the challenges using selected examples.

The focus of this chapter is on the challenges that arise when calculating a target variable for analyses of process data in an industrial environment. The subject of the chapter is "multi-stage production processes," which are common in many industrial sectors.

A central problem in this context is that defects that manifest themselves at the beginning of the production chain can often only be detected at the end—after numerous process steps, some of which are separate from one another. This makes it difficult to recognize the cause-and-effect relationships between early process parameters and quality characteristics that occur later. Consequently, it is difficult to reliably calculate a target variable and to build robust prediction and data analysis models, as relevant information must be correctly assigned across the entire process chain.

In addition, special features of batch-based production are discussed, which entail further complexity in the calculation of target variables. The methods presented in the article are illustrated using a specific example from aluminum production, but can also be transferred to other manufacturing areas with batch-based production and/or high process complexity in several process steps.

The example described in the article combines several typical challenges of industrial processes. Dimensional changes during production, batch processing, changes in aggregate states, and multi-stage process control must be taken into account. Such conditions, or parts thereof, manifest in various sectors, including the metalworking industry, the chemical industry, food processing, pharmaceutical production, and other sectors in which precise control and analysis of highly complex processes are essential.

2. The process under discussion in the examples

In the present contribution, an analysis of production data from the aluminum processing industry is carried out using key concepts from data science. The focus of the analysis examples is on the casting of aluminum ingots at AMAG Austria Metall AG.

The production chain depends on the product to be manufactured. In certain instances, it is possible for multiple systems to be utilized for the same end product.

The production process for the manufacture of aircraft sheet metal is shown schematically in **Figure 1**. The manufacturing process begins with input material and scrap sampling. The initial stage involves the melting down of the input material and its casting into ingots. The subsequent rolling process, which extends over a period of several weeks, involves a series of steps including homogenization, rolling, heat treatment, stretching, and cutting [9]. Concluding the process are quality checks, ensuring that the requirements, which vary according to the intended use of the final product, are met [10].

Defects may already be created during the casting process. For instance, non-metallic inclusions can occur in the material. The underlying causes of such defects can be traced back to the initial phase of the production process, the casting process. These defects may be attributed to the quality of the input material, the chemical composition of the alloy, or certain sensor measurements during the melting and casting process. Due to technical limitations, the detection of such defects is only feasible in the final product. This is achieved through the implementation of ultrasonic testing on the finished panels.

In this context, the first major challenge that arises in an industrial context should be mentioned, namely the calculation of a target variable that requires the tracking of an entire process chain. This is discussed in detail in the following section.

A casting batch consists of up to six individual ingots. The majority of the process data is batch-related and identical for all ingots within a batch. However, it is important to note that the quality of the products can vary considerably within a batch. The subsequent section will explore methodologies to address these challenges.

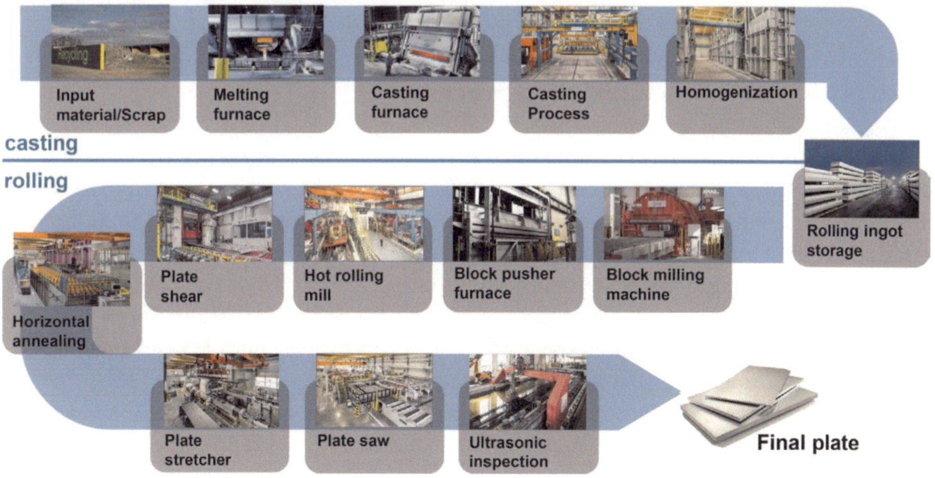

Figure 1.
Process rout.

The subsequent examples illustrate the critical importance of defining an appropriate target variable for data analysis. The concluding remarks of this chapter provide a comprehensive summary of the most important results and offer a final answer to the relevance of calculating a suitable target variable.

3. Example 1

Process fluctuations during aerospace material production can result in non-metallic inclusions. The subsequent production process involves several weeks of steps, including homogenization, rolling, heat treatment, and a final quality control check (see **Figure 1**). A range of tests are conducted as part of the quality control process, including ultrasonic testing to detect non-metallic inclusions [9, 10]. However, the inherent limitations of these methods mean that defects can only be recognized after production. If a specific number of inclusions are detected, this results in the rejection of the entire plate.

Examining historical data allows the identification of factors contributing to quality variation during the casting process and causing non-metallic inclusions. This, in turn, allows countermeasures to be implemented to reduce scrap rates, improve plant utilization, and reduce delivery times.

4. Example 2

In the process of continuous casting, liquid aluminum is continuously poured into a cooled mold where it solidifies. During the casting process, the formation of cracks within the ingot is a possibility, which can consequently result in the entire ingot being rejected. Longitudinal cracks, which are favored by inadequate casting parameters or certain alloy compositions, for example, are of particular concern in this example. These cracks typically manifest during the initial phase of the casting process. The question that arises from this is which factors (process parameters) may favor the formation of cracks in the casting ingot during the casting process [2].

5. Target variable in a multi-step process

A very common scenario in industrial processes is the occurrence of defects in certain work steps that are noticed later in the production chain. Typically, a large number of further processing steps are carried out during which the original defect remains undetected. Only during the final quality inspection, the defect is detected. In certain instances, the precise process step, which is the origin of the defect, remains unknown without further investigation. This poses a particular challenge to the company. In such instances, a full analysis of the entire process chain is essential, which requires tracing the defect through a number of systems and processes [11].

In many cases, however, the process step in which the error occurred is known. In such instances, the error must be traced back to the process step in question. This approach is a simplification of the scenario described above, but it is still highly complex. The previously described example 1 of non-metallic inclusions occurring during the casting process describes exactly this case.

5.1 Definition of the target variable

In the first step, it is necessary to define what is meant by a target variable. The target variable is the variable whose values are to be explained in data analyses. Cause-effect relationships should be established between the independent variables and the dependent variable, the target variable. The independent variables may be statistically associated with the target variable, but this does not automatically imply a causal relationship [12].

In an industrial company like AMAG, statistical models and data analysis are used to find correlations that would otherwise remain undetected. Even if a strong correlation is found between two variables, random chance and other possible distorting factors are taken into account in the decision-making process, and a technical explanation is sought together with the responsible technologists before decisions are made. Controlled experiments are also often conducted to verify causality [13, 14].

In example 1, the independent parameters may include, for instance, the parameters of the melting and casting process, the scrap groups of the input material, or the content of certain chemical elements that characterize the alloy. The target variable in this example describes the product quality in terms of non-metallic inclusions. The question, therefore, arises as to which approach is best suited for calculating the target variable.

Figure 2 shows schematically the aerospace plate production process. In one batch, up to six ingots are cast. This is shown at the top of the diagram. Process variations during casting can lead to non-metallic inclusions in the production of aerospace

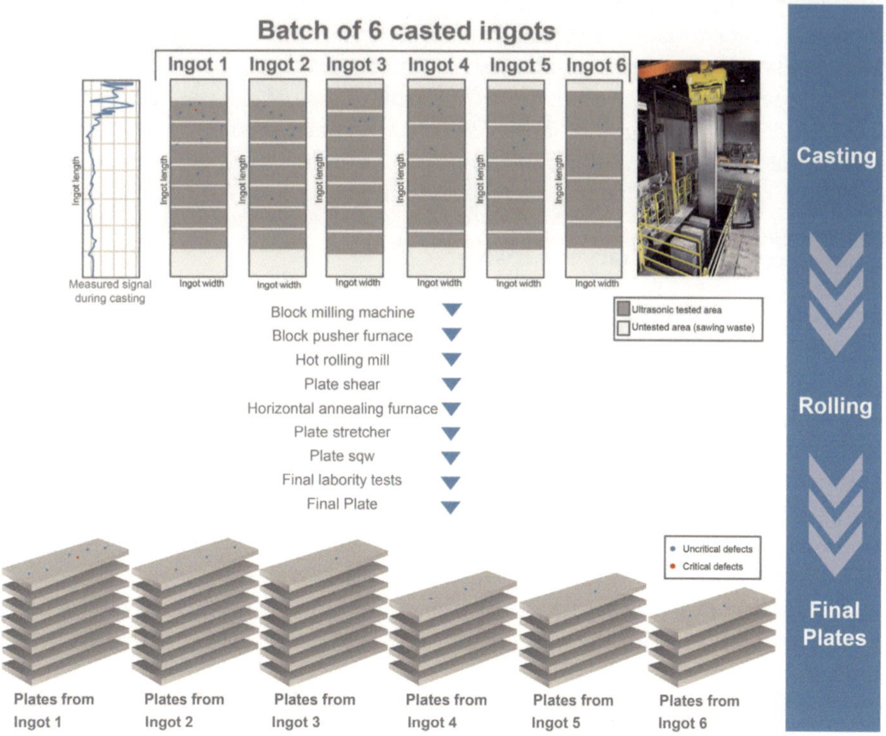

Figure 2.
Production process.

material. In the middle of the picture, the subsequent production process is shown, which takes several weeks and includes a series of steps such as homogenization, rolling, heat treatment, and final quality control. Different plate sizes are produced from each ingot, depending on the customer's requirements. In this particular instance, seven thin plates were produced from the initial ingot (ingot 1), while four thick plates were produced from the sixth ingot (ingot 6). The finished product is inspected for variations in quality using a variety of methods, including ultrasonic testing to detect non-metallic inclusions [9, 10]. Due to the inherent limitations of this method, however, defects can only be detected on the finished product after production. The ultrasonic test results are illustrated on the final plates in **Figure 2** at the bottom. Blue markers indicate uncritical findings, while red markers indicate critical findings. As already mentioned before, the presence of a substantial number of non-metallic inclusions can result in the rejection of the entire final plate.

The ultrasonic inspection facilitates the precise determination of the defect location and size, thereby establishing a foundation for the calculation of a target variable. The challenges that must be addressed to define a target variable that describes the casting quality, independent of the subsequent rolling process, are outlined below.

Ultrasonic testing is utilized to ascertain the dimensions and location of defects in the plates. However, in order to obtain a variable that represents the original casting quality before the processing steps in the rolling mill, it is necessary to trace the entire process chain. A number of aspects must be considered in numerous industrial sectors where products must be tracked over an entire process chain. In this context, the question arises as to whether the rejection rate, in example 1 defined as the proportion of plates in a batch that were rejected, is a sufficient metric for evaluating the casting quality. In a multi-step process, it is generally not readily possible to use the reject rate of the final product as a target variable. A comprehensive overview outlining a general procedure for the calculation of a target variable in a multi-step process is provided in Section 7.

The subsequent section will demonstrate why the reject rates in many cases are not suitable for defining a target variable. This is particularly evident in numerous industrial scenarios, where the number of rejects can be significantly influenced by factors such as the final format, the process route, or similar factors.

5.2 Pure reject rates as a target variable?

The initial step in this process is to ascertain the underlying database for the analysis. In examples 1 and 2, this is the process data for the casting of an entire batch, whereby all elements of the batch, i.e., all ingots, have the same process data. Consequently, it is imperative to define a target variable that accurately captures the quality of the batch. In instances where all elements (ingots) within a batch have exactly the same process data, it makes no sense to perform data analysis or train a model at the level of individual ingots, because you would be giving the analysis/model the same input for many data points (the individual ingots), but possibly different target variables. This inconsistency would lead to a poor analysis/model.

The definition of a target variable for the entire batch is predicated on the definition of a target variable for the individual ingots in the batch. In example 1, the individual ingots in a batch consist of individual plates. In this context, the question arises as to whether it is logical to define the target variable for the individual ingots via the proportion of scrap plates produced from an ingot.

Figure 3 shows the scrap rate due to non-metallic inclusions (i.e., too many or too large inclusions detected by ultrasonic testing in a plate) per ingot for different final

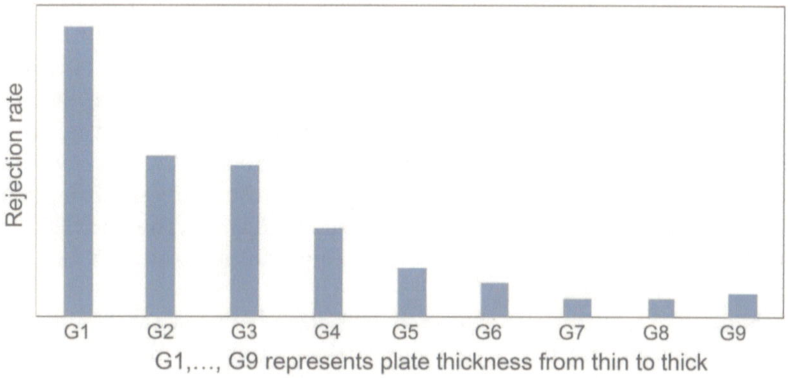

Figure 3.
Rejection rate per ingot—example 1.

plate thicknesses. In other words, the proportion of plates produced from an ingot that were rejected due to non-metallic inclusions. It is important to note that only plates of the same width and thickness format are produced from an ingot. It can be clearly seen that the scrap rate depends on the final plate thickness. The thinner the final plates, the higher the scrap rate. It is clear that the target variable describing the final casting quality must not be dependent on the final product, because when the ingot is cast, it is not yet known which final plate thickness format will be produced from the ingot. In other words, all the ingots considered for these aerospace plates have a specific ingot thickness format of x mm and can be used to produce any final plate thickness format from G1 to G9.

In the event of a significant relationship between the target variable and another variable, which is not to be included in the data analysis as a potential influencing variable, this will nevertheless have a strong influence on the analysis and will have a negative impact on the analysis result or the model. Consequently, it is imperative to explore methodologies for incorporating this parameter into the analysis. In instances where a technical cause is identified, as illustrated in Section 7, this can be incorporated into the calculation of a suitable target variable. A comprehensive elaboration of this methodology can be found in Section 5.3 under the heading "Hidden correlation."

The decision of whether to utilize the rejection rate for the definition of the target variable is not a straightforward one, and the most appropriate course of action depends on the particular circumstances of each case.

The response to this question is contingent on the particular issue under consideration and the available data. In the context of example 2, where the causes of rejects from a single piece (ingot) of a batch are investigated in the process data of the batches, the following question needs to be asked. If the information regarding the scrap due to this particular defect is available, this could be suitable for the definition of the target variable (as in example 2: scrap due to cracks in the ingots). In such instances, the proportion of cracked ingots within a batch would be calculated. However, this approach is only feasible if the scrap due to a specific defect is known; if multiple defect patterns are present in the scrap rate, this can result in a loss of interpretability by the model/analysis.

Furthermore, as previously outlined, it is imperative to ascertain the absence of a "hidden correlation" (detailed information on this can be found in Section 5.3).

In addition, it should be noted that even a single error in small batches (e.g., six pieces per batch) can significantly distort the rate (17%). This can result in high variability and instability of the analysis/model. In such cases, it can therefore be useful to categorize the scrap rate into, for example, "good," "medium," or "bad" scrap rates. Alternatively, a binary target variable can be defined, such as "batch with rejects above vs. below a certain tolerance limit." It is important to acknowledge that the majority of industrial processes are highly optimized so that very little scrap is produced in the first place (as in example 2). In such scenarios, the establishment of a binary target variable, such as "at least one scrap ingot in the batch" vs. "batch without scrap," can be defined.

Furthermore, it is relevant to consider the variation between batches, as it is only with sufficient variation that meaningful correlations can be identified (e.g., between 0% and 20% scrap). In other cases, the application of categorization is frequently beneficial. This approach is particularly relevant in contexts where industrial processes are considered to be highly efficient and optimized, and rejections are rare.

Here is an overview of the two examples. In example 2, the available data pertains exclusively to the rejection rate attributable to cracked ingots. In this instance, it is recommended to categorize the analysis into two distinct groups: The first group comprises batches that contain at least one cracked ingot, while the second group consists of batches without cracked ingots. This approach is logical, given that the reject rate per ingot is minimal and only batch-related process parameters are available for analysis. This approach contrasts with example 1, in which the exact size and position of the defect in the plates are available. This is a far better way of defining a target variable than a target variable based on the scrap rate.

5.3 Hidden connections

In the field of data analysis, the significance of "hidden correlations" is frequently underestimated, which can result in unrecognized and consequently bad performance in analyses and models, or even incorrect results.

The term "hidden correlations" is defined as follows. It is a statistical phenomenon in which there is a significant correlation between the target variable and another "external" variable, which is not a possible influencing variable. This variable should not be incorporated into the model/analysis as an additional variable because it is unknown when the process takes place (i.e., casting of the ingot in example 1), it cannot be influenced (the final sheet format is not known when the ingot is cast), and is not relevant to process optimization (only casting parameters are the cause of non-metallic inclusions). In the first example, all three of these criteria are met.

Figure 4 shows the plate thickness on the x-axis and the sum of detected defect areas per ingot on the y-axis (both variables normalized to the interval [0,1]). The trend line (blue line in the figure) acts as an indicator of the relationship between two variables. The function "geom_smooth()" in the statistical software R with the method "loess" (Locally Estimated Scatterplot Smoothing) performs a local regression for this purpose [15–19].

This non-linear technique can be employed in instances where non-linear dependencies are present. By default, a linear regression is adjusted in each local area, a process that can be controlled via the parameter "degree." In this example, the value of "degree" was set to 2. The "span" parameter specifies the proportion of data points that is taken into account for the local adjustment. Specifying "span = 0.75" would, for instance, imply that 75% of the data points would be taken into account in the calculation.

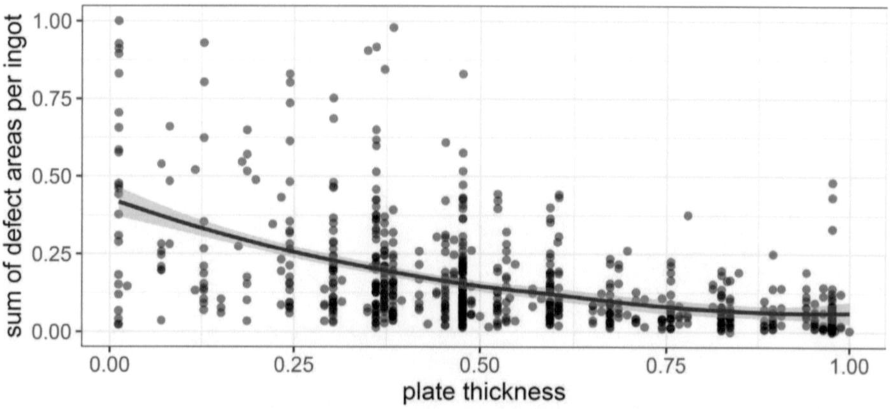

Figure 4.
Example 1—sum of defects per ingot.

The confidence interval (default: 95%) indicates the uncertainty of the estimated trend line. It is important to note that the band does not represent a prediction interval for new data points; rather, it calculates a confidence interval for the corresponding estimated y-value for each x-value [15–19]. It is notable that the band tends to be more expansive at the edges of the data, where the uncertainty is greater because there are fewer points available for local estimation.

Figure 4 clearly shows that there is a strong relationship between the sum of defect areas and the plate thickness. It is evident that this target variable is not suitable for comparison across different plate thickness formats.

The question that arises in this context is what approach can be recommended in such a case.

Assuming that the "confounding variable" is known, which represents a "hidden correlation," as is the case in example 1, there are various possibilities.

The primary option involves the division of the data into groups based on the "confounding variable," followed by the analysis of the correlations within each group. The advantage of this approach is that analyses can be carried out relatively easily without having to take the influence of the "confounding variable" into account. However, this approach is associated with a substantial reduction in the sample size for each group. This can be particularly problematic for industrial processes, where the sample size for specialty products, which are usually of particular interest for analysis, is already relatively small from the outset. In instances where the number of distinct groups is large, as in example 1, where each final plate format represents a group, comparable groups could be created, wherein each group has similar plate thickness formats. The groups $G_1, \dots, G_8$ illustrated in **Figure 5** exemplify this approach. The *cut*() function is used to divide a numeric variable "plate thickness" into intervals, which can then be used as groups [18, 19].

Another option is to neutralize the "confounding variables" using statistical approaches. For this purpose, a model is created that defines the target variable as the dependent variable and the confounding variable as the independent variable. The residuals (actual-predicted target variable) are then calculated and used as the new target variable for the analysis. This approach ensures that the further analysis only explains the part that is not already explained by the confounding variable.

In **Figure 6**, the normalization of the y-values with the smoothing curve is achieved through the subtraction of the estimate of the smoothing from the actual values.

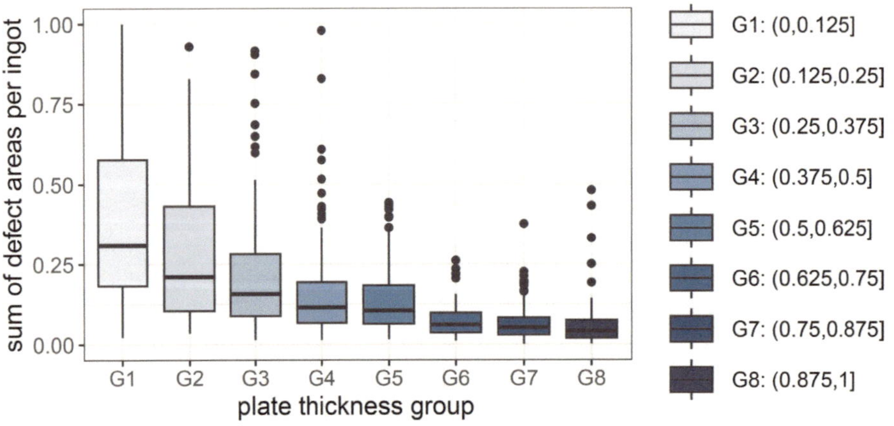

Figure 5.
Example 1—boxplot defect area per ingot.

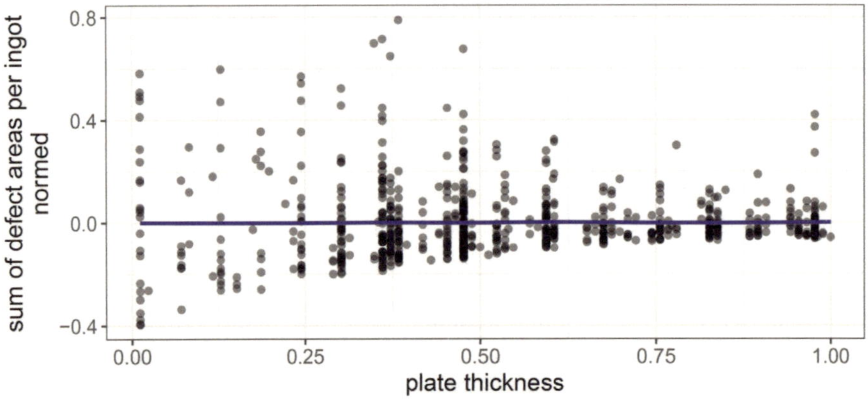

Figure 6.
Example 1—sum of defects per ingot normed.

The trend was eliminated, yet the scatter around 0 in **Figure 6** demonstrates variability contingent on the plate thickness format. These are called heteroscedastic residuals [20]. This phenomenon manifests as dependency-based variance along the x-axis. The correction of this heterogeneous variance can be achieved through a process of stabilizing the variance [20]. The aim of this procedure is to achieve a homogeneous variance along the x-axis.

The local standard deviation is estimated for each point on the basis of neighboring plate thickness values, whereby all residuals within a plate thickness window of ± 0.1 are taken into account in **Figure 7**. Subsequently, each residual is divided by the local standard deviation, resulting in a new residual series with stabilized variance. Under ideal conditions, these standardized residuals should have a constant scatter around 0 [18, 19, 21, 22].

An alternative approach involves a combination of the aforementioned methods, namely grouping and normalization, and also tends to neutralize the "confounding variable." The procedure is to form comparable groups as described above and "normalize" with the quasi-inverse distribution function. The results of this

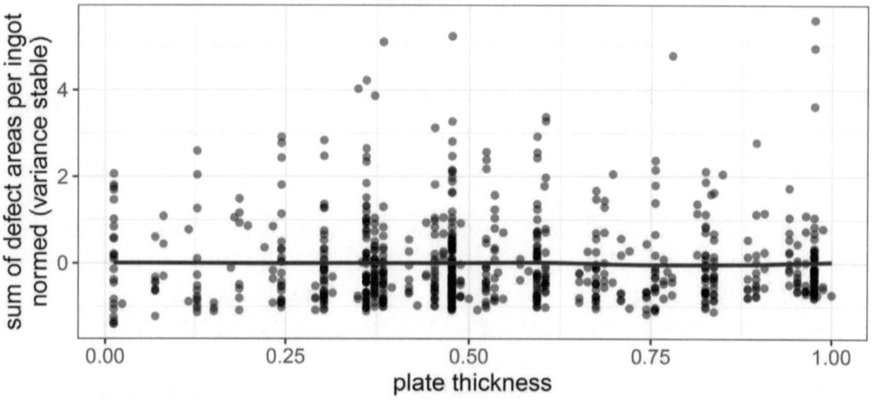

Figure 7.
Example 1 sum of defects per ingot normed and variance stable.

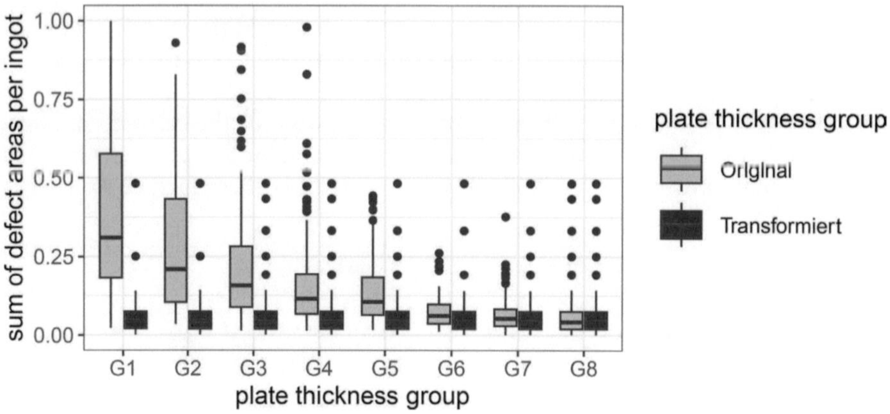

Figure 8.
Example 1—data transformation to distribution of group G8.

transformation are illustrated in **Figure 8** for example 1. The data was transformed to the distribution of the last group G_8 (target distribution of the transformation). Initially, the inverse distribution function F_{inv,G_8} of the distribution of the y-values in group G_8 was calculated. For each of the remaining groups, an empirical cumulative distribution function, F_{G_i}, was calculated using the *ecdf*() function in R on the basis of observed values of group G_i, $i = 1, \ldots 7$. The calculation of $F_{inv,G_8}(F_{G_i}(.))$ was then undertaken, converting the values of group Gi so that they retain their rank structure, but take on the distributional form of the values of group G_8 (see Probability Integral Transformation and Quantile Transformation [18, 19, 23]). **Figure 8** clearly shows that the transformed boxplots (blue) all have the same shape.

Appendix A contains a detailed synthetic example with R code, in which the individual calculations of the target variable are shown with plots and comments for interpreting the results.

The benefit of these methodologies is that the “confounding variable” can be easily neutralized using statistical methods. A notable disadvantage of these approaches is the absence of a technical explanation or interpretation that could provide a justification for these approaches. In instances where the sample size is minimal, data-driven approaches frequently encounter limitations, as estimates only attain the necessary precision with a substantial sample size. This problem also manifests itself in examples 1 and 2. In such cases, an approach that incorporates technical expertise is imperative. In the following Sections 5.4 and 7, example 1 will be used to illustrate an approach in which the "confounding variable" was neutralized by tracing the entire process chain.

The choice of the target variable cannot be generalized, as it always depends on the specific question and the respective context. Depending on the problem to be solved, a different target variable may be considered appropriate. The available data and its quality also have a significant influence on this decision. **Table 1** provides an overview of example 1 (non-metallic inclusion).

In a large number of industrial applications, only the reject rate is available. The first thing to check is whether multiple defect patterns can be found in the rejection rate and whether the feature to be analyzed can be clearly characterized by them. The reject rate can therefore be used as a target variable, provided that the above-mentioned conditions are met.

If more detailed quality characteristics are available in addition to the scrap rate, it is advisable to check whether these contain more information and thus contribute to the calculation of a more suitable target variable.

In Example 2, as shown in Section 6, the starting point for the calculation of the target variable is the information on the rejection of an ingot due to cracks, because this was the only information available. It was decided to collect further data for later

Target variable per ingot	Figure	Pro	Contra
Rejection rate	**Figure 3**	Easy available	Only feasible if no multiple defect patterns are present in the rejection rate.
			Binary information about rejection rate of plates (number of defects is not considered). ⇒ Less variety in the data.
			Highly dependent on plate thickness ⇒ No comparable groups.
Sum of defects per ingot	**Figure 4**	More detailed information about final quality	Highly dependent on plate thickness ⇒ No comparable groups.
Sum of defects per ingot normed	**Figure 6**	Elimination of trend based on plate thickness	Variability contingent on the plate thickness format (heteroscedastic residuals) ⇒ No comparable groups.[a]
Sum of defects per ingot normed and variance stable	**Figure 7**	Correction of heterogeneous variance	To get comparable groups, these standardized residuals should ideally have a constant scatter around 0.[a]
Data transformation to distribution of one group	**Figure 8**	Comparable groups	[a]

[a]*Estimates only attain the necessary precision with a substantial sample size; absence of a technical explanation or interpretation.*

Table 1.
Target variable—overview for example 1.

analyses in order to define a more precise target variable. As part of the investigation, the ingots were characterized in detail with experts and various types of cracks and their lengths were determined. It is no longer possible to generate this information for historical data. As a consequence, an evaluation on a target variable containing this additional information became impossible with historical data. It can nevertheless be advantageous to collect additional data that can be analyzed at a later date. In many cases, such data leads to new insights. Particularly for projects that are designed over a longer period of time, it is advisable to check at the start of the project whether the collection of additional data will generate added value when analyzing the data.

The early and forward-looking planning of data collection makes a significant contribution to creating the basis for well-founded analyses and long-term knowledge gain.

5.4 Definition of the target variable in processes with several consecutive work steps: General aspects in the industrial sector

In the following discussion, the steps that are relevant in many industrial areas when defining a target variable in processes with several consecutive work steps will be considered. The subsequent analysis is based on Example 1; a detailed explanation can be found in Section 7.

The initial step in this process is to calculate a target variable at the lowest unit level. In Example 1, this is represented by a target variable per plate. This is followed by a reflection on which data should be analyzed. In this instance, the focus is on process data for the individual batches. The subsequent steps are therefore to calculate a target variable per ingot and then per batch. In instances where additional unit levels are involved in the production process, it is generally advisable to follow this procedure sequentially.

In Example 1, the target variable is first calculated per ingot and then per batch. In order to carry out the required investigations into "hidden connections," it is necessary to trace the entire production process of the individual pieces and to carry out investigations into potential influencing variables (hidden connections) on the defect to be analyzed at each production step. In Example 1, it is imperative that the entire rolling process is subject to complete traceability, extending from the cast ingots to the finished plates. The question that naturally follows is how this can be achieved.

In cooperation with the technologists of the respective specialist department, "hidden connections" were identified in Example 1, as described later. Firstly, a general procedure is described that can probably be applied in many industrial areas.

Initially, it must be determined which requirements are necessary and which are fulfilled.

1. Firstly, a consistent tracking ID is required for each piece, coil, batch, plate, or part.

2. It must also be clarified whether the products are rotated, e.g., whether the start and end or top and bottom are swapped, and whether this is digitally recorded.

3. It is also essential that the position and dimensions of scrap-cut pieces are precisely recorded.

Afterward, it is advisable to ask yourself the following key questions:

1. Firstly, it should be determined what role scrap cuttings and therefore also untested areas play.
2. It should also be investigated whether products can be rotated (start/end or top/bottom).
3. Finally, it must be determined which forming steps are carried out during production, which can also have an influence on the defect's detection.
4. It must be determined whether other process parameters such as the temperature of the material play a significant role, as different densities affect different formats in hot and cold conditions. In the case of large dimensions, such as strips with a length of several kilometers, a deviation of a few percent can have a considerable effect.
5. Finally, the test method (in Example 1, the ultrasonic test) should also be analyzed for its limitations.

In the following discussion, the individual steps are analyzed in more detail using example 1.

1. Firstly, the forming steps (e.g., rolling, bending, stretching) are discussed. In example 1, the main forming steps are carried out by rolling or stretching (the material is stretched to minimize internal stresses). The process of mechanical forming has been shown to induce changes in the material, which in turn leads to alterations in the dimensions of non-metallic inclusions. FEM simulations (Finite element method) of mechanical forming can be used to model this relationship (see [24]). A detailed analysis of the parameters relating to temperatures or forming forces, for example, can be undertaken in order to facilitate a more accurate understanding of their influence on defect size [25].
2. Scrap cuts (e.g., head/end cutting or cuts during production or milling the top and bottom of the product) are addressed as a secondary topic in the investigation. These can result in defects being hidden because they are in the scrap cut and therefore not detected in the final inspection. Consequently, the number of defects detected in the product can vary depending on the extent of the scrap cuts made. It is crucial to ensure that the precise dimensions of the scrap cuts along the production chain are recorded so that the exact position of the defect in the finished product can be calculated back to the starting material, in example 1 the cast ingot. In this case, it is possible to create models/analyses separately for the section classified as "relevant" for the analysis (for example, the middle section without the start and end areas). This is particularly recommended when the error frequency varies over the course of the process of material production. In a significant number of processes, the initial stage of material production is a critical sector in which inconsistencies can accumulate. In such cases, it is advisable to carry out a separate analysis for the different areas.
3. In the subsequent course of the discussion, the topic of "rotation/repositioning of products" will be addressed. In the event of rotation or turning of products (e.g.,

when an ingot is turned around), position information can be lost if it is not explicitly tracked. In such cases, it is no longer possible to calculate the error positions back to the original material. The assignment of start and end areas of the product, for example, is no longer possible.

4. The subsequent stage of the investigation will involve determining whether the material's temperature exerts an influence on its format. It is important to note that varying densities can result in different formats in both the hot and cold states. It is important to note that, for instance, in the case of strips with a length of several kilometers, even minor deviations of a few percent can have a substantial impact. In Example 1, this is of paramount importance, as different densities affect different formats in hot and cold conditions. It is important to note that the material temperature can fluctuate significantly. Indeed, it can vary from a few hundred degrees after casting to room temperature, and even to the outside climate during storage. Furthermore, material elongation can result from approximately seven-meter-long ingots to a coil several kilometers long.

5. In the final step, a detailed analysis of the final product quality test method itself and its limitations is required. This problem is one of the essential aspects. It is evident that the measurement results can be influenced by a variety of factors. These factors include, for example, the sensor resolution or calibration, the sampling position, or even the position of the measuring sensor. This can lead to inaccuracies or bias. In many cases, only specific areas of the material are tested and not the entire final product (especially in destructive material testing). Determining the measurement accuracy, implausible and missing data, or untested areas is essential for further analysis. In example 1, for instance, there is a 3 mm zone on the bottom and top of the plate that is untested during ultrasonic testing and is subsequently milled away. It is recommended to implement strategies to deal with missing data, such as data imputation. In addition, precise recording of calibrations is required, as this is the only way to ensure that they are taken into account in the analyses (see [26]). This is important, for example, when correcting measured values or estimating measurement uncertainties.

Section 7 provides a compact description of the individual aspects using example 1. Detailed explanations can be found in the work of Schreyer et al. [25, 27].

6. Challenges when analyzing batch data

This section will address several of the most relevant aspects of batch data. As previously discussed, the concept of "small batches" is of paramount importance. When dealing with low quantities (e.g., five items in a batch) and taking into account the potential for rejection, a single error can have a substantial impact on the rejection rate (20%). This results in an increase in the target noise and an instability of the model/analysis. The categorization of the rate into distinct categories, such as "low," "medium," or "high" reject rates, can be a useful analytical approach. An alternative option is to define a binary target variable, such as "rejection rate above a certain tolerance limit." In highly optimized industrial processes, the generation of scrap is minimized from the outset. In this context, the binary target variable "at least one reject part in the batch" versus "batch without rejects" proves to be useful.

In example 2, the challenge is to define a target variable for each batch when the only information available is that an ingot of the batch is to be classified as scrap due to cracks. **Figure 9** shows an exemplary sequence of consecutively produced batches. Four to six ingots are produced per batch. Gray ingots represent produced ingots without cracks, orange ingots show cracked ingots, and white positions indicate that no ingots were produced at these positions. In this case, a binary target variable is defined that describes the status of the batch. Specifically, a distinction is made between the situation where there is at least one cracked ingot in the batch and the situation where there is no cracked ingot in the batch. The latter applies to most batches. A detailed analysis of the crack rate, which allows a distinction to be made between "low," "medium," and "high" crack rates, only makes sense if the individual groups contain a correspondingly high number of instances.

Another challenge is posed by cases with a low number of defects (examples 1 and 2), from which a low variance can be derived. In order to ensure sufficient variation between the batches and to be able to identify meaningful correlations, it is therefore often advisable to subdivide the target variable into categories for cases with a low number of defects. As industrial processes can generally be regarded as highly efficient and optimized and only rarely lead to rejections, this is a practicable approach.

An additional challenge arises in particular in situations in which a large number of batches with significant quality differences have similar process data. It is then almost impossible to identify patterns using a statistical model.

In such cases, a strong variance in the quality of individual batches can occur, which can be attributed to outlier elements within the batch (i.e., outlier elements of particularly poor or good quality compared to the other elements in the batch). However, these outliers are not due to process data relating to the entire batch, but only to data relating to the individual element of the batch. When analyzing process data relating to the entire batch, it is essential to identify these "outlier elements" and exclude them when calculating the target variables for analyzing batch data.

Figure 9 shows that there were three consecutive batches with cracks at ingot position 6. Such a sequence is referred to as a "crack-ingot sequence." The question is whether such a constellation can occur purely by chance. If this is very unlikely, the cause cannot be explained by batch-related parameters. Such cracks should not be taken into account when analyzing batch-related parameters. In the following, a probability of occurrence was therefore estimated for each sequence of consecutive cracked ingots (as in this example at position 6). In the database, 38% of the cracked ingots are a "crack-ingot sequence." For each of these ingots, the probability of occurrence of this sequence of consecutive cracked ingots is estimated by Monte Carlo

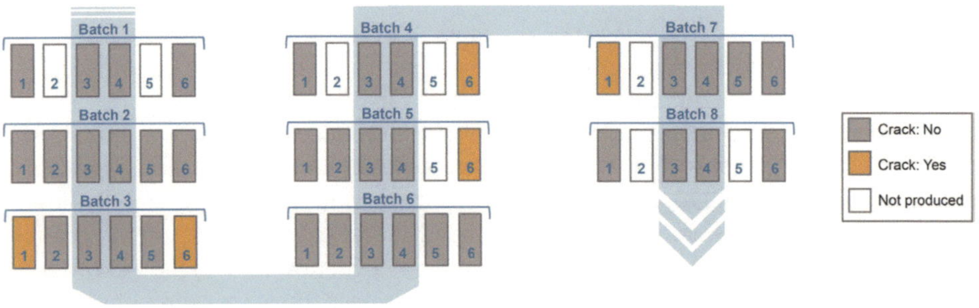

Figure 9.
Example 2—batch sequence.

simulations, assuming that the position of cracked ingots within a batch is purely random. If the probability of occurrence of this sequence is low, then these ingots are excluded from the analysis of batch-related process data [2, 19, 28].

Appendix B provides a detailed, synthetic example of how to use Monte Carlo simulations in this context, implemented in R.

A similar procedure can be observed in the definition of a target variable in example 1. A detailed description can be found in Section 7.

7. Definition of the target variable: Example 1

A detailed description of the calculation of the target variable in example 1, taking into account the entire process chain from the casting of the ingots to the final ultrasonic testing of the plates, can be found in the work of Schreyer et al. [25, 27].

To summarize, the following points in particular must be taken into account in the calculation. Firstly, it is necessary to take into account the scrap cuts mentioned in Section 5.4. Furthermore, for technical reasons, it is impossible to subject the top and bottom three millimeters in the panel thickness direction to ultrasonic testing. This situation must also be taken into account, as the re-calculation on the cast ingot results in a proportion of between 24% and 4% of the ingot in the thick direction, depending on the plate thickness, which is not ultrasonic tested. This problem was solved by estimating the defect area (using an ML model) in the ultrasonic untested area in the thickness direction, which is dependent on the plate thickness and the defects detected in the plate (see [27]).

Section 5.3 "Hidden connection" refers to another influencing variable, namely the final panel thickness. A closer look also shows that the position of the defects in the plates in the thickness direction influences their size [25, 27]. Using FEM simulations of the forming behavior and statistical methods, a transformation was defined that is used in the re-calculation of the defect size from the plates to the ingot in order to take the aforementioned effect into account [25].

Ultimately, this results in a target variable per ingot, which can then be used to determine a target variable per batch. Similar to the second example, outlier ingots also occur within a batch that are characterized by significantly poorer or better quality compared to all other ingots in the same batch. In this case, the outliers must be calculated using Monte Carlo simulations as described in example 2 in Section 6. They are then no longer taken into account when calculating the target variable per batch (see [27]). The target variable per batch, which results from the median of the target variable per ingot without outliers, is referred to below as the quality measure per batch (results for quality measure per ingot see **Figure 10**). Given that the quality measure is based on the exact defect positions calculated back to the ingot, it is possible to calculate a target variable analogously for different ingot sections. This provides the crucial benefit that alterations in quality during the casting process can be considered, as is typical of numerous industrial procedures. The initial phase, specifically, poses significant difficulties and is frequently associated with an increase in product defects. Consequently, a quality criterion is then defined for each batch section [3, 27].

A comparison of the different target variables is now presented below. The investigation focuses on a signal that was recorded during the casting process. From a technical perspective, it is known that this signal has an influence on non-metallic inclusions. It is known that batches with higher signal values are associated with a lower number of non-metallic inclusions, which in turn means better quality. The results for the various target variables and the p-value for each are shown in **Figure 11** (The p-value was calculated using a non-parametric test [29]).

The first figure shows the analysis with the reject rate per batch as the target variable. There is no difference between batches with a high and low reject rate (p-value = 0.86). The analysis yielded no evidence to suggest that the signal influenced the reject rate in relation to non-metallic inclusions.

The upper figure shows the analysis for the target variable "Sum of defects per ingot normed and variance stable" from **Figure 7**, and the median per batch was calculated. It can be seen that the two groups with high and low target variables do not differ significantly (p-value = 0.29). Once more, no influence of the signal on the formation of non-metallic inclusions could be determined.

Furthermore, the calculation of the "Transformation to distribution of group G8" (see **Figure 8**) and the determination of the median per batch show no significant differences between the groups with a high and low target variable (p-value = 0.09), as illustrated in the plot located in the bottom right corner.

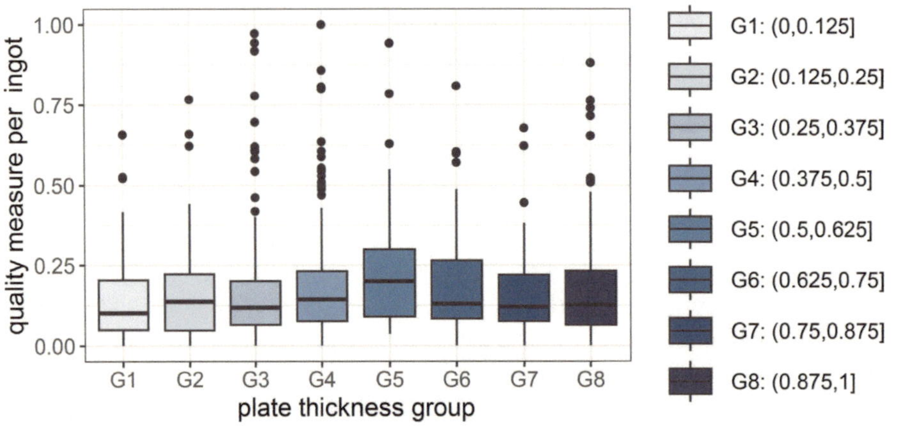

Figure 10.
Quality measure per ingot.

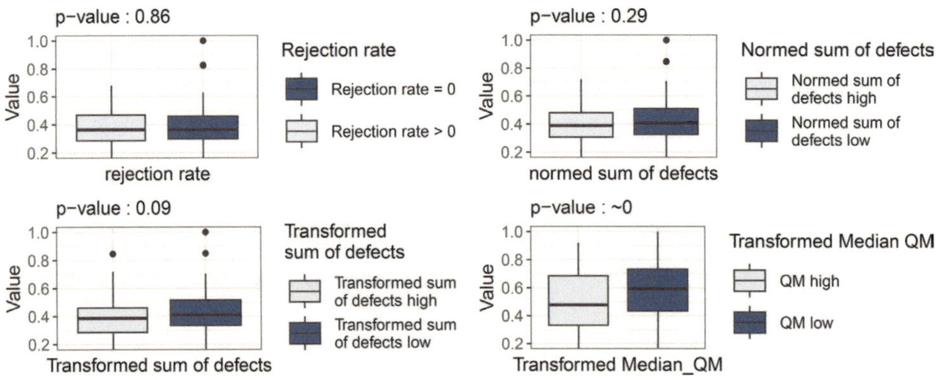

Figure 11.
Comparison of the different target variables from Sections 5.3 and 7.

DOI: http://dx.doi.org/10.5772/intechopen.1011564

Finally, in the lower left area of the plot, there is a representation of the quality measure per batch section, which was described at the beginning of this section, taking into account the entire process chain (results for quality measure per ingot see **Figure 10**). The quality measure for each batch section is derived from the quality measure per ingot, with the exclusion of any outlier ingots within a batch, for a specific phase of the casting process (in **Figure 10**, the section not including the start and end phases of casting is shown). There is a highly significant difference between the two groups (p-value 0.0). Batches that have a low quality measure (batches of good quality) have significantly higher values of the selected signal. As already mentioned, this is also the case from a technical perspective.

It is thus clear that a meaningful target variable that is free of "hidden connections" is an essential component of the analysis. The evidence for the influence of the selected signals on non-metallic inclusions can only be provided under the premise that a meaningful target variable is available.

8. Defining target variables in industry: A collaborative, iterative approach

The definition of a suitable target variable is of central importance in any data-driven project, particularly in an industrial context where processes are complex and data landscapes are challenging. However, it is a false impression that a target variable can be clearly and conclusively determined in a single step.

In practice, a structured starting point (possibly as part of a kick-off workshop) between data scientists and domain experts is often helpful in order to develop a common understanding of the project objective, formulate initial hypotheses on the target variable, and identify possible directions for the analysis.

The following questions can serve as a template/suggestion for a structured starting point (in the context of a kick-off workshop, for example) when determining a target variable:

1. Project objective and context:

   At the beginning, a common understanding of the overarching project objective should be established: For example, is it about increasing quality, efficiency, or reducing costs? It is important to clarify which processes, products, or decisions are in focus and which specific decisions the analysis should support in the future.

2. Collection of target variable ideas:

   Potential target variables are then identified. Which key figures or quality characteristics are important in the company and could be considered as target variables?

3. Formulating hypotheses:

   For each target variable idea, it is important to examine the conditions under which it would make sense. What are the underlying assumptions, and what physical, technical, or metrological limitations need to be taken into account? Known domain knowledge about possible influencing variables is particularly essential.

4. Understanding the production process:

   A basic understanding of the process chain is essential: Which systems and processing steps does the material go through until the relevant characteristics are measured? This is the only way to evaluate correlations between process parameters and target values.

5. Checking the data situation:

   The availability and quality of the data are crucial for feasibility. It must be clarified whether sufficient historical data is available, how complete and reliable it is, and which pre-processing steps would be necessary.

6. Defining the first steps:

   Finally, specific target variable hypotheses should be selected for in-depth analysis. It should be noted which open questions still need to be coordinated with specialist departments such as technology, quality assurance, or IT.

However, it should be noted that the actual definition of the target variables is undertaken as part of a longer, iterative process. Subsequently, the initial hypotheses formulated and discussed are then subjected to rigorous testing by data experts. Furthermore, consultations with the technology, quality assurance, or production departments are necessary to ensure technical validity.

There is no universal checklist that is suitable for all industrial processes. Each industrial process has its own physical, operational, and economic framework conditions. For example, the target values that are appropriate for a melting and rolling process can differ fundamentally from those for a packaging or logistics application.

Therefore, close, repeated coordination between domain-specific knowledge and data-analytical evaluation is particularly important, in addition to structural guiding questions. This collaboration is an essential component of a successful analysis process. It is the only way to create a target variable that is both meaningful and technically feasible, thereby creating real added value for the company.

9. Conclusion: Wrong target variable, wrong decisions

A fundamental challenge in data analysis and machine learning involves the definition of an appropriate target variable. This aspect exerts a substantial influence on the analysis result and consequently on the decisions based on it.

The following aspects must be considered when defining a target variable: The target variable is defined as the variable whose values are to be explained in data analyses. In the examples presented here, the focus is on the optimization of industrial processes with the aim of reducing scrap.

In the initial phase, the database of potential influencing variables must be identified in order to determine the target variable, in such a way that a causal relationship between the independent variables in this database and the target variable can be established. It is imperative to have a precise understanding of the process, the objectives, and the available data to ensure a correct definition of the target variable. It is evident that the definition of the target variable is not the exclusive responsibility of the data scientist. Indeed, the process necessitates close collaboration between data scientists and technical experts.

In certain instances, the rejection rate can be utilized as a criterion for defining the target variable. However, it should be noted that further calculation steps are generally required (see Section 5.2), particularly in instances where a target variable is defined per batch (see Section 6). In several cases, the pure rejection rate has been found to be an inadequate metric for defining the target variable, particularly in processes comprising multiple successive work steps (see Section 5.4). In such cases, so-called "hidden connections" often occur. This statistical phenomenon involves the presence of a substantial correlation between the target variable and an "external" variable, which is not a possible influencing variable. There exist general transformation methods that are suitable for neutralizing so-called "hidden connections." Further detailed explanations can be found in Section 5.3. However, it should be noted that the efficacy of this approach is contingent upon the quantity of observations. Data-driven methods are only able to yield satisfactory results when a sufficient number of observations are available. In other cases, with low sample size, an alternative approach to neutralizing the so-called "confounding variable" is recommended, in which the entire course of the production process is traced back (see Section 5.4 and Section 7).

In Section 7, a comparison is drawn between the various definitions of the target variable using a selected example. The aim of this comparison is to provide a practical illustration of the concepts discussed. The focus of this comparison is on a signal from the casting process, the influence of which on product quality is already known from a technical perspective. As part of the comparison, the pure scrap rate was used as the target variable, followed by a "normed and variance stable" target variable and a "distribution-transformed" target variable (detailed information on this can be found in Section 5.3). In conclusion, a target variable was utilized that serves to neutralize the confounding variable by tracing the entire production process. This example illustrates that the influence of the selected signal on product quality can only be demonstrated for the target variable if the confounding variable is neutralized by tracing the entire process chain. The present chapter demonstrates that a precise definition of the target variable is of crucial importance in order to identify influencing variables.

In the event of an inadequate definition of the target variable, what is the resultant consequence?

If the target variable is selected incorrectly, this will result in the model/analysis being trained on an incorrect target. This may result in relevant correlations and patterns not being identified or even incorrectly interpreted. Inadequate selection of the target variable is frequently the consequence of an insufficient understanding of the underlying process. Consequently, effective collaboration with technical experts is of central importance.

The definition of the target variable is not a minor technical aspect, but rather a critical success factor of every analysis and every machine learning model. If this aspect is not given adequate consideration, even highly developed algorithms are ineffective. In extreme cases, this can result in an incorrect assessment of the situation and consequent wrong decisions.

A. Appendix

```
library(dplyr) # Load required package
library(ggplot2)
set.seed(42) # Set seed for reproducibility

n_products <- 1000 # Number of products
product_ids <- 1:n_products # Generate unique product IDs

# Generate product classes G1 to G10 randomly
prod_classes <- sample(paste0("G", 1:10), n_products, TRUE)

# Convert product classes to numeric (G1 = 1, ..., G10 = 10)
product_class_num <- as.numeric(gsub("G", "", prod_classes))

# Define a quadratic relationship for the mean number of defects
# E.g.: mean = a * (10 - class)^2 + noise_offset
a <- 0.9 # scaling factor for shape
noise_offset <- 5 # base level of defects
mean_defects <- a * (10 - product_class_num)^2 + noise_offset

# Define class-dependent standard dev. (higher at lower classes)
# e.g., sd = b * sqrt(mean)
std_dev <- sqrt(mean_defects)

# Generate normally distributed number of defects (not clipped!)
n_defects <- round(rnorm(n_products, mean_defects, std_dev))

# Combine into dataframe
product_data <- data.frame(
  ID = product_ids,
  Product_Class = factor(prod_classes, levels=paste0("G", 1:10)),
  Product_Class_Num = as.numeric(gsub("G", "", prod_classes)),
  Number_of_Defects = n_defects)

# Define plotting funktions
Scatter_func <- function(data, x, y, Typ, tit, tit_x, tit_y){
  p <- ggplot(data, aes(x = x, y = y, color = Typ)) +
    # geom_jitter() is used to avoid overlapping
    geom_jitter(width = 0.2, alpha = 0.5) +
    geom_smooth(method = "loess", degree = 2, se = FALSE) +
    scale_x_continuous(breaks = 1:10, labels = paste0("G",1:10)) +
    labs(tit = tit, x = tit_x, y = tit_y) + theme_bw()
  return(p)}

Boxplot_func <- function(data, x, y, fill, tit, tit_x, tit_y){
  if(length(fill)==1){
    p <- ggplot(data, aes(x = x, y = y)) +
         geom_boxplot(fill = fill, color = "black")
```

```
  } else{
     p <- ggplot(data, aes(x = x, y = y, fill = fill)) +
          geom_boxplot(color = "black")
  }
  p <- p + labs(tit = tit, x = tit_x, y = tit_y) + theme_bw()
  return(p)}

# ---------------------------------------------------------------
# 1. Scatterplot with numeric x for loess
Scatter_func(product_data, product_data$Product_Class_Num, product
    _data$Number_of_Defects, "original Data", "Scatterplot of
    Number of Defects per Product, Grouped by Product Class", "
    Product Class", "Number of Defects")
# Shows individual products with number of defects on the y-axis,
# grouped by product class on the x-axis (G1 to G10).
# LOESS smoothing line shows the overall trend in the data:
# The number of defects decreases as product class increases.

# ---------------------------------------------------------------
# 2. Create boxplot of number of defects grouped by product class
Boxplot_func(product_data, product_data$Product_Class, product_
    data$Number_of_Defects, "steelblue", "Scatterplot of Number of
     Defects per Product, Grouped by Product Class", "Product
    Class", "Number of Defects")
# Shows the the number of defects for product class G1 to G10.
# x-axis: product classes (G1 = low quality, G10 = high quality).
# y-axis: number of defects per product.
# The number of defects decreases with increasing product class.

# ---------------------------------------------------------------
# 3. Calculate normed number of defects grouped by product class
# Calculation of the LOESS smoothing curve with ggplot2
smooth_model <- Scatter_func(product_data, product_data$Product_
    Class_Num, product_data$Number_of_Defects, "transformed data",
    "", "", "")

# Extracting the LOESS estimates
fit <- loess(Number_of_Defects ~Product_Class_Num, product_data)
product_data$trend <- predict(fit, newdata = product_data)

# Normalisation of the Number_of_Defects by subtracting the trend
product_data$normalized_Number_of_Defects <- product_data$Number_
    of_Defects - product_data$trend

Scatter_func(product_data, product_data$Product_Class_Num, product
    _data$normalized_Number_of_Defects, "transformed data", "
    Scatterplot of normalized Number of Defects per Product,
    Grouped by Product Class", "Product Class", "normalized Number
    of Defects")
```

```
# Normalization -> comparison of products independent of class.
# Different Variance per groups -> has to be taken into account.

# ————————————————————————————————————————
# 4. Number of defects normed + variance stable, grouped by class
# Trend with LOESS
fit <- loess(Product_Class_Num ~Number_of_Defects, data = product
    _data)

# Estimation of LOESS values (trend line)
product_data$trend <- predict(fit, newdata = product_data)

# Residuals Calculation (difference between actual values & trend)
product_data$residuals <- product_data$Product_Class_Num - product
    _data$trend

# Local dispersion (in sliding window)
window_size <- 10
product_data$local_sd <- NA

for (i in seq_len(nrow(product_data))) {
    # Define a window around the current point
    h_i <- product_data$Number_of_Defects[ i]
    window_idx <- which(abs(product_data$Number_of_Defects - h_i) <
        0.1) # e.g. all neighbours at a distance < 1
    product_data$local_sd[ i] <- sd(product_data$residuals[ window_idx
        ], na.rm = TRUE)
}

# Normalisation: Stabilise scattering
product_data$standardized_residuals <- product_data$residuals /
    product_data$local_sd

Scatter_func(product_data, product_data$Product_Class_Num,
product
    _data$standardized_residuals, "transformed data", "Scatterplot
    of normalized Number of Defects per Product, Grouped by
    Product Class", "Product Class", "normalized Number of Defects
    ")
# Each residual is divided by the local standard deviation.
# Ideal: standardized residuals have constant scatter around 0.
# Line trends up or down -> residual structure remains
# and the model or classification logic may be improved.

# ————————————————————————————————————————
# 5. Transform with inverse distribution function
product_data_sub <- subset(product_data, select=c(ID, Number_of_
    Defects, Product_Clas, Product_Class_Nums))
product_data_sub$Typ = "Original"
```

```
# Calculation of the target distribution, transformation to G10
df_target <- product_data_sub %>% filter(Product_Class == "G10")

f_inv <- approxfun(x=seq(1/nrow(df_target), 1, by=1/nrow(df_target
    )), y=sort(df_target$Number_of_Defects), method = "constant",
    yleft = min(df_target$Number_of_Defects), yright = max(df_
    target$Number_of_Defects))

df_transformation <- data.frame()
for(gr in unique(product_data_sub$Product_Class)){
    dfhelp <- product_data_sub %>% filter(Product_Class == gr)
    if(gr == "G10"){ # no Transformation
      dfhelp$Typ <- "Transformed"
      df_transformation <- rbind(df_transformation, dfhelp)
    }
    # Transformation
    g <- ecdf(dfhelp$Number_of_Defects)
    dfhelp$Number_of_Defects <- f_inv(g(dfhelp$Number_of_Defects))
    dfhelp$Typ <- "Transformed"
    df_transformation <- rbind(df_transformation, dfhelp)
}
dfplot <- rbind(product_data_sub, df_transformation)

Boxplot_func(dfplot, dfplot$Product_Class, dfplot$Number_of_
    Defects, dfplot$Typ,
"Scatterplot of Number of Defects per Product (Transform with
    inverse distribution function),\nGrouped by Product Class", "
    Product Class", "Transform Number of Defects")
# Transformed to distribution of group G10 (target distribution).
# For Typ = "Transformed": boxplots (blue) all have the same shape
    .
Scatter_func(dfplot, dfplot$Product_Class_Num, dfplot$Number_of_
    Defects, "transformed data", "Scatterplot of normalized Number
    of Defects per Product, Grouped by Product Class", "Product
    Class", "Transform Number of Defects")
```

B. Appendix

```
# Function to generate a series of simulated batches
gen_batches <- function(n_batches, n_cracks, n_seq2, n_seq3, n_
     seq4) {
   # Data frame with 6 columns, n_batches rows, with 0 = no crack
   batches <- data.frame(matrix(0, nrow = n_batches, ncol = 6))
   colnames(batches) <- paste0("ingot", 1:6)

   # Randomly select positions, assign the value 1 = cracked ingot
   crack_pos <- sample(n_batches * 6, n_cracks)
   row_idx <- (crack_pos - 1) %/% 6 + 1
   col_idx <- (crack_pos - 1) %% 6 + 1
```

```
  # Assign the value 1 to the selected positions
  for(i in seq_along(crack_pos)) batches[row_idx[i],col_idx[i]] <-1

  # Function to add sequences of cracked ingots in consecutive
      rows within the same column
  add_seq <- function(batches, seq_len, n_seq) {
    for (i in 1:n_seq) {
      repeat {
        row <- sample(1:(nrow(batches) - seq_len + 1), 1)
        col <- sample(1:ncol(batches), 1)
        if (all(batches[row:(row + seq_len - 1), col] == 0)) {
          batches[row:(row + seq_len - 1), col] <- 1
          break
        }
      }
    }
    batches
  }

  # Add sequences of cracked ingots
  if (n_seq2 > 0) batches <- add_seq(batches, 2, n_seq2)
  if (n_seq3 > 0) batches <- add_seq(batches, 3, n_seq3)
  if (n_seq4 > 0) batches <- add_seq(batches, 4, n_seq4)
  batches
}

# Function to count sequences of consecutive 1s in each column
count_seq <- function(batches) {
  seqs <- list()
  for (col in 1:ncol(batches)) {
  col_data <- batches[, col]
  seq_lengths <- rle(col_data)$lengths
  seq_values <- rle(col_data)$values
  one_seqs <- seq_lengths[seq_values == 1]
  if (length(one_seqs) > 0) seqs[[paste0("ingot", col)]] <- one_
     seqs
  }
  seqs
}

# Function to count sequences of a given length
count_seq_len <- function(seqs, len) {
  sum(sapply(seqs, function(x) sum(x == len)))
}

# Function to find all sequences of consecutive 1s
find_all_seq <- function(batches) {
  seqs <- list()
  for (col in 1:ncol(batches)) {
    col_data <- batches[, col]
```

```
      seq_lengths <- rle(col_data)$lengths
      seq_values <- rle(col_data)$values
      start_idx <- 1
      for (i in 1:length(seq_lengths)){
        if (seq_values[i] == 1 && seq_lengths[i] > 1){
          seqs <- append(seqs, list(list(row = start_idx, col = col,
              length = seq_lengths[i])))
        }
        start_idx <- start_idx + seq_lengths[i]
      }
  }
  seqs
}

# Function for Monte Carlo simulation
# Random batch simulation with given length and number of cracks.
    Number and length of sequence of cracked ingots are determined
monte_carlo_sim_len <- function(n_sim, n_batches, n_cracks, seq_
    len){
  num_seq_list <- replicate(n_sim, {
    batches <- gen_batches(n_batches, n_cracks, 0, 0, 0)
    seqs <- count_seq(batches)
    count_seq_len(seqs, seq_len)
  })
  mean(num_seq_list)
}

# ————————————————————————————————————————
# Example usage
set.seed(123) # for reproducibility
batch_ex <- gen_batches(100, 20, 3, 2, 1)
print(batch_ex) # example batch

# Calculate the sequences of consecutive 1s
seqs <- count_seq(batch_ex)

# Calculate the number of sequences of different lengths
text <- "Count of consecutive 1s sequences of length"
cat(text," 2:", count_seq_len(seqs, 2), "\n")
cat(text," 3:", count_seq_len(seqs, 3), "\n")
cat(text," 4:", count_seq_len(seqs, 4), "\n")
cat("Total number of 1s:", sum(batch_ex == 1), "\n")

# Find all sequences of consecutive 1s in batch_ex
all_seqs <- find_all_seq(batch_ex)

# Perform Monte Carlo simulation
# For each sequence of cracked ingots in batch_ex, the +-x lines
   before and after are selected. For each partial data set, a
   Monte Carlo simulation is then made with num_sim runs, where n
```

```
    _batches and n_cracks are based on the partial data set
window_size <- 15 # +-x lines selected before and after
num_sim <- 1000

set.seed(12)
for (seq in all_seqs) {
  window_start <- max(1, seq$row - window_size)
  window_end <- min(nrow(batch_ex), seq$row + window_size)
  batch_ex_subset <- batch_ex[ window_start:window_end, ]
  num_batches <- nrow(batch_ex_subset)
  num_cracks <- sum(batch_ex_subset == 1)
  avg_num_seqs <- monte_carlo_sim_len(num_sim, num_batches, num_
      cracks, seq$length)
  cat("Column:", seq$col, "Sequence length:", seq$length, "
      Probability of longer sequence in window:", avg_num_seqs, "
      Number of 1s in window:", num_cracks, "Rows:", seq$row, "-",
        seq$row + seq$length - 1, "\n")
}

set.seed(12)
# In the present modelling, a threshold value is now defined from
    which a sequence of consecutive cracked ingots has a low
    probability of occurrence (selected threshold value = 0.5).
    The following code outputs those rows and columns that fall
    below the threshold value and must be removed from the data
    set before data analyses can begin.

for (seq in all_seqs) {
  window_start <- max(1, seq$row - window_size)
  window_end <- min(nrow(batch_ex), seq$row + window_size)
  batch_ex_subset <- batch_ex[ window_start:window_end, ]
  num_batches <- nrow(batch_ex_subset)
  num_cracks <- sum(batch_ex_subset == 1)
  avg_num_seqs <- monte_carlo_sim_len(num_sim, num_batches, num_
      cracks, seq$length)
  if (avg_num_seqs < 0.5) {
    cat("Probability of longer sequence in window:", avg_num_seqs,
        " < 0.5 -> delete column ", seq$col, " and Rows: ", seq$
        row, "-", seq$row + seq$length - 1, "\n")
  }
}
```

Author details

Manuela Larissa Schreyer
Austria Metall GmbH, Ranshofen, Austria

*Address all correspondence to: manuela.schreyer@amag.at

References

[1] Lee J, Kao HA, Yang S. Service innovation and smart analytics for industry 4.0 and big data environment. Procedia CIRP. 2014;**16**:3-8. DOI: 10.1016/j.procir.2014.02.001

[2] Schreyer M, Gerber A, Neubert S. Data analysis of production data for continuous casting of aluminium rolling ingots. In: THERMEC; 2-7 July 2023; Wien. Vol. 968. Bäch, Switzerland: Key Engineering Materials; 2023. pp. 95-101

[3] Tschimpke MJ, Trutschnig W, Schreyer M, Neubert S, Gerber A. Statistical methods for prediction of the quality of aluminium ingots. In: THERMEC; 2-7 July 2023; Wien. Vol. 968. Bäch, Switzerland: Key Engineering Materialsa; 2023. pp. 109-116

[4] Elmasri R, Navathe SB. Fundamentals of Database Systems. 6th ed. London, United Kingdom: Pearson; 2010. 1200 p

[5] Mineraud J, Mazhelis O, Su X, Tarkoma S. A gap analysis of internet-of-things platforms. Computer Communications; 2016;**89-90**:5-16. DOI: 10.1016/j.comcom.2016.03.015

[6] Armbrust M, Fox A, Griffith R, Joseph A, Katz R, Konwinski A, et al. A view of cloud computing. Communications of the ACM. 2010;**53**:50-58. DOI: 10.1145/1721654.1721672

[7] Microsoft. Azure Machine Learning Documentation [Internet]. 2023. Available from: https://docs.microsoft.com/en-us/azure/machine-learning/ [Accessed: April 22, 2025]

[8] Microsoft. Power BI Documentation [Internet]. 2023. Available from: https://docs.microsoft.com/en-us/power-bi/ [Accessed: April 22, 2025]

[9] Vasudevan AK, Doherty RD. Aluminum Alloys—Contemporary Research and Applications. 1st ed. Amsterdam: Elsevier; 2012

[10] Prillhofer B, Antrekowitsch H, Böttcher H, Enright P. Nonmetallic inclusions in the secondary aluminium industry for the production of aerospace alloys. In: TMS; 9-13 March 2008; New Orleans. Pittsburgh, Pennsylvania, USA: Light Metals; 2008. pp. 603-608

[11] Montgomery DC. Statistical Quality Control: A Modern Introduction. 7th ed. Hoboken, New Jersey, USA: Wiley; 2013

[12] Seehafer M, Nörtemann S, Offtermatt J, Transchel F, Kiermaier A, Külheim R, et al. Actuarial data science: Maschinelles Lernen in der Versicherung. In: Actuarial Data Science. Berlin: De Gruyter; 2021. pp. 305-319

[13] Neubert S, Schreyer M, Gerber A, Pucher P. Umsetzung von Big-Data-Analysen zur Verbesserung der Walzbarrenqualität. Hannover, Germany: ALUMINIUM; 2023

[14] Schreyer M, Gerber A, Neubert S, Tschimpke M, Trutschnig W. Interactive visual data analysis for quality optimization in aluminum casting. In: Visualization & Visual Analytics (VIS). Los Alamitos, California, USA: IEEE TVCG; 2025

[15] Cleveland WS. Visualizing Data. 1st ed. Summit, New Jersey, USA: Hobart Press; 1993. 360 p

[16] Wickham H, Grolemund G. R for Data Science: Import, Tidy, Transform, Visualize, and Model Data. Sebastopol, California, USA: O'Reilly Media; 2016. Available from: https://cloudera2017.

wordpress.com/wp-content/uploads/2019/01/r-for-data-science-import-tidy-transform-visualize-and-model-data.pdf [Accessed: May 20, 2025]

[17] Fahrmeir L, Kneib T, Lang S. Regression: Modelle, Methoden und Anwendungen. Berlin: Springer-Verlag; 2007

[18] Wickham H. ggplot2: Elegant Graphics for Data Analysis. Berlin, Germany: Springer-Verlag; 2016. DOI: 10.1007/978-3-319-24277-4

[19] R Core Team. R: A Language and Environment for Statistical Computing. Vienna, Austria: R Foundation for Statistical Computing; 2023

[20] Faraway JJ. Linear Models with R. 2nd ed. New York: Chapman & Hall/CRC Texts in Statistical Science; 2014. DOI: 10.4324/9780203507278

[21] Cleveland WS, Devlin SJ. Locally weighted regression: An approach to regression analysis by local fitting. Journal of the American Statistical Association. 1988;**83**(403):596-610. DOI: 10.2307/2289282

[22] Loader C. Local Regression and Likelihood. 1st ed. New York: Springer; 1999. DOI: 10.1007/b98858

[23] Rüschendorf L. Mathematical Risk Analysis: Dependence, Risk Bounds, Optimal Allocations and Portfolios. Berlin, Germany: Springer; 2013. DOI: 10.1007/978-3-642-33590-7

[24] Valberg HS. Applied Metal Forming: Including FEM Analysis. Cambridge: Cambridge University Press; 2010. DOI: 10.1017/CBO9780511801907

[25] Schreyer M, Gerber A, Neubert S, Peter S. Hybrid Modeling: Combining Physics-Based Simulations and Data Science for Target Variable Estimation. In Preparation. Basel, Schweiz: MDPI; 2025

[26] Montgomery DC. Introduction to Statistical Quality Control. Hoboken, New Jersey, USA: Wiley; 2012

[27] Schreyer M, Tschimpke M, Gerber A, Neubert S, Trutschnig W. Applied statistics in industry: Defining an appropriate target variable and analysing factors affecting aluminium ingot quality. In: SMPS; 3-6 September 2024; Salzburg. Cham, Switzerland: Springer; 2024. pp. 457-465. DOI: 10.1007/978-3-031-65993-5_56

[28] Kroese DP, Brereton T, Taimre T, Botev ZI. Why the Monte Carlo method is so important today. Wiley Interdisciplinary Reviews: Computational Statistics. 2014;**6**:386-392. DOI: 10.1002/wics.1314

[29] Burchett WW, Ellis AR, Harrar SW, Bathke AC. Nonparametric inference for multivariate data: The R package npmv. Journal of Statistical Software. 2017; **76**(4):1-18. DOI: 10.18637/jss.v076.i04

Section 2

Advanced Machine Learning and Model Optimization

Chapter 3

Perspective Chapter: Optimized Random Forests for Effective and Efficient Healthcare Data Analytics

Fawagreh Khaled

Abstract

It is clear that machine learning (ML) has influenced every aspect of our lives! From reviewing the weather report to seeking a loan or a credit card, machine learning is utilized in nearly every facet of our everyday lives. This chapter examines ML through its algorithms and applications. Particular attention is focused on ML applications within the healthcare data analytics sector, encompassing new and emerging diseases. The chapter highlights the importance of random forest as a powerful machine learning classification technique for several diseases. Enhancing the efficiency and performance of random forest by utilizing only a portion of the model (via a technique known as pruning) has shown success in two approaches: CLUstering-based diverse random forest (CLUB-DRF) and evolutionary game theoretic approach to random forest pruning (eGAP). Owing to pruning, both CLUB-DRF and eGAP exhibit substantially reduced model sizes compared to the unpruned random forest, while consistently achieving better predictive performance. We experimentally illustrate the effectiveness of these two approaches on three diseases.

Keywords: healthcare data analytics, machine learning, random forest, CLUB-DRF, eGAP

1. Introduction

Healthcare data analytics, often referred to as clinical data analytics, involves the collection and analysis of information from multiple sources (such as information obtained from electronic health records, healthcare billing claims, institutional cost reports, and patient satisfaction survey responses) to assist organizations in enhancing care quality, reducing care costs, and improving the patient experience. As indicated in [1], numerous researchers have carried out studies demonstrating that using healthcare data analytics technologies has allowed them to lower mortality rates, healthcare expenses, and medical complications in different hospitals. Additionally, healthcare analytics can lower treatment costs, prevent avoidable diseases, forecast epidemic outbreaks, prevent needless fatalities, and enhance overall quality of life [2]. According to Grand View Research, the global healthcare analytics market is projected to experience significant growth, reaching $167 billion by 2030. To enhance healthcare as outlined previously, healthcare analytics has emerged as a prominent field of interest and garnered attention from various areas, including databases, data mining, information retrieval, image processing, medical researchers, and healthcare professionals [1]. This chapter will utilize a fundamental task in machine learning called classification to enhance the traditional random forest's performance on medical datasets, focusing on both accuracy and classification speed.

2. Machine learning: An overview

Machine learning (ML), a core area of artificial intelligence (AI), focuses on developing systems that learn patterns from data rather than relying on explicitly programmed rules. Rooted in computational learning theory and pattern recognition, ML has evolved into a discipline capable of producing both predictive and descriptive models. ML algorithms are commonly grouped into supervised and unsupervised approaches. In supervised learning, the goal is to establish a functional relationship between a set of input variables, X, and a corresponding output variable, Y, enabling the model to predict outcomes for previously unseen data. Classification is a prominent example of supervised learning; it relies on labeled datasets to train models that can subsequently infer the class labels of new, unlabeled instances. Using such labeled training data, a classification algorithm constructs a model – known as a classifier – illustrated in **Figure 1**.

After the model demonstrates its capability to categorize unfamiliar data in the testing dataset, as illustrated in **Figure 2**, it is sent to the field.

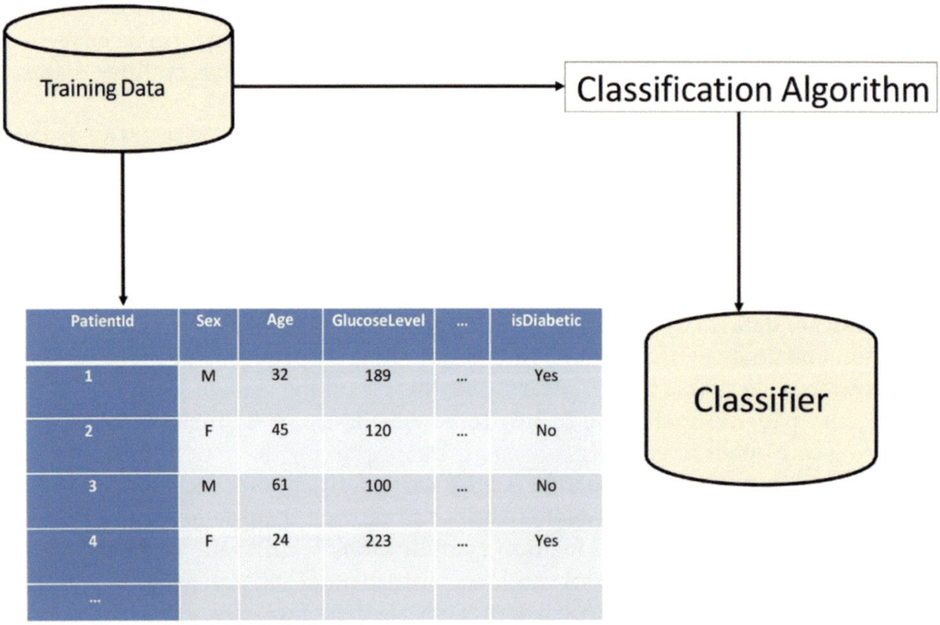

Figure 1.
Classifier construction workflow.

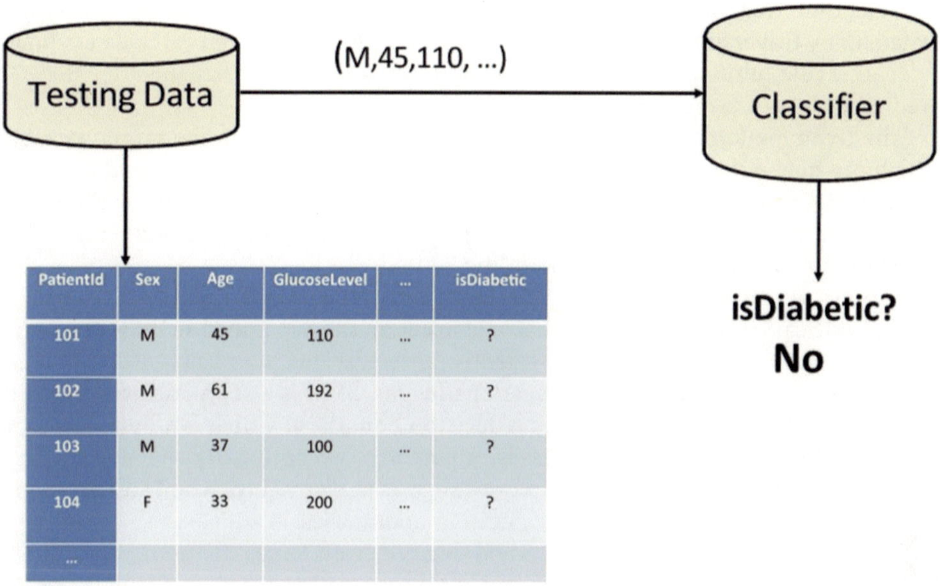

Figure 2.
Prediction workflow.

Unsupervised algorithms seek to reveal concealed patterns in unlabeled data without having extensive knowledge of their traits. An example of unsupervised algorithms is clustering, a method used to categorize objects with unknown similarity traits by dividing a varied set of objects into smaller groups of similar ones.

2.1 Machine learning algorithms

In this subsection, we provide readers with a brief summary of several frequently utilized machine learning techniques. This is not meant to serve as an all-encompassing examination of machine learning algorithms in any way. It merely acts as guidance for interested readers to delve deeper into these methods in the literature.

Linear regression is the process of identifying a line that accurately represents the given data points, enabling the line to forecast output values for unseen inputs based on the assumption that those outputs will fall on or near the line. Usually, one target variable/feature is employed for the line fitting, whereas the remaining features serve as independent variables. Linear regression is straightforward and easily understood.

Logistic regression employs the logistic (sigmoid) function to estimate the probability of an outcome, which can then be mapped to one of two or more categorical classes. Unlike linear regression – which is designed to predict continuous variables – logistic regression is specifically used for modeling discrete outcomes. Accordingly, linear regression is best suited for regression tasks, whereas logistic regression is widely applied in classification problems. One of its advantages is its simplicity, both in implementation and interpretation.

A decision tree, in contrast, represents a non-linear predictive model. It classifies instances by traversing a hierarchical structure in which each internal node evaluates a decision rule, ultimately guiding the instance to a leaf node that specifies the predicted class or target value.

The tree type (whether classification/regression) is based on the target variable, which can hold either a discrete value or a continuous value (usually a real number). In the former case, the tree is referred to as a classification tree, while in the latter case, it is referred to as a regression tree. The primary benefit of decision trees is their interpretability and ease of understanding.

Support vector machine (SVM) is a linear model that, while capable of addressing both classification and regression tasks, is predominantly applied in classification scenarios. Not only does it function effectively for various practical issues, but it can also address both linear and non-linear challenges. SVM is a sophisticated modeling technique; it operates by identifying a decision boundary, which is a hyperplane, to differentiate or classify any two classes. It performs exceptionally well even with data that has high dimensions. Techniques such as the kernel trick and soft boundary enable SVM to represent non-linear decision boundaries.

Naive Bayes is a classification method derived from Bayes' theorem, assuming that the features are independent of one another. In other terms, a Naive Bayes classifier presumes no interaction among features (that is, no independent feature influences any other independent feature). Naive Bayes is recognized for its scalability regarding the quantity of predictors and data points. It is also perfect for generating real-time forecasts.

k-nearest neighbor, or k–NN, is a supervised learning method that addresses both regression and classification tasks. It relies on the premise that points in the same category are those that are located close to one another. In other terms, similar items are those that are close to one another. In contrast to other algorithms, KNN can effortlessly handle multi-class classification problems.

k-means is a clustering algorithm in unsupervised machine learning developed by MacQueen et al. [3] during the late 1960s. It is regarded not only as one of the earliest clustering algorithms but also as the most popular, primarily because of its efficiency, simplicity, and empirical success [4].

Random forest (RF) is a supervised ensemble learning technique used for both classification and regression, widely recognized for its reliability and strong predictive performance relative to other ensemble approaches. To further enhance its accuracy, researchers have proposed multiple variants that incorporate different strategies to refine particular components of the algorithm. Several studies have applied RF in practice [5–10]. A brief overview of the method is provided below.

2.2 Random forest

Random forest (RF), developed by Breiman [11], is a supervised ensemble learning technique used for tackling classification and regression tasks. To create a varied collection of decision trees with regulated differences, RF incorporates Breiman's bootstrap aggregating (bagging) technique [12], along with the random feature selection method introduced by [13, 14] and Amit and Geman [15].

Every decision tree in RF is built using a sample taken from the training dataset. Through bagging, the sample is obtained by sampling with replacement from the training dataset, which means that, statistically speaking, about 63.2% of instances are expected to appear at least once in the sample. Instances that are part of the sample are referred to as in-bag instances, while the rest of the instances (approximately 36.8%) are known as out-of-bag (OOB) instances.

To maintain diversity in every decision tree, a goodness metric (like the Gini index or information gain) is applied at each node across all trees to choose the optimal split feature from a group of randomly chosen features (where n represents the total number of features, as is typically the case). Every tree is left unpruned and is allowed to grow to its maximum potential. To avoid trees consuming excessive memory, especially in high-dimensional datasets, a maximum depth is typically established.

2.3 Machine learning applications

Machine learning applications are not only playing a greater role in our daily lives but are also becoming routine in various areas of contemporary society. They are expanding quickly and now extensively span all sectors. Besides the healthcare data analytics area that will be explored thoroughly in the following section, machine learning applications also encompass, but are not limited to, financial data analytics [16, 17], filtering of email spam and malware [18, 19], autonomous vehicles [20, 21], traffic forecasting [22, 23], recognition of speech and images [24, 25], and automatic translation of languages [26, 27].

3. Machine learning in health data analytics

Here, we briefly describe research conducted by several researchers who leverage machine learning algorithms for better health data analytics in order to analyze vast datasets, improve diagnostics, predict patient outcomes, and personalize treatment.

As highlighted in the abstract, this study employs an enhanced RF–based classification approach to boost both accuracy and inference speed across multiple diseases. In related work [6], we proposed an ensemble regression framework derived from CLUB-DRF, a pruned RF model designed for efficiency and high predictive performance. Experimental results on three medical datasets, each representing a distinct disease, demonstrated the method's strong accuracy and significantly faster execution.

The study in [28] applies modern machine-learning and predictive-analytics techniques to healthcare data to forecast disease trends, identify high-risk patients, and improve resource allocation. Using data from EHRs and public-health records, the work demonstrates that predictive models can support earlier interventions and more informed clinical decisions. The paper highlights the growing role of data-driven methods in improving healthcare efficiency and patient outcomes.

An improved method for correcting partial-volume effects in ASL MRI by modeling the contributions of different tissue types within each voxel was investigated in [29]. The approach produces more accurate cerebral blood-flow estimates, especially near tissue boundaries, and improves the overall reliability of ASL perfusion measurements.

The paper in [30] presents a healthcare-analytics system that uses a Ridge-Adaline model combined with a Stochastic Gradient Descent (SGD) classifier to improve early disease detection. The authors integrate regularization methods

(Ridge regression, LASSO) with an Adaline-SGD classifier to enhance convergence and classification accuracy, achieving around 92% accuracy in their experiments.

Higher medication-regimen complexity was found to correlate with an increased likelihood of mortality in ICU patients, and incorporating this measure offered a modest improvement to standard severity-prediction models [31].

Finally, machine-learning models were investigated in [32] to classify patients with influenza-like illness and identify those at risk of developing severe outcomes during emerging disease outbreaks. The results show that ML-based classification can support early triage and improve preparedness for novel infectious threats.

4. Pruned random forests

Here, we introduce two efficient pruning techniques for RF that we previously developed and published. In the next section of our experimental study, these techniques will be applied to examine their performance in health decision-making regarding both effectiveness (i.e., predictive accuracy) and efficiency (i.e., inference time).

4.1 CLUB-DRF

A well-established principle in ensemble classification is that ensembles tend to perform better when the individual classifiers in the ensemble exhibit a high level of diversity [33–35]. Because clustering has been used extensively as a diversity technique in many applications [36–38], we believe that it likely has the potential to diversify trees in RF. This explains why we have used it in our approach, CLUB-DRF.

The acronym CLUB-DRF stands for CLUstering-based diverse random forest [8]. By employing clustering techniques, CLUB-DRF identifies a subset of trees from a conventional RF. Using only a limited number of trees in the RF, CLUB-DRF often achieves even greater classification accuracy. In healthcare analytics, CLUB-DRF was applied to enhance the precision of various regression medical datasets [6]. In this chapter, we will assess its capability on some classification medical datasets. CLUB-DRF groups trees according to their predictive similarity on the training dataset. Afterward, the top-performing tree is chosen from every cluster, creating a pruned RF. The number of trees selected matches the number of clusters. For example, if the number of clusters is 5, then the resulting pruned RF will have 5 trees.

In summary, the CLUB-DRF approach can be outlined in the following algorithm, with T indicating the training data set and S denoting the size of the parent RF to be generated. The constant k denotes the number of clusters to be formed, specified as a multiple of 5 within the range of 5 to 50:

Algorithm CLUB-DRF(T, S, k)

```
Input:
    T // Training data
    S // Size of random forest
    k // Number of clusters
```

```
Output:
    Tclubdrf // Ordered list representing CLUB-DRF

Begin
    Create empty super ordered list AllPredictions
    Create empty ordered list Trf to represent parentRF
    Create empty ordered list Tclubdrf to represent CLUB-DRF

    // Step 1: Train random forest
    TrF ← TrainRandomForest(T, S)

    // Step 2: Collect predictions from each tree
    For each tree t in Trf, do
      Predictions ← Predict(t, T)
      Add (t, predictions) to AllPredictions
    End For

    // Step 3: Cluster trees based on predictions
    If datasetType == "classification" then
      {cluster1, cluster2, . . ., clusterk} ← KModesCluster
      (AllPredictions, k)
    Else
      {cluster1, cluster2, . . ., clusterk} ← KMeansCluster
      (AllPredictions, k)
    End If

    // Step 4: Select representative trees
    For each cluster c in {cluster1, cluster2, . . .,
    clusterk}, do
      repTree ← SelectRepresentativeTree(c)
      Add repTree to Tclubdrf
    End For

    Return Tclubdrf
      End
```

The last step in the algorithm above is to choose a representative from each cluster (SelectRepresentativeTree(c)). To accomplish this, three different variations can be used and are elaborated upon below.

4.1.1 Best representative on training CLUB-DRF

In this variant, we assess all clusters by measuring how accurately their trees predict the training data. The tree that achieves the highest accuracy within its cluster is selected as its representative. As outlined in the previous steps, this selected tree is then added to $T_{clubdrf}$ to construct the CLUB-DRF model. This is the version used in the experimental evaluations presented in Section 5.

4.1.2 Best representative on OOB CLUB-DRF

In this variant, the representative tree for each cluster is selected based on its performance on the out-of-bag (OOB) samples rather than its accuracy on the training data. The OOB samples, which constitute roughly 36% of the total dataset, consist of the instances not included in the bootstrap sample used to build the tree. Because these samples are not seen during training, they offer a more objective and unbiased estimate of the tree's predictive capability compared to the training data.

4.1.3 Random representative CLUB-DRF

In this variant, we randomly choose a prediction list from each cluster and select the corresponding tree without evaluating its effectiveness. As accuracy was not a criterion for choosing the representative in this variation, in contrast to the earlier two variations that have been overfitted on the training and OOB samples respectively, this variation avoids overfitting issues.

4.2 eGAP

eGAP [5] integrates the clustering method from CLUB-DRF with the evolutionary game theory approach known as Replicator Dynamics (RD) [39]. Using this technique, an ensemble of RF is developed by eGAP as follows. Trees with high similarity in an initial RF are clustered first. Through the addition and removal of trees via RD, clusters expand and contract by assessing the predictive accuracy of each subforest, which is a group of trees, against the predictive accuracy of the whole forest. The starting count of trees in every cluster matches the count of trees in the smallest cluster. Trees that weren't sampled initially are used to expand the clusters.

In brief, the eGAP approach can be outlined in the following algorithm, where T denotes the training dataset, S represents the size of the parentRF that will be generated, k signifies the number of clusters to be formed, and RDIterations indicate the number of RD iterations to be conducted on the active clusters:

Algorithm eGAP(T, S, k, RDIterations)

```
Input:
    T    // Training data
    S    // Size of random forest
    k    // Number of clusters
    RDIterations     // Number of refinement iterations

Output:
    TeGAP    // Ordered list representing eGAP

Begin
    Create empty ordered list TeGAP
```

```
// Step 1: Train random forest
TrF ← TrainRandomForest (T, S)

// Step 2: Collect predictions from each tree
AllPredictions ← empty list
For each tree t in TrF, do
  predictions ← Predict (t, T)
  Add (t, predictions) to AllPredictions
End For

// Step 3: Cluster trees based on predictions
{cluster1, cluster2, . . ., clusterk} ← Cluster
(AllPredictions, k)

// Step 4: Determine the smallest cluster size
minSize ← SizeOfSmallestCluster({cluster1, . . .,
clusterk})

// Step 5: Create k working and idle clusters
wkClusters ← empty list
idleClusters ← empty list

For each cluster c in {cluster1, . . ., clusterk}, do
  wkCluster ← SelectFirstNTrees(c, minSize)
  idleCluster ← RemainingTrees(c)
  Add wkCluster to wkClusters
  Add idleCluster to idleClusters
End For

// Step 6: Refinement iterations
For i from 1 to RDIterations, do
  For each nextwkCluster in wkClusters, do
    wkClustersPerformance ← EvaluateAllTrees
    (wkClusters)
    nextwkClusterPerformance ← EvaluateCluster
    (nextwkCluster)

    If nextwkClusterPerformance is better than
    wkClustersPerformance, then
      bestTree←Remove best tree from corresponding
      idle cluster
      Add bestTree to nextwkCluster
    Else
      worstTree←Remove worst tree from nextwkCluster
      Add worstTree to corresponding idle cluster
    End If
  End For
End For
```

```
        // Step 7: Populate TeGAP from final working clusters
        For each wkCluster in wkClusters, do
        Append wkCluster.trees to TeGAP
        End For
         Return TeGAP
    End
```

After outlining the algorithms of CLUB-DRF and eGAP, the next section evaluates the effectiveness and efficiency of each method when applied to health datasets.

5. Experimental study

This section showcases the effectiveness and efficiency of the proposed methods: CLUB-DRF and eGAP, validated through an extensive experimental analysis on three classification datasets representing three diseases within the health sector, namely, Alzheimer's, Mpox, and Parkinson's. While previous work of ours investigated the efficiency of these methods on datasets related to some diseases, this is the first time that these methods are tested on classification datasets for Alzheimer's, Mpox, and Parkinson's. The Parkinson's dataset used in [5] and all the healthcare-related datasets used in [6] (which also included Parkinson's) were completely regression datasets.

5.1 Diseases

5.1.1 Alzheimer's

Alzheimer's disease is the most common form of dementia, a progressive brain disorder that gradually impairs memory, thinking, and behavior. It typically begins after age 60 and worsens over time, eventually interfering with daily tasks like eating, speaking, or recognizing loved ones. In the past five years (2020–2024), an estimated 9.5 million to 10 million people globally have died from Alzheimer's disease and other forms of dementia.

5.1.2 Mpox

Mpox is a viral infection caused by the monkeypox virus, a pathogen closely related to the smallpox virus. Transmission occurs through close contact with infected individuals, animals, or contaminated surfaces and materials. In the past five years (2020 - 2024), there have been over 1,100 deaths attributed to Mpox, according to recent reports.

5.1.3 Parkinson's

Parkinson's disease is a long-lasting, progressive neurological condition that mainly impacts movement. It is caused by the deterioration of dopamine-producing neurons in an area of the brain known as the substantia nigra. While it's difficult to pinpoint the exact number of deaths specifically caused by Parkinson's disease in the past five years, global estimates suggest that Parkinson's disease has contributed to the deaths of hundreds of thousands of people annually.

5.2 Datasets

The datasets are typically small to medium in size. As a result, a simple ML model, such as RF, is preferable. This contrasts with deep learning models, which usually require larger datasets to function effectively. All datasets were sourced from Kaggle [40], a prominent online platform and community for data science and machine learning. Luckily, these datasets have already been pre-processed, ready to be used, and do not have any missing values. **Table 1** provides additional details regarding these datasets that will be used in the experiments.

The class label for all the datasets is binary, which can be either 0 (negative) or 1 (positive). These class labels are called *Diagnosis, MonkeyPox,* and *Class* for the datasets Alzheimers_disease, mpox, and Parkinsons_disease, respectively.

Across all experiments, the parentRF consisted of 1,000 trees. Because the number of RD iterations was intentionally set to match the size of parentRF, the evolutionary process involved 1000 RD iterations to expand or contract the clusters.

For the holdout evaluation, which represents the simplest form of cross-validation, each dataset was partitioned into separate training and testing subsets. Two-thirds of the data (66%) were allocated for training, while the remaining one-third (34%) was used for testing. The split was generated randomly using a uniform distribution, ensuring that every instance had an equal chance of being assigned to either set.

For a small dataset like Parkinson's, the risk of overfitting is already handled by CLUB-DRF and eGAP. CLUB-DRF reduces overfitting through cluster-based diversity and localized learning, while eGAP reduces overfitting mainly through evolutionary pruning and diversity optimization. For very small datasets, eGAP is generally more robust, while CLUB-DRF may need careful tuning to avoid splitting data too thinly.

5.3 Performance metrics

Although the experiments generated cluster counts in multiples of five, ranging from 5 to 50, the results presented in the following subsections reflect only the best-performing cluster configurations used to construct CLUB-DRF and eGAP.

Table 2 shows the performance of CLUB-DRF and eGAP on all the datasets for several metrics, including accuracy, area under curve (AUC), F-Measure, pruning

Name	Type	Number of features	Number of instances
Alzheimers_disease	classification	34	2149
mpox_disease	classification	10	25000
Parkinsons_disease	classification	754	756

Table 1.
Datasets.

level, and inference time per instance (ITPI) (in microseconds). ITPI is calculated as the total time taken to predict all the instances in the testing dataset, divided by the total number of instances in the testing dataset.

The pruning level represents the proportion by which the original ensemble – referred to as parentRF – is reduced when forming CLUB-DRF or eGAP. For instance, if the parentRF contains 500 trees and the resulting CLUB-DRF consists of 50 trees, then the pruning level is calculated as $100\% - \frac{50}{500} \times 100\% = 90\%$. This indicates that, relative to the parentRF, the CLUB-DRF model is reduced in size by 90%.

Based on the key performance indicator (percentage accuracy), **Table 2** shows that both have identical performance on one dataset (mpox_disease), while CLUB-DRF is superior on the other two datasets. Based on these results, we can say that the two methods have approximately comparable performance. However, CLUB-DRF has the added advantage of reduced space and lower inference time due to having a higher pruning level than eGAP.

As demonstrated in the table, CLUB-DRF achieved a high 99.5% pruning level on the mpox_disease and Parkinsons_disease datasets because only one tree was selected from each cluster, yielding a pruned ensemble of only 5 trees. With a pruned ensemble of 15 trees, CLUB-DRF achieved a slightly lower pruning level of 98.5% on the Alzheimers_disease dataset. By taking a closer look at **Table 2**, notice that for all datasets, a high pruning level of at least 90% has been achieved by both CLUB-DRF and eGAP. Considering the key performance metrics presented in **Table 2**, bar charts illustrating these metrics are provided in **Figure 3**.

It is worth mentioning that the ability of CLUB-DRF and eGAP to achieve a high pruning level is not restricted to a single domain, such as healthcare. They can also generalize well to other domains, such as financial, industrial, or environmental, as long as the datasets are structured with sufficient instances to form meaningful clusters. For unstructured or highly complex datasets, preprocessing or dimensionality reduction is needed before applying CLUB-DRF.

The performance of CLUB-DRF and eGAP was also compared with parentRF and with a random forest of identical size to eGAP, called RF, as demonstrated in **Table 3**. By comparing it with **Table 2**, it is obvious that CLUB-DRF and eGAP have performed better on all the datasets.

Performance metrics of parentRF and RF across datasets, presented as bar charts in **Figure 4**, are shown for comparison with **Figure 3**.

Dataset	Clusters	Accuracy	AUC	F-Measure	Pruning level	ITPI
CLUB-DRF						
Alzheimers_disease	15	**93.87%**	**0.93**	**0.94**	**98.5%**	**179**
mpox_disease	5	**67.43%**	**0.61**	**0.67**	**99.50%**	**55**
Parkinsons_disease	5	**86.74%**	**0.77**	**0.87**	**99.50%**	**82**
eGAP						
Alzheimers_disease	5	**93.75%**	**0.93**	**0.94**	**90.60%**	**1183**
mpox_disease	5	**67.43%**	**0.61**	**0.67**	**97.50%**	**305**
Parkinsons_disease	5	**86.13%**	**0.76**	**0.86**	**96.30%**	**640**

Table 2.
Performance metrics of CLUB-DRF and eGAP.

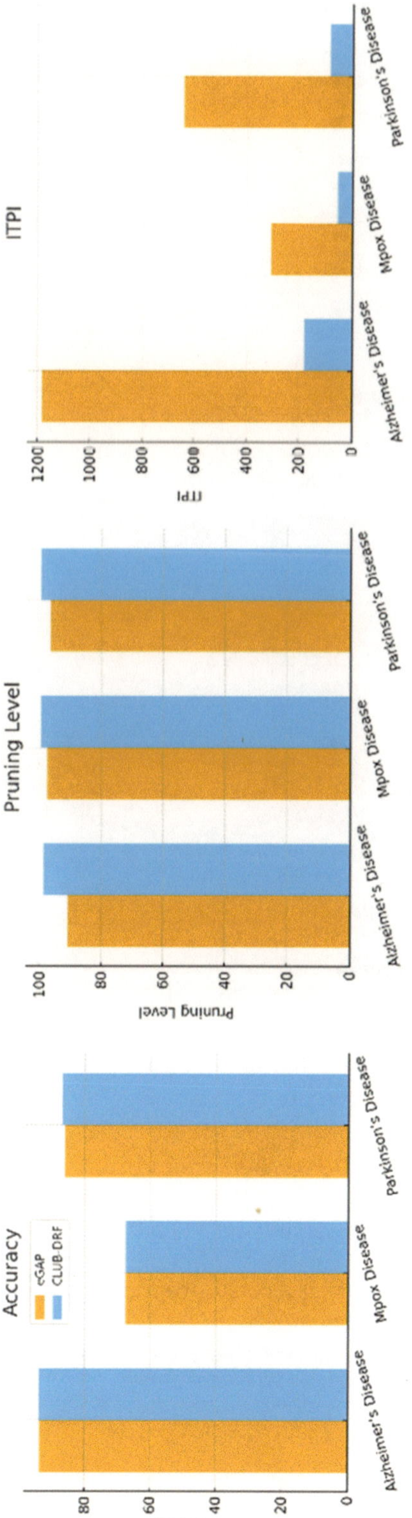

Figure 3.
Performance comparison of CLUB-DRF and eGAP across datasets.

Dataset	Accuracy	AUC	F-Measure	ITPI
parentRF				
Alzheimers_disease	93.41%	0.92	0.93	11531
mpox_disease	67.29%	0.61	0.67	4285
Parkinsons_disease	85.30%	0.75	0.85	1035
RF				
Alzheimers_disease	93.57%	0.93	0.94	1130
mpox_disease	67.37%	0.61	0.67	183
Parkinsons_disease	85.48%	0.75	0.85	640

Table 3.
Performance metrics of parentRF and RF.

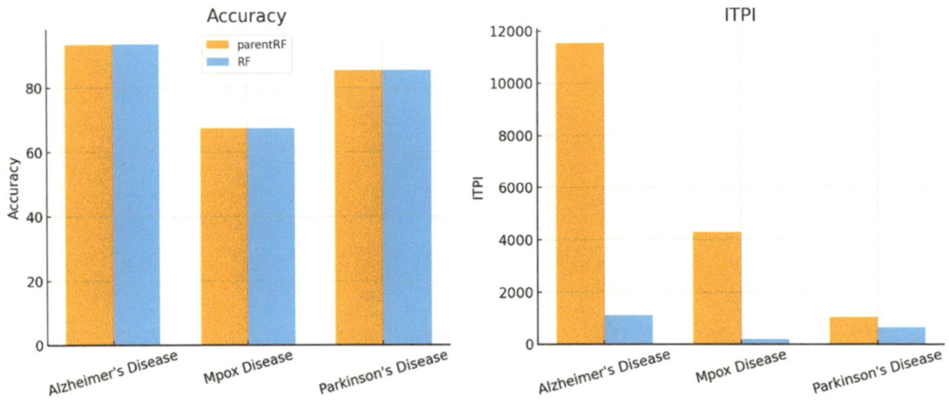

Figure 4.
Performance metrics of parentRF and RF.

6. Big o complexity analysis

6.1 CLUB-DRF

Typically, CLUB-DRF consists of:

- Training the base random forest (RF)
- Clustering RF trees using K-Means (or similar)
- Constructing DRF by selecting a cluster representative from each cluster
- Making predictions using the new clustered ensemble DRF

Let:

- n = training instances
- S = parent forest size (trees)

- k = clusters
- m = final pruned ensemble size
- T_{tree} = time to train one tree
- I_{clust} = number of clustering iterations until convergence

Simply put, and without getting into too much detail, the overall time complexity of CLUB-DRF is

$$O(S \,.\, T_{tree} + S \,.\, n + I_{clust} \,.\, S \,.\, k \,.\, n + m \,.\, n)$$

6.2 eGAP

Typically, eGAP consists of:

- Training the base random forest (RF)
- Clustering RF trees using K-Means (or similar)
- Constructing the initial working and idle clusters
- Evolution of the working clusters using RD, hence, creating eGAP
- Making predictions using the new clustered RD-based ensemble eGAP

Let:

- n = training instances
- S = parent forest size (trees)
- T_{tree} = time to train one tree
- I = number of replicator-dynamics iterations.

Since training the base RF is done in $O(S \cdot T_{tree})$, and the evolutionary pruning (RD) is done in $O(I \cdot n \cdot S)$, the overall time complexity of eGAP is, therefore,

$$O(S \cdot Ttree + I \cdot n \cdot S)$$

7. Benchmarking with LightGBM

LightGBM (short for Light Gradient Boosting Machine) is a machine learning framework developed by Microsoft that is designed for fast, efficient, and accurate gradient boosting on decision trees. It is widely used for both classification and regression tasks, and is particularly popular in Kaggle competitions and industry applications due to its speed and performance. In this section, we compare the performance of LightGBM with CLUB-DRF and eGAP on similar datasets.

The authors in [41] processed EEG recordings from Alzheimer's and frontotemporal dementia patients by extracting complexity-based signal features for three different conditions and then used the gradient-boosting algorithm LightGBM to improve automated discrimination between these conditions. For these three conditions, LightGBM achieved a classification accuracy of 83.06%, 80.67%, and 92.27%, respectively. With reference to **Table 2**, it can be observed that CLUB-DRF and eGAP achieve higher performances of 93.87% and 93.75%, respectively.

A symptom-based prediction system for Mpox cases was developed in [42] by applying multiple boosting ensemble learning models (including LightGBM) and comparing their performance on public data. Their system achieved a classification accuracy of 68.67%, while, as shown in **Table 2**, both CLUB-DRF and eGAP attained slightly lower accuracies of 67.43%.

In [43], a method is proposed for diagnosing Parkinson's disease using patients' voice signals, where multiple classifiers – including LightGBM – were combined through a hard-voting ensemble, and SHAP analysis was applied to interpret the influence of each vocal feature on the prediction. The proposed method achieved an overall accuracy of 85.42%, while, as shown in **Table 2,** CLUB-DRF and eGAP achieved higher accuracies of 86.74% and 86.13%, respectively.

8. Conclusion and future work

Accurate prediction in healthcare analytics is essential for enhancing patient outcomes, optimizing resource allocation, and reducing healthcare costs. Reliable predictive models enable early detection of diseases, support personalized treatment plans, and minimize the risk of medical errors. At a systems level, accurate forecasts inform hospital capacity planning, supply chain management, and public health interventions, ensuring timely and effective responses to emerging health threats. Given that even minor inaccuracies can have significant clinical and financial consequences, achieving high predictive accuracy is critical to building trust in data-driven healthcare decision-making.

Overall, ML-driven methods have demonstrated better computational outcomes in health decision-making contexts. Specifically, RFs have significantly surpassed other algorithms in terms of accuracy performance. Current literature indicates opportunities for enhancement in RF algorithms. The pruned RF methods, CLUB-DRF and eGAP, have been developed and have demonstrated promising results in healthcare applications. Therefore, this chapter intends to (1) outline the efficacy of RFs in health decision-making areas; (2) implement CLUB-DRF and eGAP algorithms for health modeling; and (3) present experimental proof regarding the effectiveness and efficiency of utilizing these pruned RF models in three classification health datasets.

Based on the performance metrics presented in **Table 2**, both CLUB-DRF and eGAP exhibit comparable performance and are therefore well-suited for healthcare decision-making tasks. However, CLUB-DRF offers the added advantage of reduced space requirements due to its higher pruning level and, consequently, lower inference time. These experimental findings suggest that CLUB-DRF and eGAP can enhance the performance in healthcare decision-making activities. Significantly, these pruned RF models are reduced in size and more efficient without compromising their reliability. Further research can examine the use of CLUB-DRF and eGAP to boost accuracy and efficiency in other areas, including but not limited to retail, manufacturing and industry, transportation and logistics, and education.

Author details

Fawagreh Khaled
Prince Mohammad Bin Fahd University, Khobar, Saudi Arabia

*Address all correspondence to: kfawagreh@pmu.edu.sa

References

[1] Reddy CK, Aggarwal CC. Healthcare Data Analytics. Chapman and Hall/ CRC; 2015

[2] Sarada J, Lakshmi M. An introduction to data analytics in healthcare industry. International Journal of Advanced Scientific Technologies, Engineering and Management Sciences. 2017;**3**(1): 169–173

[3] MacQueen J, et al. Some methods for classification and analysis of multivariate observations. In: Proceedings of the fifth Berkeley symposium on mathematical statistics and probability; volume **1**; California, USA: 1967. p. 14

[4] Jain AK. Data clustering: 50 years beyond k-means. Pattern Recognition Letters. 2010;**31**(8):651–666

[5] Fawagreh K, Gaber MM. eGAP: An evolutionary game theoretic approach to random forest pruning. Big Data and Cognitive Computing. 2020;**4**(4):37

[6] Fawagreh K, Gaber MM. Resource-efficient fast prediction in healthcare data analytics: A pruned Random Forest regression approach. Computing. 2020;**102**(5):1187–1198

[7] Fawagreh K, Gaber MM, Elyan E. Diversified random forests using random subspaces. In: International Conference on Intelligent Data Engineering and Automated Learning; Springer; 2014. p. 85–92

[8] Fawagreh K, Gaber MM, Elyan E. CLUB-DRF: A clustering approach to extreme pruning of random forests. In: International Conference on Innovative Techniques and Applications of Artificial Intelligence. Springer; 2015. p. 59–73

[9] Fawagreh K, Gaber MM, Elyan E. An outlier ranking tree selection approach to extreme pruning of random forests. In: International Conference on Engineering Applications of Neural Networks; Springer; 2016. p. 267–282

[10] Fawgreh K, Gaber MM, Elyan E. A replicator dynamics approach to collective feature engineering in random forests. In: International Conference on Innovative Techniques and Applications of Artificial Intelligence; Springer; 2015. p. 25–41

[11] Breiman L. Random forests. Machine Learning. 2001;**45**(1):5–32

[12] Breiman L. Bagging predictors. Machine Learning. 1996;**24**(2):123–140

[13] Tin Kam H. Random decision forests. In: Proceedings of 3rd international conference on document analysis and recognition; vol. **1**; IEEE; 1995. p. 278–282

[14] Tin Kam H. The random subspace method for constructing decision forests. IEEE Transactions on Pattern Analysis and Machine Intelligence. 1998;**20**(8):832–844

[15] Amit Y, Geman D. Shape quantization and recognition with randomized trees. Neural Computation. 1997;**9**(7):1545–1588

[16] Van Liebergen B, et al. Machine learning: A revolution in risk management and compliance? Journal

of Financial Transformation. 2017;**45**:60–67

[17] Snihovyi O, Kobets V, Ivanov O. Implementation of robo-advisor services for different risk attitude investment decisions using machine learning techniques. In: International Conference on Information and Communication Technologies in Education, Research, and Industrial Applications; Springer; 2018. p. 298–321

[18] Guzella TS, Caminhas WM. A review of machine learning approaches to spam filtering. Expert Systems with Applications. 2009;**36**(7):10206–10222

[19] Blanzieri E, Bryl A. A survey of learning-based techniques of email spam filtering. Artificial Intelligence Review. 2008;**29**(1):63–92

[20] Stilgoe J. Machine learning, social learning and the Governance of Self-driving cars. Social Studies of Science. 2018;**48**(1):25–56

[21] Maqueda AI, Loquercio A, Gallego G, García N, Muzza DS. Event-based vision meets deep learning on steering prediction for self-driving cars. In: Proceedings of the IEEE Conference on Computer Vision and Pattern Recognition; 2018. p. 5419–5427

[22] Rzeszótko J, Nguyen Sinh Hoa. Machine learning for traffic prediction. Fundamenta Informaticae. 2012;**119**(3-4):407–420

[23] Boukerche A, Wang J. Machine learning-based traffic prediction models for Intelligent Transportation Systems. Computer Networks. 2020;**181**:107530

[24] Srinivasan G, Panda P, Roy K. Spilinc: Spiking liquid- ensemble computing for unsupervised speech and image recognition. Frontiers in Neuro-Science. 2018;**12**:524

[25] Deng L, Xiao L. Machine learning paradigms for speech recognition: An overview. IEEE Transactions on Audio, Speech, and Language Processing. 2013;**21**(5):1060–1089

[26] Tenni J, Lehtola A, Bounsaythip C, Jaaranen K. Machine learning of language translation rules. In: IEEE SMC'99 Conference Proceedings. 1999 IEEE International Conference on Systems, Man, and Cybernetics (Cat. No. 99CH37028); Vol. **5**; IEEE; 1999. p. 171–177

[27] Baroni M, Bernardini S. A new approach to the study of translationese: Machine–Learning the difference between original and translated text. Literary and Linguistic Computing. 2006;**21**(3):259–274

[28] Nwoke J. Healthcare data analytics and predictive modelling: Enhancing outcomes in Resource Allocation, disease prevalence and High-Risk Populations. International Journal of Health Sciences. 2024;**7**:1–35

[29] Chappell MA, Groves AR, Whitcher B, Woolrich MW. Partial volume correction in arterial spin labeling perfusion MRI. NeuroImage. 2021;**239**:118267

[30] Deepa N, Prabadevi B, Maddikunta PK, Gadekallu TR, Baker T, Khan MA. An AI-based intelligent system for healthcare analysis using Ridge-Adaline Stochastic gradient descent classifier. The Journal of Supercomputing. 2021;**77**:1998–2017

[31] Sikora A, Devlin JW, Yu M, Zhang T, Chen X, Smith SE, Murray B,

Buckley MS, Rowe S, Murphy DJ. Evaluation of medication regimen complexity as a predictor for mortality. Scientific Reports. 2023;**13**:10784

[32] Chiu HYR, et al. Machine learning for emerging infectious disease field forecasting. Scientific Reports 2022;**12**:17711

[33] Kuncheva LI, Whitaker CJ. Measures of diversity in classifier ensembles and their relationship with the ensemble accuracy. Machine Learning. 2003;**51**(2):181–207

[34] Brown G, Wyatt J, Harris R, Yao X. Diversity creation methods: A survey and categorisation. Information Fusion. 2005;**6**(1):5–20

[35] Tang EK, Suganthan PN, Yao X. An analysis of diversity measures. Machine Learning. 2006;**65**(1):247–271

[36] Jian L, Yi K, Zhang Q. Clustering with diversity. In: International Colloquium on Automata, Languages, and Programming Berlin, Heidelberg. Springer; 2010. p. 188–200

[37] Lee J, Sun Y, Nabar R, Lou H-L. Cluster-based transmit diversity scheme for mimo ofdm systems. In: Vehicular Technology Conference, 2008. VTC 2008-Fall. IEEE 68th. IEEE, 2008. p. 1–5

[38] Sharpton T, Jospin G, Dongying W, Langille M, Pollard K, Eisen J. Sifting through genomes with iterative-sequence clustering produces a large, phylogenetically diverse protein-family resource. BMC Bioinformatics. 2012;**13**(1):264

[39] Peter S, Sigmund K. Replicator dynamics. Journal of Theoretical Biology. 1983;**100**(3):533–538

[40] Kaggle. Kaggle. 2024. Google LLC. Available from: https://www.kaggle.com

[41] Miltiadous A, et al. Enhanced Alzheimer's disease and Frontotemporal Dementia EEG Detection: Combining lightGBM Gradient Boosting with Complexity Features. In: 2023 IEEE 36th International Symposium on Computer-Based Medical Systems (CBMS). IEEE; 2023

[42] Rahu M-U-R, Liu Q, Rahu AG. Accurate prediction of monkeypox disease cases by analyzing symptoms with ensemble learning boosting methods and using ML techniques. SSRN Preprint, 2024, Available from: https://ssrn.com/abstract=4978187

[43] Ghaheri P, et al. Diagnosis of Parkinson's disease based on voice signals using SHAP and hard voting ensemble method. Computer Methods in Biomechanics and Biomedical Engineering 2024;**27**:1858–1874

Chapter 4

Data Augmentation and Graph Regularization for Adversarial Training

Samet Bayram and Kenneth Barner

Abstract

This chapter explores innovative regularization strategies designed to enhance the resilience and accuracy of deep learning models against adversarial attacks, focusing particularly on graph-based methods. At the forefront is Graph Regularized Adversarial Training (GReAT), a pioneering approach that integrates graph-based regularization with adversarial training to exploit the underlying data structure for improved model robustness. By leveraging relationships among related samples, including augmented ones, GReAT significantly enhances performance. This chapter introduces enhanced versions of GReAT (Augmented GReAT) that incorporate standard data augmentation techniques. These extensions further enrich model training by diversifying the training examples within the graph framework. These methods aim to fortify models against sophisticated adversarial perturbations and improve generalization to new unseen datasets. Our comprehensive evaluations on benchmark datasets such as CIFAR-10 and SVHN demonstrate that these techniques, particularly Augmented GReAT, outperform traditional adversarial training methods. Augmented GReAT shows significant performance gains, achieving up to a 12% increase against PGD attacks on CIFAR-10 and 6.3% on SVHN. This chapter details the underlying theories and implementation of these augmented graph-based regularization techniques and thoroughly analyzes their impact through extensive experimental results. By integrating graph structures and data augmentation into the training process, we showcase significant advancements in neural networks' robustness and predictive accuracy, setting new benchmarks in the field.

Keywords: graph theory, adversarial machine learning, deep learning, robustness, data augmentation, image classification

1. Introduction

Deep learning (DL) has achieved impressive results in image and text classification, speech recognition, image generation, and natural language processing [1–3]. Supervised learning, where models are trained on labeled datasets, is particularly successful. It aims to predict new, unseen data based on patterns learned from labeled data, with deep neural networks adjusting weights and biases through back-propagation.

Semi-supervised learning combines supervised and unsupervised techniques [4]. Here, models are trained on datasets with both labeled and unlabeled instances, using labeled data to predict new unseen data. This approach is useful when labeled data are limited, but unlabeled data are abundant. Algorithms such as label propagation [5, 6], pseudo-labeling [7], transductive SVMs [8], and self-training [9] are commonly used, with label propagation showing outstanding performance.

Despite their success, deep learning models are vulnerable to adversarial examples, crafted by adding small perturbations to input data that cause misclassification while appearing similar to the original [10–12]. This vulnerability has spurred significant research on adversarial attacks and defenses. Adversarial attacks such as PGD [13], CW [11], BIM [14], and others demonstrate the susceptibility of AI systems, especially in image classification [11, 14–20].

Data augmentation, a technique to improve model generalization by generating additional training samples, includes transformations such as rotations, scaling, and cropping [21]. Adversarial examples can also be seen as a form of data augmentation [22]. By incorporating adversarial perturbations, models can be trained to recognize and withstand these modified inputs, thus enhancing their robustness.

Adversarial defense mechanisms fall into three categories. The first focuses on preprocessing techniques to remove adversarial perturbations, such as feature denoising [23], Fourier filtering [24], and random resizing/padding [25]. The second focuses on neural network architecture and training processes, including modifications of the activation function [26], distillation [27], and new loss functions [28]. The third combines these approaches.

The authors of [29] introduce TAAT and ATA, which leverage topological information to maintain consistency between natural and adversarial examples, along with a Knowledge-Guided training scheme for stability and efficiency. TRADES [30] decomposes prediction errors into natural and boundary errors, using a differentiable upper bound for its defense method.

Adversarial logit pairing (ALP) [31] improves accuracy on adversarial examples by encouraging logit similarity, while TLA training [32] uses metric learning to enhance robustness. Adversarial Contrastive Learning (ACL) [33] integrates adversarial perturbations into a contrastive learning framework for robustness and label efficiency.

Unlabeled samples are effective in improving deep learning performance [5, 34, 35] and adversarial robustness [36]. Motivated by this, earlier, we proposed Graph-Regularized Adversarial Training (GReAT) to enhance robustness [37]. GReAT uses structural information from input data, constructing a graph with clean data and adversarial neighborhoods to incorporate structural information into training.

In this chapter, we extend GReAT by incorporating standard data augmentation techniques, enriching the diversity of training examples within the graph framework. This Augmented GReAT approach aims to improve model robustness against adversarial attacks further while enhancing generalization to new, unseen datasets.

We evaluated Augmented GReAT on TensorFlow's flower dataset [38], CIFAR-10 [39], and SVHN [40] datasets, comparing it with state-of-the-art methods. The results show that Augmented GReAT consistently outperforms the baselines in accuracy and robustness. Our contributions include:

- Integrating graph structure and standard data augmentation into adversarial training;

- Enhancing feature extraction by incorporating neighboring information and augmented samples;

- Leveraging training sample structures and augmented data to enhance learning capabilities;
- Demonstrating significant advantages over state-of-the-art methods in robustness and generalization.

2. Background and related works

This section discusses the relevant background and related work, focusing on data augmentation, deep learning and semi-supervised learning, adversarial learning, and graph-based semi-supervised learning.

2.1 Data augmentation techniques

Data augmentation involves artificially increasing the size of a dataset by applying various transformations to existing samples. Data augmentation techniques, such as geometric transformations, noise addition, and color adjustments, enhance training data diversity and model generalization. Geometric transformations alter spatial properties (*e.g.*, scaling, flipping, rotations, translation), color transformations modify color properties (*e.g.*, brightness, contrast, color shifting, saturation), and noise injection adds noise (*e.g.*, Gaussian, salt-and pepper, speckle, Poisson) to improve robustness. This technique enhances the generalization and robustness of machine learning models by exposing them to a wider range of data variations.

2.2 Deep learning and semi-supervised learning

Deep learning models operate as complex non-linear mapping systems between inputs and outputs. They consist of several layers of neurons linked by activation functions. These networks extract features from input data and use them to predict labels. Training neural networks involves extensive labeled datasets, allowing them to learn and improve their performance over time through backpropagation algorithms.

The traditional DL prediction process can be described by the following equation:

$$\boldsymbol{Y} = f(\boldsymbol{X}, \boldsymbol{\theta}, \boldsymbol{b}), \tag{1}$$

where $\boldsymbol{X}$ is the input data passed into the neural network function f, $\boldsymbol{\theta}$ are the weights of the neural connections, and $\boldsymbol{b}$ are the biases. The output $\boldsymbol{Y}$ is the prediction generated by the neural network after processing the input data through its layers of neurons.

Semi-supervised learning leverages both labeled and unlabeled data to train the model. The prediction process for semi-supervised learning is expressed as:

$$\boldsymbol{Y} = f(\boldsymbol{X}_l, \boldsymbol{X}_{ul}, \boldsymbol{\theta}, \boldsymbol{b}), \tag{2}$$

where $\boldsymbol{X}_l$ represents the labeled data and $\boldsymbol{X}_{ul}$ denotes the unlabeled data. The weights $\boldsymbol{\theta}$ and biases $\boldsymbol{b}$ are similar to those used in supervised learning. The output $\boldsymbol{Y}$ is the model's prediction after processing labeled and unlabeled data through its neuron layers. In semi-supervised learning, a label assignment procedure is typically applied to the unlabeled data, using a smoothing function or similarity metrics to assign labels from the most similar labeled samples to the unlabeled ones [6].

2.3 Adversarial learning

Adversarial learning is a key area of research in machine learning, focused on enhancing model robustness against intentional perturbations. These perturbations, often subtle, can significantly impair model performance, leading to erroneous predictions with potentially severe consequences in areas such as autonomous driving, healthcare, and finance [10, 13].

The main goal of adversarial learning is to create models that can withstand adversarial attacks, which exploit model vulnerabilities [10].

2.3.1 Adversarial examples as data augmentation

Adversarial examples are artificial data points that introduce slight perturbations to natural instances to mislead a model into making incorrect predictions. These examples are crucial for understanding and improving model robustness, often used as a form of data augmentation during training.

Given a natural data instance $\boldsymbol{x}$ with a true label y, an adversarial example $\boldsymbol{x}'$ is generated to be almost identical to $\boldsymbol{x}$ according to a specific distance metric, but leads the model to predict an incorrect label, such that $f(\boldsymbol{x}') \neq y$ [41]. Formally, an adversarial example is defined as:

$$\boldsymbol{x}' : D(\boldsymbol{x}', \boldsymbol{x}) < \varepsilon, \;\; f(\boldsymbol{x}') \neq y, \tag{3}$$

where $D(\cdot,\cdot)$ denotes a distance metric, such as the $\|\cdot\|_2$ norm, and ε is a small threshold.

The Fast Gradient Sign Method (FGSM) [10] is a popular technique to generate adversarial examples. It perturbs the input data by adjusting each pixel in the direction of the gradient of the loss function with respect to the input, scaled by a small factor. This process is formalized as:

$$\boldsymbol{x}' = \boldsymbol{x} + \varepsilon \cdot \text{sign}(\nabla_{\boldsymbol{x}} \ell(\theta, \boldsymbol{x}, y)), \tag{4}$$

where $\nabla_{\boldsymbol{x}} \ell(\theta, \boldsymbol{x}, y)$ represents the gradient of the loss function ℓ with respect to the input $\boldsymbol{x}$, and ε is the magnitude of the perturbation.

Another effective method is Projected Gradient Descent (PGD) [13], which iteratively applies small perturbations and projects the resulting adversarial example back onto the valid input space defined by a norm-ball constraint:

$$\boldsymbol{x}'_{t+1} = \text{Proj}_{\boldsymbol{x}+\mathcal{B}}\left(\boldsymbol{x}'_t + \alpha \cdot \text{sign}(\nabla_{\boldsymbol{x}'} \ell(\theta, \boldsymbol{x}', y))\right), \tag{5}$$

where α is the step size, and $\text{Proj}_{\boldsymbol{x}+\mathcal{B}}$ denotes the projection onto the norm-ball $\mathcal{B}$ centered at $\boldsymbol{x}$.

Adversarial training is formalized as a min-max optimization problem aimed at finding the optimal model parameters θ that minimize the loss over the worst-case adversarial examples:

$$\boldsymbol{\theta}^* = \arg\min_{\theta \in \Theta} \frac{1}{L} \sum_{i=1}^{L} \max_{D(\boldsymbol{x}'_i, \boldsymbol{x}_i) < \varepsilon} \ell_{adv}\left(\theta, \boldsymbol{x}'_i, y_i\right). \tag{6}$$

This approach enhances the model's defense against known attacks and its robustness to previously unseen perturbations, making adversarial training a cornerstone of defense strategies in adversarial learning.

2.4 Graph-based semi-supervised learning

Graph-based semi-supervised learning effectively utilizes both labeled and unlabeled data to train deep learning (DL) models [34, 35, 42–45]. This approach combines a small set of labeled data with a larger set of unlabeled data to learn the underlying graph structure of the dataset. In this context, a graph is represented as $G = (V, E, W)$, where V are the data points (vertices), E are the edges connecting these points, and W is the edge weight matrix that captures the similarity between the data points. The edges of a graph are constructed on the basis of a similarity metric. Graph-based semi-supervised learning aims to use this graph structure and the labeled data to infer labels for the unlabeled data points. This is typically achieved by propagating labels from labeled to unlabeled data points through the similarity graph that spans the entire dataset [6, 45–47].

In graph-based semi-supervised learning, label propagation is a widely used technique for classifying nodes within a graph when only a few nodes are labeled. This method starts with the labeled nodes and propagates their labels to neighboring nodes. The labels are iteratively spread until the process converges, resulting in a fully labeled graph. The loss function for graph-based semi-supervised learning is given by [6]:

$$\sum_{i=1}^{L} \ell(\theta, \boldsymbol{x}_i, y_i) + \lambda \sum_{i,j} w_{i,j} \|h(\boldsymbol{x}_i) - h(\boldsymbol{x}_j)\|^2, \tag{7}$$

where the first term denotes the standard supervised loss, and the second term represents the neighborhood loss penalty. Here, $w_{i,j}$ captures the similarity between different instances, and λ controls the influence of neighborhood regularization. When $\lambda = 0$, the loss term reduces to the standard supervised loss. The penalty magnitude depends on the similarity between instance $\mathbf{x}_i$ and its neighbors. Additionally, h is a lookup table containing all samples and similarity weights, which can be obtained through a closed-form solution, as described in [47].

The authors of [42] proposed replacing the lookup tables with sample embeddings, extending the regularization term in Eq. (7) to $\lambda \sum_{i,j} \alpha_{i,j} \|g_\theta(\boldsymbol{x}_i) - g_\theta(\boldsymbol{x}_j)\|^2$, where $g_\theta(\cdot)$ denotes the embeddings of the sample generated by a neural network. Transitioning from h to g imposes stronger constraints on the neural network, as observed in [6].

We extend Eq. (7) by replacing the lookup table term with an embedding-based regularization component that defines a general neighbor similarity metric:

$$\sum_{i=1}^{L} \ell(\theta, \boldsymbol{x}_i, y_i) + \lambda \sum_{i=1} w_i \mathrm{D}\big(g_\theta(\boldsymbol{x}_i), \mathrm{N}(g_\theta(\boldsymbol{x}_i))\big). \tag{8}$$

In Eq. (8), N denotes the neighbors of a given sample $\boldsymbol{x}_i$, w_i represents the edge weights between the sample $\boldsymbol{x}_i$ and its neighbors, and D represents the distance metric between embeddings.

This framework provides a more flexible and general approach to integrating neighbor similarity metrics into graph-based semi-supervised learning, thereby enhancing the model's capacity to generalize effectively from labeled *and* unlabeled data.

3. Graph regularized adversarial training (GReAT)

3.1 Introduction to GReAT

In this section, we integrate the adversarial learning process [13] into the graph-based semi-supervised learning framework [6, 42, 45] to take advantage of both adversarial training and semi-supervised learning. The main framework of GReAT augmented with standard data augmentation is shown in **Figure 1**.

The feature space encompasses clean samples and adversarial examples created through adversarial regularization and neighbor similarities. Clean samples consist of original labeled training samples and standard augmented samples that we can show as $\boldsymbol{x} = \boldsymbol{x}_{org} + \boldsymbol{x}_{aug}$, where $\boldsymbol{x}_{org}$ are original samples and $\boldsymbol{x}_{aug}$ are augmented samples. The feature space is crucial for identifying nearest-neighbor samples. When we feed a batch of input samples to the neural network, it includes the original samples and their corresponding neighbors. In the final layer of the neural network, we derive a sample embedding for each of these samples.

The training objective for regularization includes two components: the supervised loss and the neighbor loss, which accounts for neighbor-related loss. In other words, it considers the impact of neighbors on the overall training objective. Thus,

$$\mathcal{L}_{GReAT} = \mathcal{L}_{adv} + \lambda \mathcal{L}_N, \tag{9}$$

where $\mathcal{L}_{adv}$ represents the supervised loss from training labels of clean samples and their adversarially perturbed versions, and $\mathcal{L}_N$ represents the neighbor loss, which includes the loss from the clean training samples and adversarially perturbed samples.

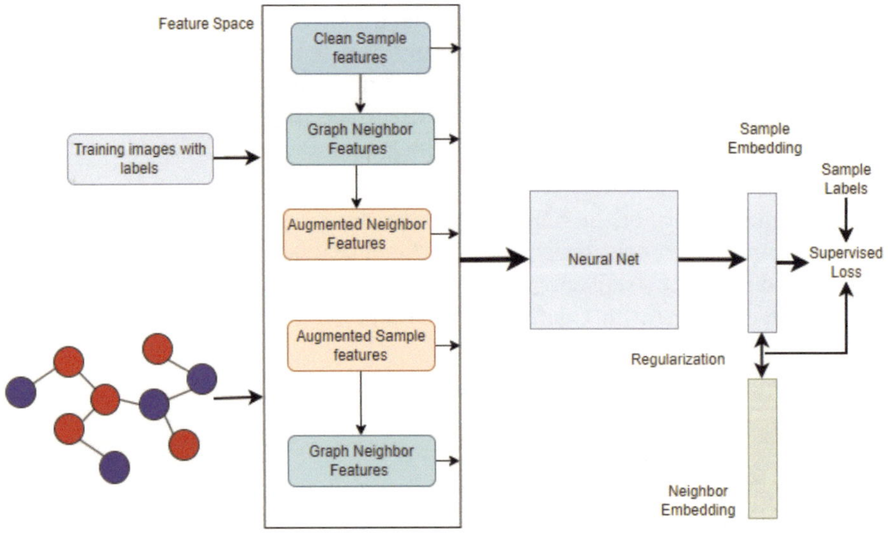

Figure 1.
Augmented GReAT framework.

We consider similar instances as neighbors of sample $\boldsymbol{x}$ in the graph regularized semi-supervised learning case. In our case, we consider an adversarial example, $\boldsymbol{x}'$, in addition to a neighbor of sample $\boldsymbol{x}$. Next, we extend Eq. (8) by including adversarial and adversarial neighbor losses as new regularizer terms. Formally, the unpacked form of Eq. (9) is:

$$\begin{aligned}\mathscr{L}_{GReAT}(\Theta) = &\sum_{i=1}^{L} \ell(\theta, \boldsymbol{x}_i, y_i) \\ &+\alpha_{11} \sum_{i=1}^{L} \ell_N(y_i, x_i, \mathrm{N}(x_i)) \\ &+\alpha_{22} \sum_{i=1}^{L} \ell_N(y_i, x'_i, \mathrm{N}(x'_i)) \\ &+\alpha_3 \sum_{i=1}^{L} \ell(\theta, \mathrm{N}_{adv}(x_i), y_i).\end{aligned} \tag{10}$$

In the above equation, $\mathrm{N}(\mathbf{x})$ represents neighbors of sample $\boldsymbol{x}$. The neighbors could be clean or adversarially perturbed samples. Thus, $\mathrm{N}(\boldsymbol{x}')$ represents the neighbors of adversarial example $\boldsymbol{x}'$. Its neighbors could be clean samples and adversarial examples. Specifically, $\mathrm{N}_{adv}(\boldsymbol{x})$ represents the adversarial neighbor of the sample $\boldsymbol{x}$. The adversarial neighbors have the same label as the original sample $\boldsymbol{x}$, similar to the standard adversarial training.

We obtain adversarial examples using PGD as described in [13]. Note that the $\alpha_{11}, \alpha_{22}, \alpha_3$ hyperparameters determine the contributions of different neighborhood types, which are shown in **Figure 2** as sub-graph types. The α terms can be tuned according to performance on clean and adversarially perturbed testing inputs. The pseudo-code of GReAT method is given in the Algorithm 1. Furthermore, a detailed explanation of the embedding of neighbor nodes and graph construction between clean and adversarial examples is shown in Section 3.3.

Algorithm 1: Graph Regularized Adversarial Training (GReAT).

Input: Labeled data $\boldsymbol{X}_l$, unlabeled data $\boldsymbol{X}_{ul}$, model parameters Θ, hyperparameters α_{11}, α_{22}, α_3, λ
Output: Trained model Θ^*
Train classifier $f(\boldsymbol{X}_l, \Theta)$ on labeled data using supervised loss ℓ
Generate adversarial examples $\boldsymbol{X}_{adv}$
Propagate labels of $\boldsymbol{X}_l$ to $\boldsymbol{X}_{ul}$ using label propagation on graph
Construct graph $\mathcal{G}$ with nodes $\boldsymbol{X}_l, \boldsymbol{X}_{ul}, \boldsymbol{X}_{adv}$
Compute neighbor set $\mathrm{N}(\boldsymbol{x})$, $\mathrm{N}(\boldsymbol{x}')$, $\mathrm{N}_{adv}(\boldsymbol{x})$ for each sample $\boldsymbol{x}, \boldsymbol{x}'$
Train model using loss $\mathscr{L}_{GReAT}$ defined in Eq. (10)
return Θ^*

3.2 Related previous methods

Creating graph embeddings using deep neural networks (DNNs) is a well-known method, [42]. Furthermore, the propagation of unlabeled graph embeddings using transductive methods, [6, 46], is efficient and well-studied. Neural Graph Machines (NGMs), [45], are a commonly used example of label propagation and graph embeddings, along with supervised learning. The proposed training objective takes

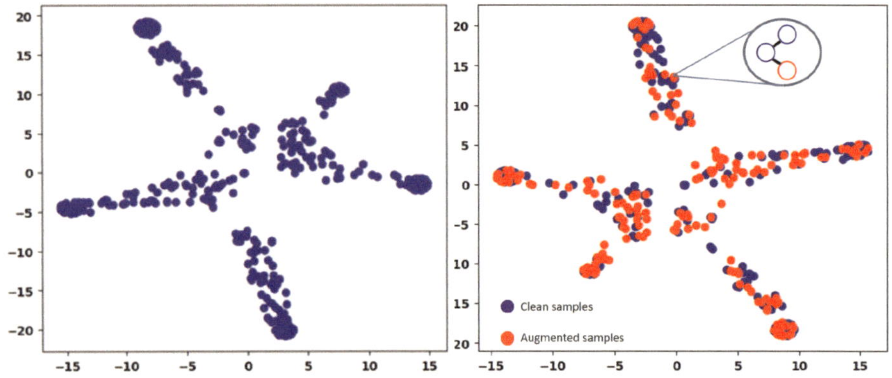

Figure 2.
Samples in embedding space. The figure on the left represents all the samples in the validation data set. The figure on the right shows some clean samples and their augmented neighbors.

advantage of these frameworks and provides more robust image classifiers. Therefore, the training objective can be considered a combination of nonlinear label propagation and a graph-regularized version of adversarial training.

3.3 Graph construction

We use a pre-trained model, DenseNet121, [48], to generate image embeddings as a feature extractor. The pre-trained model has weights obtained by training on ImageNet. The pre-trained model is more complex than the model we use to train and test the proposed regularization algorithm in our simulations. Numerous studies show that deep DNNs are better feature extractors than shallow networks [49, 50]. Another significant advantage of using larger pre-trained models is to reduce computational costs while obtaining high-quality embeddings. The process of creating embeddings is illustrated in **Figure 3**.

Generating appropriate inputs to the neural network plays an important role in making the correct predictions. As noted above, we use a pre-trained DL model to create node embeddings. We generate embeddings of clean and augmented samples to obtain the neighborhood relationship between clean and augmented samples. The overall graph construction process is shown in **Figure 4**.

Similarly, generating embeddings of the same size is crucial to measuring the similarities between samples. Since the size of the embeddings is the same, we can visualize clean and augmented samples in the embedding space using the [51] t-distributed stochastic neighbor embedding (t-SNE) method.

In **Figure 2**, we use t-SNE (t-distributed stochastic neighbor embedding) to create a visual representation of the validation data set obtained from TensorFlow's flower dataset. The primary purpose of this visualization is to provide insight into the distribution and relationships among the data points. The figure's left panel displays all the

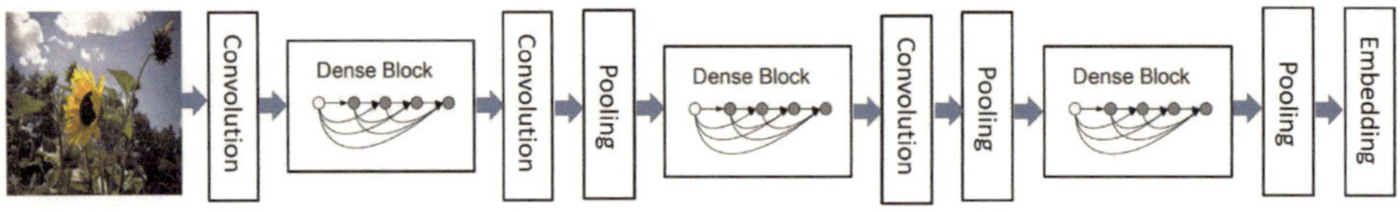

Figure 3.
Densenet121 for generating image embeddings.

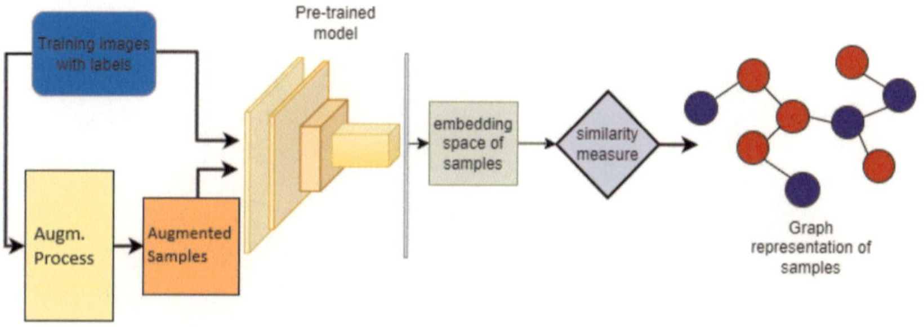

Figure 4.
Graph creation from embedding of clean and adversarial examples.

samples that constitute the validation data set. It is important to note that this data set encompasses samples of five distinct classes. Each class represents a specific category or data type within the dataset, and the samples within each class share certain common characteristics or features.

Visualizing the embeddings highlights a strong connection between individual samples and their neighbors, effectively distinguishing between various classes. We use strong neighborhood connections to learn better and create more robust models. Consequently, we use these node embeddings as input features to the neural network by creating an adjacency embedding matrix, as shown in **Figure 5**. In particular, we use the label propagation method [7] to propagate the information from the labeled data points to the unlabeled instances, which improves the model performance on both clean and augmented samples.

Sample sub-graph of training instances are shown in **Figure 5**. These examples might be labeled or unlabeled since we generate embeddings for each sample and create the graph based on the similarity between embeddings. Note that a labeled sample may have one neighbor or none, for instance, if the similarity measure of the embeddings cannot

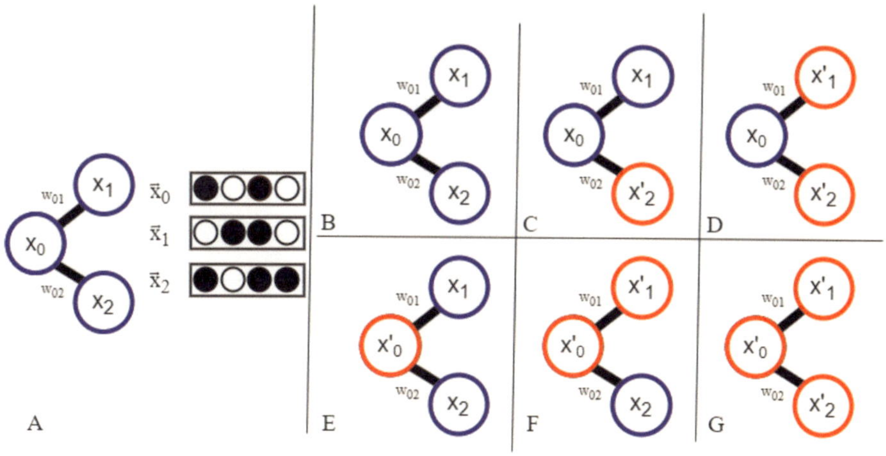

Figure 5.
A: A sample with two neighbors showing their sub-graph and feature inputs. Blue nodes represent clean samples, and red nodes represent augmented samples. B–G show how clean samples and augmented samples may link on the graph structure.

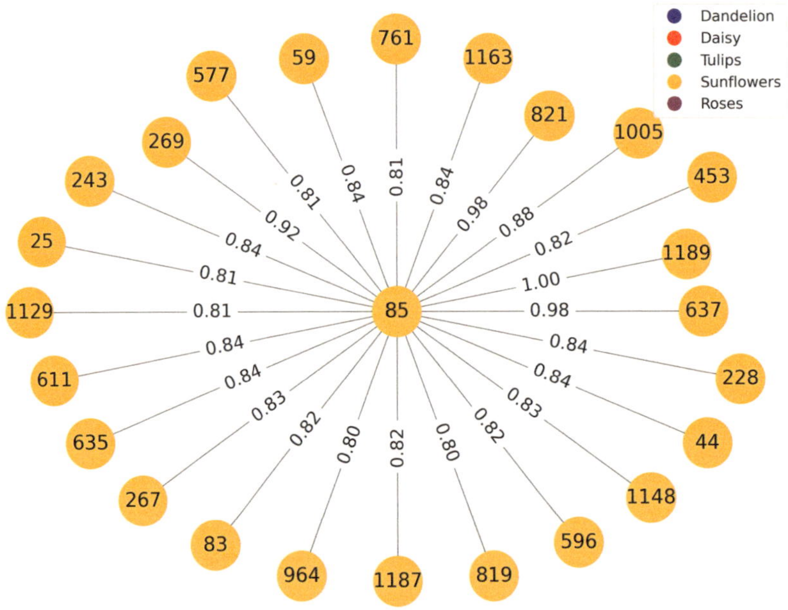

Figure 6.
Node 85 and its neighbors (threshold: 0.8).

Figure 7.
Visualization of Node 85 image and its top 5 nearest neighbors.

pass the similarity threshold. In that case, the labeled sample goes through the neural network as a regular input without graph regularization. A visual example of a sub-graph is demonstrated in **Figure 6**.

The sub-graph in **Figure 6** shows a node and its most similar neighbors. We limit the number of neighbors for each sample (node) for the training set before the training because it directly affects the training set's size and computation time. In this example, all neighbor nodes are classified as the main node. However, there could be some cases in which there are misclassified neighbors. **Figure** 7 shows the image of Node 85 and its top 5 nearest neighbors. As we can see, there are different augmented samples among Node 85's nearest neighbors.

3.4 Optimization process

The training starts by taking a minibatch of samples and their corresponding edges. Instead of utilizing the entire dataset in one batch, the procedure randomly picks a subset of edges for each iteration, introducing variability and randomness, which benefits the learning process. In addition, to further enhance training, edges are selected from a nearby region to increase the likelihood of including certain edges. This approach helps minimize noise and accelerates the learning process. Like other benchmark models [29], the Stochastic Gradient Descent (SGD) algorithm is employed to update network weights using the cross-entropy loss function. Additionally, we include the GReAT model trained with the Adam optimizer in our benchmark. Notably, we observe that the use of the Adam optimizer yields a superior performance compared to SGD in our experiments.

Note that the overall open form of the cost function in the following is equivalent to Eq. (8). The cost function incorporates the cost of supervised loss from labeled clean and labeled adversarial examples and neighbor losses. That is, the cost includes different neighbor types/edges, as shown in **Figure 5**. Formally,

$$\begin{aligned}
\mathcal{L}_{GReAT}(\Theta) = & \sum_{i=1}^{L} \ell(\theta, \boldsymbol{x}_i, y_i) + \sum_{i=1}^{L} \ell(\theta, \boldsymbol{x}'_i, y_i), \\
& + \lambda \left[\alpha_{11} \sum_{i=1}^{L} w_a \mathrm{D}(g_\theta(x_i), \mathrm{N}(g_\theta(x_i))) \right. \\
& + \alpha_{12} \sum_{i=1}^{L} w_b \mathrm{D}(g_\theta(x_i), \mathrm{N}(g_\theta(x'_i))) \\
& + \alpha_{21} \sum_{i=1}^{L} w_c \mathrm{D}(g_\theta(x'_i), \mathrm{N}(g_\theta(x_i))) \\
& \left. + \alpha_{22} \sum_{i=1}^{L} w_d \mathrm{D}(g_\theta(x'_i), \mathrm{N}(g_\theta(x'_i))) \right],
\end{aligned} \tag{11}$$

where w_a, w_b, w_c, w_d represent the similarity weights between the samples and their neighbors calculated by cosine similarity measurement.

The similarity weights for each sample and its neighbors are potentially unique, ranging from zero to one. A sample and its neighbor are considered dissimilar if the similarity weight is close to zero. To calculate the neighbor loss, we use D to represent the distance between a sample and its neighbor, using the norms L_1 and L_2 as distance metrics. The hyperparameters α_{11}, α_{12}, α_{21}, and α_{22} determine the contributions of different types of edges. In our simulations, we set all α values to one to include all edges in the training process. This new objective function enables using SGD with clean and adversarial examples and their neighbors in mini-batch training.

3.5 Complexity analysis

The proposed method integrates graph regularization into its training process, applying it to both labeled and unlabeled data instances within the graph, including benign and adversarial examples. The computational complexity of each training epoch depends on the number of edges in the graph, denoted as E_c. To evaluate the complexity of the training, we can express it as $O(count(E_c))$. It is important to note that E_c is directly proportional to several factors. Firstly, it scales with the number of neighboring data points considered, indicating that more neighbors will increase the complexity. Secondly, it is influenced by a parameter that determines the selection of the most similar neighbors, further affecting the computational load. The step size used for adversarial regularization is also linked to E_c.

4. Experiments

We conducted experiments to demonstrate the performance of the proposed Augmented GReAT method. Each experiment is performed on clean datasets with a fixed number of epochs and training steps. The typical hyperparameters are kept constant to ensure fair comparisons with other state-of-the-art methods. The base CNN model is first trained and then regularized using the proposed loss function. We use a copy of the base model to obtain the regularized model each time, preserving the original base model. Once the models are trained, we test each model on the same clean and adversarially perturbed test data to measure their generalization and robustness performances.

4.1 Datasets

Data sets from the Canadian Institute for Advanced Research (CIFAR-10) [39], Street View House Numbers (SVHN) [40], and Flowers [38] are used to evaluate the methods. The CIFAR-10 dataset consists of 60,000 images with 10 classes, and each class contains fixed-size 32×32 three-channel RGB images. To further assess the robust generalizability of our proposed method, we performed evaluations using the SVHN dataset, which comprises 73,257 training samples and 26,032 testing samples. The Flowers dataset contains 3670 images with five classes, each consisting of high-resolution RGB images. The image sizes are not fixed in the Flowers dataset, so resizing is required as one of the pre-processing steps.

The class distributions of the images are balanced in both datasets. We divide each dataset into train-validation-test sets in an 80%-10%-10% split, respectively. For our simulations, we exclusively use the flowers dataset for the ablation study, as existing benchmark methods do not incorporate flowers. Within the ablation study, we reduce the training set to 20% and 50% to observe model performance with fewer labeled samples.

4.2 Pre-processing steps

Several essential pre-processing steps are necessary to prepare batches for training. After generating image embeddings, we compute the similarity between each embedding and organize training batches based on this similarity metric.

4.2.1 Similarity measurement

Identifying the nearest neighbors for a given sample requires assessing the similarity among the embeddings. Various metrics, such as Euclidean distance, cosine similarity, and Structural Similarity Index Measure (SSIM), are available. We opt for cosine similarity due to its effectiveness in quantifying similarity among image embeddings in a multidimensional space. Cosine similarity is formally defined as:

$$Cos\left(x_i, x_j\right) = \frac{x_i \cdot x_j}{\|x_i\| * \|x_j\|}. \tag{12}$$

4.2.2 Similarity weights

Similarity weights range from 0 to 1, depending on the angle between pairs of vectors. Overlapping embeddings exhibit a weight of 1 when their angle is zero. Conversely, orthogonal vectors result in dissimilarity, with a weight of 0. A predefined similarity threshold is utilized to identify neighbors, excluding embeddings below this threshold from consideration.

4.2.3 Training batches

Once the graph structure is established with clean samples and adversarial examples, training batches are generated for input into the neural network model. Each batch includes samples, their identified neighbors, and adversarial neighbors. The number of neighbors per sample is predetermined, although alternative strategies may be employed. In our simulations, we set this number to 2.

4.2.4 Standard augmented samples generation

For the CIFAR-10 dataset, pixel values are normalized between 0 and 1. Augmentation techniques include random erasing, left-to-right flips, and Gaussian noise. The random erasing parameters are set to minval = 0.02 and maxval = 0.2 for the erasure area, and minval = 10 and maxval = 20 for the mask. Gaussian noise parameters have a mean of 0.0 and a standard deviation of 0.01.

4.2.5 Adversarial examples generation

During training, we adopt the conventional ℓ_∞ threat model with a radius of 8/255. Adversarial examples are generated using the PGD attack, iterating 10 steps with a step size of 2/255 across all datasets.

4.3 Network architecture

We used ResNet-18 [52] as the default baseline model architecture for our experiments. We employ the SGD optimizer to train all models with a momentum of 0.9 and the weight decay set to 0.0005. The training batch size is set to 128. We maintain consistency by using the same baseline model architecture and training parameters across all methods for a fair comparison. The Adam optimizer is configured with a learning rate of 0.001.

5. Results and analysis

5.1 Ablation study: augmented verses non-augmented datasets

In this ablation study, we compare the performance of models trained on augmented and non-augmented datasets under different training scenarios using the CIFAR-10 dataset, with 5% for training, 2% for validation, and 2% for testing, and employing the ResNet-18 model for training. The model trained with data augmentation (*base (aug) model*) demonstrates improved generalization and robustness over the non-augmented model (*base (no aug) model*), as discussed in the context of standard training. Additionally, incorporating graph regularization with augmentation (*graph reg (aug)*) further enhances performance, preserving relationships in the feature space and improving resistance to adversarial attacks. The choice of using a smaller training dataset allows us to observe the effects of augmented versus non-augmented training more distinctly. These results are depicted in **Figure 8**, which shows accuracy performances with increasing perturbation sizes. They are detailed in **Table 1**, which provides numerical accuracies for clean and adversarially perturbed test sets with 0.2 perturbation size.

5.1.1 Standard training: augmented versus not augmented models

In standard training, the model trained with the augmented dataset (*base (aug) model*) outperforms the model trained without augmentation (*base (no aug) model*) as expected. Augmentation increases the diversity of the training data and helps the

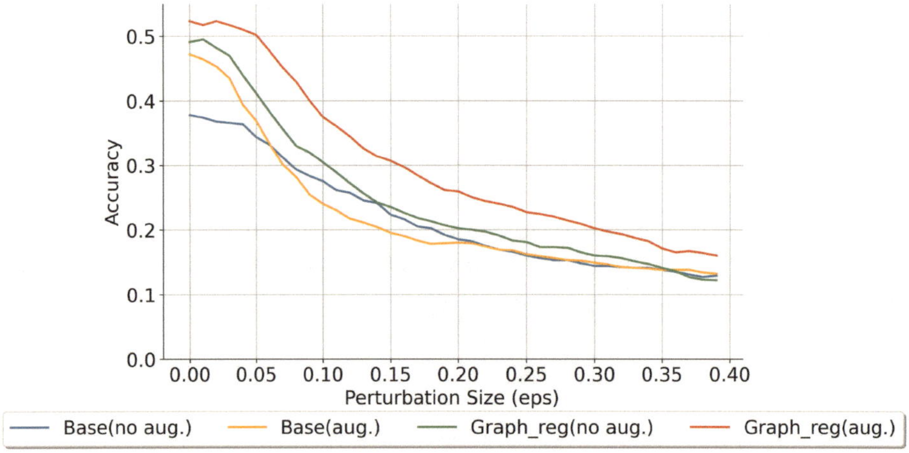

Figure 8.
Accuracy vs. attack strength.

Testing	Base (no aug)	Base aug	Graph reg (no aug)	Graph reg (aug)
Base test	37.8	47.2	49.0	**52.3**
Adversarial test	18.5	18.9	20.2	**25.9**

Bold accuracies show the best and the second best performances for each column (test method).

Table 1.
Accuracy results for models.

model generalize better to unseen data by learning more robust features, reducing overfitting, and improving overall performance on the test set.

5.1.2 Graph regularization: augmented versus not augmented models

When applying graph regularization during training, the augmented model with regularization (*graph reg (aug)*) shows superior performance compared to both the non-augmented models and the augmented model without regularization. Graph regularization helps preserve the relationships between samples in the feature space, which enhances the model's ability to generalize by maintaining smoothness in the data manifold. The combination of augmentation and regularization further boosts this effect, leading to better generalization and robustness.

5.1.3 Robustness: augmented versus not augmented models

In terms of robustness against adversarially perturbed test samples, the *graph reg (aug)* model shows the strongest resistance against variations and perturbations in the test data as shown in **Figure 8**. The integration of data augmentation introduces a variety of scenarios during training, which helps the model become less sensitive to changes in input data. Graph regularization further enhances this robustness by enforcing smoothness and consistency in the learned feature space. Consequently, the *graph reg (aug)* model demonstrates superior robustness compared to both the *base (aug)* and *base (no aug)* models.

5.2 Comparison with state-of-the-art models

We compare the robust accuracy of our proposed method with various baseline models under different attack methods, specifically FGSM and PGD-100, applied to the CIFAR-10 and SVHN datasets. The evaluations use the ℓ_∞ norm with $\varepsilon = 8/255$. All models are based on the ResNet-18 architecture. The best checkpoint is selected based on the achievement of the highest robust accuracy on the test set.

Table 2 presents the robustness results for the CIFAR-10 dataset, highlighting the performance of various methods in defending against adversarial attacks from FGSM and PGD-100. Although the original GReAT method outperforms other approaches in terms of robust accuracy, its natural accuracy is slightly lower than that of some other methods. However, the new Augmented GReAT method closes this gap and surpasses other methods in natural accuracy and robustness. Specifically, Augmented GReAT (ADAM) achieves the highest scores, demonstrating the effectiveness of integrating standard data augmentation techniques with GReAT in enhancing the robustness and overall performance of CIFAR-10 classification models against adversarial attacks.

Table 3 displays the natural accuracy and robustness results for the SVHN dataset, showing the accuracy of various methods when faced with adversarial attacks from FGSM and PGD-100. The original GReAT method significantly improves robust accuracy compared to other methods while maintaining comparable natural accuracy. The new Augmented GReAT method further enhances performance, achieving the highest scores in both natural and robust accuracy.

CIFAR-10, $l_{inf} = 8/255$, untargeted attack			
Method	**Natural Acc**	**FGSM**	**PGD-100**
AT [13]	82.97	57.77	51.35
ALP [31]	84.86	57.55	51.57
TLA [32]	83.49	58.17	51.96
ACL [33]	83.26	57.54	51.51
TRADES [30]	83.74	59.54	52.73
ATA [29]	83.41	57.96	52.39
TAAT [29]	83.12	59.91	54.45
GReAT (SGD)	82.64	62.78	60.58
GReAT (ADAM)	82.89	**72.47**	**71.31**
Augmented GReAT (SGD)	**85.12**	63.11	60.97
Augmented GReAT (ADAM)	**85.62**	**72.9**	**71.47**

Bold accuracies show the best and the second best performances for each column (test method).

Table 2.
Robust Benchmark under l_{inf} type attack for CIFAR-10.

SVHN, $l_{inf} = 8/255$, untargeted attack			
Method	**Natural Acc**	**FGSM**	**PGD-100**
AT [13]	90.5	65.08	52.87
ALP [31]	90.67	65.51	54.07
TLA [32]	90.63	64.66	52.96
ACL [33]	90.33	63.57	52.07
TRADES [30]	90.38	73.31	57.94
ATA [29]	89.11	62.81	53.75
TAAT [29]	90.44	72.59	59.91
GReAT (SGD)	90.24	74.47	63.45
GReAT (ADAM)	90.54	**75.81**	**65.66**
Augmented GReAT (SGD)	**90.71**	75.01	63.67
Augmented GReAT (ADAM)	**91.12**	**76.23**	**65.9**

Bold accuracies show the best and the second best performances for each column (test method).

Table 3.
Robust Benchmark under l_{inf} type attack for SVHN.

6. Conclusion

This chapter presented an enhanced version of the Augmented Graph Regularized Adversarial Training Method (Augmented GReAT) to improve classifier robustness by incorporating standard data augmentation techniques. We leveraged classical adversarial training with graph regularization to further enhance the robustness of deep learning classifiers. We bolstered the model's capacity to withstand adversarial attacks by employing graph-based constraints to regularize the training process. Our comprehensive evaluations, shown in **Tables 2** and **3**, demonstrate that the Augmented GReAT method achieves superior performance in both natural and robust accuracy compared to other state-of-the-art methods. Specifically, Augmented GReAT (ADAM) outperforms all methods, showcasing the effectiveness of combining graph structures with data augmentation in enhancing the robustness and generalization of deep learning classifiers. This strategy is a valuable tool in adversarial training, significantly advancing neural networks' robustness and predictive accuracy against sophisticated adversarial perturbations.

Author details

Samet Bayram* and Kenneth Barner
Electrical and Computer Engineering Department, University of Delaware, Newark, DE, USA

*Address all correspondence to: sbayram@udel.edu

References

[1] Liu C, Dong Y, Xiang W, Yang X, Su H, Zhu J, et al. A comprehensive study on robustness of image classification models. Benchmarking and Rethinking. 2023. Available from: https://arxiv.org/abs/2302.14301

[2] Mauricio J, Domingues I, Bernardino J. Comparing vision transformers and convolutional neural networks for image classification: A literature review. Applied Sciences. 2023;**13**(9):306-322. Available from: https://www.mdpi.com/2076-3417/13/9/5521

[3] Taye MM. Understanding of machine learning with deep learning: Architectures, workflow, applications and future directions. Computers. 2023; **12**(5):26. Available from: https://www.mdpi.com/2073-431X/12/5/91

[4] Li S, Kou P, Ma M, Yang H, Huang S, Yang Z. Application of semi-supervised learning in image classification: Research on fusion of labeled and unlabeled data. IEEE Access. 2024;**12**:27331-27343

[5] Bengio Y, Delalleau O, Le Roux N. Label propagation and quadratic criterion. In: Semi-Supervised Learning. Cambridge, Massachusetts, USA: The MIT Press; 2006. DOI: 10.7551/mitpress/6173.003.0016

[6] Yang Z, Cohen WW, Salakhutdinov R. Revisiting Semi-Supervised Learning with Graph Embeddings. arXiv; 2016. ArXiv: 1603.08861 [cs]. Available from: http://arxiv.org/abs/1603.08861

[7] Lee DH. Pseudo-label: The simple and efficient semi-supervised learning method for deep neural networks. In: ICML 2013 Workshop: Challenges in Representation Learning (WREPL). Atlanta, USA: ICML Conference; 2013

[8] Joachims T. Transductive inference for text classification using support vector machines. In: ICML '99: Proceedings of the Sixteenth International Conference on Machine Learning. San Francisco, CA, USA: Morgan Kaufmann Publishers Inc.; 1999. pp. 200-209

[9] Amini MR, Feofanov V, Pauletto L, Devijver E, Maximov Y. Self-Training: A Survey. arXiv; 2022. Available from: https://arxiv.org/abs/2202.12040

[10] Goodfellow I, Shlens J, Szegedy C. Explaining and harnessing adversarial examples. In: International Conference on Learning Representations. San Diego, CA, USA: ICLR Conference; 2015. Available from: http://arxiv.org/abs/1412.6572

[11] Carlini N, Wagner D. Towards evaluating the robustness of neural networks. In: 2017 IEEE Symposium on Security and Privacy (SP). San Jose, CA, USA: IEEE, SP; 2017. pp. 39-57

[12] Nguyen A, Yosinski J, Clune J. Deep Neural Networks Are Easily Fooled: High Confidence Predictions for Unrecognizable Images. Boston, Massachusetts, USA: CVPR; 2015

[13] Madry A, Makelov A, Schmidt L, Tsipras D, Vladu A. Towards Deep Learning Models Resistant to Adversarial Attacks. Vancouver, BC, Canada: ICLR; 2018

[14] Kurakin A, Goodfellow IJ, Bengio S. Adversarial Examples in the Physical World. CoRR. International Joint Conferences on Artificial Intelligence Organization (IJCAI); 2016. pp. 4925-4926. Available from: http://arxiv.org/abs/1607.02533

[15] Szegedy C, Zaremba W, Sutskever I, Bruna J, Erhan D, Goodfellow I, et al. Intriguing Properties of Neural Networks. Banff, AB, Canada: ICLR; 2014

[16] Biggio B, Roli F. Wild patterns: Ten years after the rise of adversarial machine learning. Pattern Recognition. 2018;**84**:317-331. DOI: 10.1016/j.patcog.2018.07.023

[17] Moosavi-Dezfooli SM, Fawzi A, Frossard P. DeepFool: A Simple and Accurate Method to Fool Deep Neural Networks. Las Vegas, NV, USA: CVPR; 2016

[18] Sharif M, Bhagavatula S, Bauer L, Reiter MK. Accessorize to a crime: Real and stealthy attacks on state-of-the-art face recognition. In: Proceedings of the 2016 ACM SIGSAC Conference on Computer and Communications Security. CCS '16. New York, NY, USA: Association for Computing Machinery; 2016. pp. 1528-1540. DOI: 10.1145/2976749.2978392

[19] Eykholt K, Evtimov I, Fernandes E, Li B, Rahmati A, Xiao C, et al. Robust Physical-World Attacks on Deep Learning Models. Salt Lake City, Utah, USA: CVPR; 2018

[20] Bayram S, Barner K. A Black-Box Attack on Optical Character Recognition Systems. arXiv. 2022. Available from: https://arxiv.org/abs/2208.14302

[21] Shorten C, Khoshgoftaar TM. A survey on image data augmentation for deep learning. Journal of Big Data. 2019;**6**:1-48. Available from: https://api.semanticscholar.org/CorpusID:195811894

[22] Luo R, Wang Y, Wang Y. Rethinking the Effect of Data Augmentation in Adversarial Contrastive Learning. Kigali, Rwanda: ICLR; 2023. Available from: https://arxiv.org/abs/2303.01289

[23] Xie C, Wu Y, Lvd M, Yuille AL, He K. Feature denoising for improving adversarial robustness. In: Proceedings of the IEEE/CVF Conference on Computer Vision and Pattern Recognition. Long Beach, CA, USA: CVPR; 2019. pp. 501-509

[24] Bafna M, Murtagh J, Vyas N. Thwarting Adversarial Examples: An L_0-RobustSparse Fourier Transform. arXiv preprint arXiv:181205013. 2018

[25] Xie C, Wang J, Zhang Z, Ren Z, Yuille A. Mitigating adversarial effects through randomization. arXiv preprint arXiv:171101991. 2017

[26] Wang B, Lin AT, Zhu W, Yin P, Bertozzi AL, Osher SJ. Adversarial defense via data dependent activation function and total variation minimization. arXiv preprint arXiv:180908516. 2018

[27] Papernot N, McDaniel P, Wu X, Jha S, Swami A. Distillation as a defense to adversarial perturbations against deep neural networks. In: 2016 IEEE Symposium on Security and Privacy (SP). San Jose, CA, USA: IEEE; 2016. pp. 582-597

[28] Chen HY, Liang JH, Chang SC, Pan JY, Chen YT, Wei W, et al. Improving adversarial robustness via guided complement entropy. In: Proceedings of the IEEE/CVF International Conference on Computer Vision. Seoul, Korea: ICCV; 2019. pp. 4881-4889

[29] Kuang H, Liu H, Lin X, Ji R. Defense against adversarial attacks using topology aligning adversarial training. IEEE Transactions on Information Forensics and Security. 2024;**19**:1-1

[30] Zhang H, Yu Y, Jiao J, Xing EP, Ghaoui LE, Jordan MI. Theoretically principled trade-off between robustness and accuracy. In: ICML. Vol. 97 of Proceedings of Machine Learning Research. Long Beach, California, USA: PMLR; 2019. pp. 7472-7482

[31] Kannan H, Kurakin A, Goodfellow I. Adversarial Logit Pairing. Montreal, Canada: NIPS; 2018

[32] Mao C, Zhong Z, Yang J, Vondrick C, Ray B. Metric learning for adversarial robustness. In: NeurIPS. Vancouver, Canada: NIPS; 2019. pp. 478-489

[33] Jiang Z, Chen T, Chen T, Wang Z. Robust Pre-Training by Adversarial Contrastive Learning. Virtual: NIPS; 2020

[34] Zhou D, Huang J, Schölkopf B. Learning from labeled and unlabeled data on a directed graph. In: Proceedings of the 22nd International Conference on Machine learning - ICML '05; Bonn, Germany. Bonn, Germany: ICML; 2005. pp. 1036-1043. Available from: http://portal.acm.org/citation.cfm?doid=1102351.1102482

[35] Belkin M, Niyogi P, Sindhwani V. Manifold regularization: A geometric framework for learning from labeled and unlabeled examples. Journal of Machine Learning Research. 2006;7(85):2399-2434. Available from: http://jmlr.org/papers/v7/belkin06a.html

[36] Carmon Y, Raghunathan A, Schmidt L, Duchi JC, Liang PS. Unlabeled data improves adversarial robustness. In: Advances in Neural Information Processing Systems. Vol. 32. Vancouver, Canada: Curran Associates, Inc.; 2019

[37] Bayram S, Barner K. GReAT: A graph regularized adversarial training method. IEEE Access. 2024;**12**:63130-63141

[38] TensorFlow. Flowers; 2019. Available from: http://download.tensorflow.org/example-images/flower-photos.tgz

[39] Krizhevsky A, Nair V, Hinton G. CIFAR10 Dataset. Canada: Canadian Institute for Advanced Research; 2009

[40] Netzer Y, Wang T, Coates A, Bissacco A, Wu B, Ng AY. Reading digits in natural images with unsupervised feature learning. In: NIPS Workshop on Deep Learning and Unsupervised Feature Learning. Granada, Spain: NIPS; 2011. Available from: http://ufldl.stanford.edu/housenumbers

[41] Ren K, Zheng T, Qin Z, Liu X. Adversarial attacks and defenses in deep learning. Engineering. 2020;**6**(3):346-360

[42] Weston J, Ratle F, Collobert R. Deep learning via semi-supervised embedding. In: Proceedings of the 25th International Conference on Machine Learning. ICML '08. New York, NY, USA: Association for Computing Machinery; 2008. pp. 1168-1175. DOI: 10.1145/1390156.1390303

[43] Agarwal N, Liu H, Murthy S, Sen A, Wang X. A social identity approach to identify familiar strangers in a social network. Proceedings of the International AAAI Conference on Web and Social Media. 2009;**3**(1):2-9. Available from: https://ojs.aaai.org/index.php/ICWSM/article/view/13946

[44] Jacob Y, Denoyer L, Gallinari P. Learning latent representations of nodes for classifying in heterogeneous social networks. In: Proceedings of the 7th ACM International Conference on Web Search and Data Mining. New York, New York, USA: ACM; 2014. pp. 373-382. Available from: https://dl.acm.org/doi/10.1145/2556195.2556225

[45] Bui TD, Ravi S, Ramavajjala V. Neural graph learning: Training neural networks using graphs. In: Proceedings of the Eleventh ACM International Conference on Web Search and Data Mining. Marina Del Rey, CA, USA: ACM; 2018. pp. 64-71. Available from: https://dl.acm.org/doi/10.1145/3159652.3159731

[46] Zhu X, Lafferty J, Rosenfeld R. Semi-Supervised Learning with Graphs. USA: Carnegie Mellon University; 2005. p. AAI3179046

[47] Zhou D, Bousquet O, Lal TN, Weston J, Schölkopf B. Learning with Local and Global Consistency. San Francisco, CA, USA: ACM Digital Library; 2004. p. 8

[48] Huang G, Liu Z, van der Maaten L, Weinberger KQ. Densely Connected Convolutional Networks. arXiv. 2016. Available from: https://arxiv.org/abs/1608.06993

[49] Krizhevsky A. Learning Multiple Layers of Features from Tiny Images. Canada: University of Toronto; 2009

[50] Mhaskar H, Liao Q, Poggio TA. When and why are deep networks better than shallow ones? In: Singh SP, Markovitch S, editors. AAAI. San Francisco, California, USA: AAAI Press; 2017. pp. 2343-2349. Available from: http://dblp.uni-trier.de/db/conf/aaai/aaai2017.htmlMhaskarLP17

[51] van der Maaten L, Hinton G. Visualizing data using t-SNE. Journal of Machine Learning Research. 2008;**9**: 2579-2605. Available from: http://www.jmlr.org/papers/v9/vandermaaten08a.html

[52] He K, Zhang X, Ren S, Sun J. Deep Residual Learning for Image Recognition. Las Vegas, USA: CVPR; 2016

Section 3

Deep Learning and Intelligent Systems Applications

Chapter 5

Discriminative-Encoder GAN and Lightweight CNN for Interpretable Plant Disease Detection and Deployable Diagnosis

Md. Abid Hasan Rafi, Pijush Kanti Roy Partho, Pankaj Bhowmik, Md. Delowar Hossain and Tangina Sultana

Abstract

The application of intelligent decision-making tools to enhance the identification of plant diseases represents a significant advancement in precision farming. A viable diagnostic system in this domain involves more than advanced algorithms; it requires the careful integration of diagnostic accuracy, computational efficiency, and interpretability for real-world deployment. We offer a unified framework that combines baseline deep learning architectures with explainable AI (XAI) approaches to enable high-performance predictions and transparent, trustworthy decision-making, addressing these interrelated challenges. At the core of this system lies a lightweight convolutional neural network augmented with attention mechanisms designed to achieve strong classification performance while significantly reducing model complexity. To enhance the generalization and transferability of learned features, a discriminative-encoder Generative Adversarial Network (GAN) is employed, generating synthetic representations that, when paired with classical machine learning classifiers, demonstrate superior capability in capturing subtle disease patterns. The technology makes data easier to understand and adds a level of transparency that is crucial for practical use by employing gradient-based visual explanation methods that closely align with expert opinions. A wide variety of crop species have undergone extensive validation of the entire diagnostic process, which has consistently demonstrated high accuracy and computational efficiency across a range of environmental conditions. The technology is implemented using an interactive interface that provides clear and easy-to-understand visual feedback, as well as real-time forecasts, making it straightforward for agricultural specialists to utilize. This work has led to tremendous progress in developing new, interpretable, and scalable precision agriculture technologies.

Keywords: plant disease, lightweight CNN, adversarial learning, explainable AI, attention mechanism

1. Introduction

Plant disease detection represents a critical challenge in agricultural technology, with significant implications for global food security and crop yield optimization [1]. Recent progress in deep learning has shown promising outcomes in laboratory environments, yet substantial gaps remain in transitioning these technologies to practical field applications [2]. Three persistent challenges hinder widespread adoption: the inherent trade-off between model accuracy and computational efficiency [3, 4], limited availability of annotated training data for rare diseases [5, 6], and insufficient model interpretability for agricultural stakeholders [7, 8].

Current plant disease detection systems use different methods to address these problems. Lightweight convolutional architectures [4, 9] have shown potential for efficient deployment, though they often sacrifice accuracy compared to deeper models [10, 11]. Generative adversarial networks have emerged as powerful tools for data augmentation [12, 13], while explainability methods [7] continue to evolve toward domain-specific applications [8, 14]. Despite these advances, no unified framework has successfully addressed all three challenges simultaneously while maintaining state-of-the-art performance across diverse agricultural scenarios. This work makes four principal contributions to the field of automated plant disease detection:

- A lightweight convolutional neural network (CNN) architecture combining depthwise separable convolutions with attention mechanisms, achieving 98.18% accuracy with only lower parameters (a reduction from ResNet-50 [1, 10]).
- The discriminative-encoder GAN (DE-GAN) framework, which unifies synthetic data generation with discriminative learning (99.36% accuracy across all classes [5, 6, 13]).
- A domain-specific interpretability pipeline improving diagnostic utility over conventional methods [8, 14]
- Comprehensive validation demonstrating superior performance in both controlled and field conditions [2, 15].

Our methodological innovations address the fundamental limitations of current systems through three synergistic advances. The lightweight CNN architecture establishes new benchmarks for efficient deployment without compromising accuracy. The DE-GAN framework simultaneously overcomes data scarcity while enhancing feature learning. Finally, our specialized interpretability pipeline bridges the gap between algorithmic predictions and practical agricultural decision-making.

The rest of this chapter is divided as follows: In Section 2, we review the essential work done to identify plant diseases; Section 3 details our methodological framework; Section 4 presents experimental approaches; Section 5 explores results analysis; Section 6 discusses the dataset coverage; and Section 7 presents the deployment feasibility. Finally, in Section 8, we discuss the implications of this chapter and outline potential next steps.

2. Background research

Recent advancements in deep learning have revolutionized plant disease detection, offering scalable and precise solutions for agricultural monitoring. This section reviews key methodologies, from CNN-based systems to generative augmentation, highlighting their strengths and limitations.

2.1 Overview of deep learning in plant disease detection

Deep learning has made an enormous impact in the field of plant disease diagnosis. Different architectures and data augmentation methodologies have shown excellent outcomes in a wide range of plants and circumstances. Among these, Generative Adversarial Networks (GANs) have emerged as particularly impactful tools for enhancing model generalizability and addressing data limitations. For instance, the study by Lokesh et al. [5] utilized CycleGAN-based augmentation to achieve 99.51% accuracy in cassava leaf disease classification, highlighting the potential of generative models to enrich dataset diversity. However, even though they work well, these kinds of methods make us wonder if they can be used on diverse types of plants and diseases.

2.2 CNN-based approaches

Convolutional Neural Networks (CNNs) remain foundational to plant disease detection efforts. Traditional CNN-based pipelines have shown consistent success, as demonstrated by Srinath et al. [10], who developed a VGG19-based detection system with an accessible web interface. Similarly, Maniyar and Budihal [6] enhanced classification performance (98.29% accuracy) by integrating CNNs with GAN-generated synthetic data. On the other hand, Reddy et al. [1] conducted a comparative study that showed high-performing pretrained models, like ResNet-50, could get state-of-the-art results (99.8%) without using data augmentation, which suggests that the architecture of the model is significant for how well it can classify things.

There have also been attempts to make architectures more suited to the needs of plant disease detection. For instance, the PLDD-CANN framework proposed by Kanagaraj et al. [2] showed that it might boost performance by up to 27.46% compared to traditional approaches, which shows how domain-specific architectural improvements can be helpful. Additionally, mobile-focused solutions like that of Saranathan et al. [11] underscore the growing interest in real-time, edge-deployable applications.

2.3 GAN-augmented techniques

The incorporation of GANs into training pipelines has further improved model robustness and accuracy. Recent GAN-driven research has pushed performance boundaries even further. For example, Deshpande and Patidar [12] employed a Deep Convolutional Neural Network (DCNN) augmented by GANs to reach 99.74% accuracy in tomato disease classification, whereas Zhao et al. [13] addressed dataset imbalance using DoubleGAN, achieving 99.53% accuracy. The WGP-ESR GAN introduced by Harinadha and Krishna Mohan [15] generated highly realistic leaf images, enabling classifiers to generalize better and attain 99.69% accuracy on downstream tasks.

Moreover, lightweight and computationally efficient models have demonstrated surprising effectiveness when paired with GAN-based augmentation. A parallel DCNN architecture proposed by Deshpande and Patidar [9] achieved 99.14% accuracy using GAN-augmented samples, and Pandian et al. [4] showed that even a simple five-layer CNN, when trained with synthetic data, could reach an accuracy of 98.41%.

2.4 Hybrid and lightweight architectures

Innovative hybrid frameworks are being explored to balance performance and efficiency. The Tranvolution detection network proposed by Zhang et al. [14] combines CNN and GAN modules to address the challenges of small-scale object detection, achieving a mean Average Precision (mAP) of 50.3%. Meanwhile, Pandian et al. [4] demonstrated that traditional CNN pipelines can remain competitive, achieving 98.5% accuracy even without the use of generative augmentation.

2.5 Evaluation and deployment considerations

Along with newly extending concepts, it is essential to do the proper evaluations in different situations. The thorough review by Mustofa et al. [17] looked all known deep learning models and highlighted the importance of being able to work well in different lighting, occlusion, and background situations. The study by Selvam and Joy [16] also contributed by integrating Mask R-CNN with multivariate feature selection, generating 95. About 06% accuracy in complex feature settings. Furthermore, Shivaprasad and Wadhawan [3] introduced a new dataset containing 38 disease classes and achieved 99.07% training accuracy using MobileNet, underscoring the importance of both model and dataset quality.

An increasing number of studies show that both traditional and generative deep learning methods can produce very accurate models for finding plant diseases. Often, the choice of strategy is based on practical issues like the size of the dataset, the availability of computing resources, and the setting in which the strategy will be used. Building upon these insights, our work proposes a hybrid framework that synergizes the strengths of lightweight CNNs and GAN-based data enhancement to deliver a robust and efficient solution for plant disease classification.

3. Methodology

Our proposed methodology integrates lightweight deep learning architectures with explainable AI techniques to deliver both high accuracy and model interpretability for plant disease classification. The pipeline begins with standardized image preprocessing and lightweight CNN feature extraction, augmented with spatial attention mechanisms to enhance diagnostic focus. Then, two parallel learning streams are utilized: a CNN-based attention architecture for real-time inference, and a GAN-based discriminative encoder for synthetic data generation and feature learning. Finally, an explainable AI pipeline, explicitly tailored for tomato disease classification, provides interpretable visualizations using Grad-CAM. The entire pipeline, shown in **Figure 1**, is optimized for low-latency, edge-compatible deployment.

3.1 Proposed lightweight CNN with attention-based XAI

The lightweight CNN architecture was specifically designed to balance diagnostic accuracy with computational efficiency for edge deployment scenarios. The model processes 128×128 RGB input images through three sequential depthwise separable convolution blocks defined by Eq. (1):

$$\mathcal{F}(x) = \text{DSConv}_{128}(\text{DSConv}_{64}(\text{DSConv}_{32}(x))) \tag{1}$$

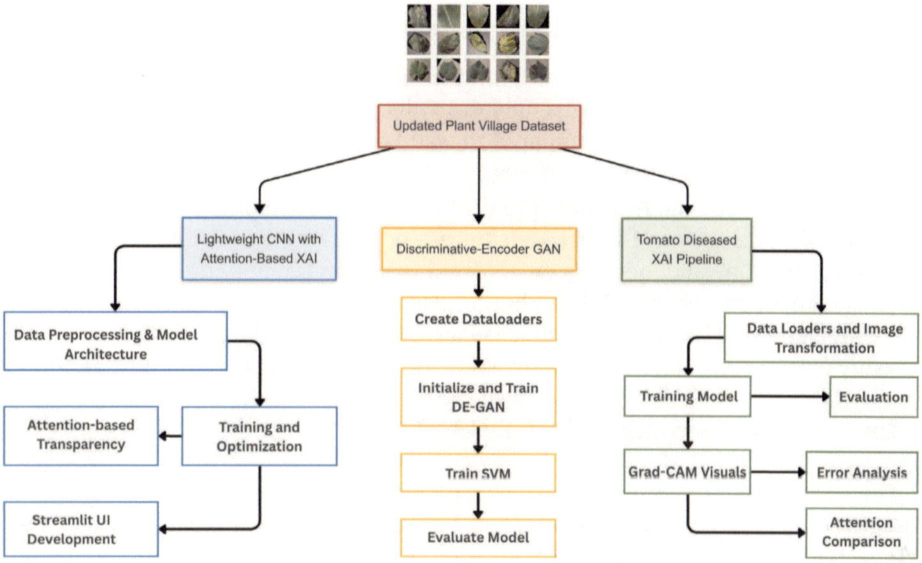

Figure 1.
Diagram of proposed methodology showing the complete pipeline from image preprocessing to explainable AI visualization. The architecture integrates both lightweight CNNs and GAN-based components for comprehensive plant disease analysis.

where $\mathcal{F}(x)$ represents the complete feature transformation, and each DSConv_n block (with n output channels) consists of two key operations defined in Eqs. (2) and (3):

$$\mathcal{DW}(x) = \sum_{c=1}^{C} w_c * x_c \quad \text{(Depthwise convolution)} \tag{2}$$

where $\mathcal{DW}(x)$ processes each input channel x_c (total C channels) independently with channel-specific kernel w_c, followed by:

$$\mathcal{PW}(x) = W_{1\times1} * x \quad \text{(Pointwise convolution)} \tag{3}$$

where $\mathcal{PW}(x)$ combines channels using learnable weights $W_{1\times1}$ (a 1×1 convolution).

The architecture progressively increases feature depth from 32 to 128 channels while maintaining spatial resolution through zero-padding. Each block incorporates batch normalization and ReLU activation before 2×2 max pooling, with dropout ($p = 0.3$ where p is the dropout probability) applied in the final fully connected layer to prevent overfitting.

A critical innovation in our architecture is the attention mechanism implemented between the convolution blocks and the classification head. The attention module computes spatial importance weights through:

$$\mathbf{A} = \sigma(W_a * \mathcal{F}) \tag{4}$$

where $\mathbf{A}$ is the attention map, σ is the sigmoid activation, W_a are learnable attention weights, and $\mathcal{F}$ are input features. This attention map is element-wise multiplied ($\odot$) with the feature maps:

$$\mathbf{F}' = \mathcal{F} \odot \mathbf{A} \tag{5}$$

yielding attention-weighted features $\mathbf{F}'$ that emphasize diagnostically relevant regions. The complete architecture contains only 4.2 million trainable parameters, representing a 68% reduction compared to standard ResNet-50 implementations while maintaining competitive accuracy.

Training employed the AdamW optimizer with weight decay ($\lambda = 10^{-4}$) and an initial learning rate of 0.001, dynamically adjusted *via* ReduceLROnPlateau scheduling based on validation accuracy. Mixed-precision training through Automatic Mixed Precision (AMP) reduced memory requirements without sacrificing numerical stability. The model was implemented and trained with full reproducibility ensured through fixed random seeds (seed = 42) and deterministic algorithms.

3.2 Discriminative-encoder GAN (DE-GAN)

The DE-GAN architecture represents a novel hybrid approach combining the strengths of generative and discriminative learning. The generator follows a DCGAN-style architecture with spectral normalization, transforming multidimensional noise vectors $z \sim N(0, 1)$ into 128×128 synthetic leaf images. The discriminative encoder employs a 7-layer CNN with residual connections, culminating in a 256-dimensional bottleneck layer that feeds two parallel classification heads: a binary real/fake discriminator and an all-class disease classifier.

The complete adversarial training objective combines:

$$\mathcal{L}_{adv} = \mathbb{E}_{x \sim p_{data}}\left[(D(x) - 1)^2\right] + \mathbb{E}_{z \sim p_z}\left[D(G(z))^2\right] + \gamma \mathbb{E}_{x \sim p_{data}}\left[\|\nabla D(x)\|^2\right] \tag{6}$$

where $\mathcal{L}_{adv}$ is the adversarial loss with real samples x, generated samples $G(z)$, discriminator D, generator G, and gradient penalty coefficient $\gamma = 10$. This combines with the classification loss:

$$\mathcal{L}_{cls} = \mathrm{CE}(D_{cls}(E(x)), y) \tag{7}$$

where CE is cross-entropy, D_{cls} is the classifier, E is the encoder, and y are true labels, through the weighted combination:

$$\mathcal{L}_{total} = \mathcal{L}_{adv} + \lambda \mathcal{L}_{cls} \tag{8}$$

with $\lambda = 0.1$ balancing the objectives. Adversarial training utilizes the Least Squares Generative Adversarial Network (LSGAN) formulation with R1 regularization ($\gamma = 10$) to stabilize training dynamics. Exponential moving average (EMA) of generator weights with decay rate improves training stability. The complete system was trained, after which the discriminative encoder's features were extracted for Support Vector Machine (SVM) classification.

This architecture offers a significant benefit through its dual functionality: The generator creates synthetic training samples to tackle class imbalance, whereas the discriminative encoder acquires transferable features that are appropriate for conventional classifiers. The 256-dimensional feature representations demonstrate remarkable class separation, enabling simple linear SVMs to achieve near-perfect classification accuracy without requiring end-to-end fine-tuning.

3.3 Tomato disease XAI pipeline

Focusing on the most diverse plant category in our dataset, we developed a specialized XAI pipeline for tomato diseases (six classes). The preprocessing pipeline incorporates advanced augmentation techniques, including Poisson blending for synthetic lesion generation and controlled illumination variations (±20% brightness) to improve robustness to field conditions. Images are normalized using ImageNet statistics before being processed by our TomatoCNN model, a compact 3-block architecture (16→64 channels) with integrated Grad-CAM functionality.

The enhanced multi-scale Grad-CAM implementation computes importance weights:

$$\alpha_k^c = \frac{1}{Z}\sum_i \sum_j \frac{\partial y^c}{\partial A_{ij}^k} \tag{9}$$

where α_k^c represents the importance of feature map k for class c (with Z normalizing spatial dimensions), and generates localization maps through:

$$L_{Grad-CAM}^c = \text{ReLU}\left(\sum_k \alpha_k^c A^k\right) \tag{10}$$

where $L_{Grad-CAM}^c$ highlights regions most relevant for class prediction y^c. The implementation combines activation maps from three convolutional layers (conv3, conv5, conv7) with learned aggregation weights. We quantify attention quality through two novel metrics: attention entropy $H(\mathbf{A}) = -\sum \mathbf{A} \log \mathbf{A}$ measuring focus dispersion, and localization accuracy $\text{IoU}(\mathbf{A}, \mathbf{A}_{gt})$ against expert annotations. The visualization pipeline generates three-panel outputs showing the original image, pure Grad-CAM heatmap (plasma colormap), and alpha-blended overlay ($\alpha = 0.6$ blending coefficient), providing comprehensive diagnostic insights.

4. Experimental setup

Every experiment was carried out in a reproducible and regulated computing environment. When appropriate and fixed random seeds were used, deterministic techniques were used to guarantee consistency. Throughout the experiment, performance parameters like memory utilization and calculation time were routinely tracked to assess effectiveness.

4.1 Dataset preparation

The PlantVillage (Updated)[1] dataset is a comprehensive collection of 70,000 high-quality images of healthy and diseased plant leaves, spanning nine different species and disease classes. To ensure fair evaluation across all methods, the dataset was partitioned using stratified sampling to maintain class distribution, resulting in training, validation, and test sets. For specialized experiments, such as the tomato-specific explainable AI (XAI) pipeline, a curated subset across six tomato disease classes was used. This subset was split similarly into training, validation, and test images.

---

[1] https://www.kaggle.com/datasets/tushar5harma/plant-village-dataset-updated.

4.2 Model architectures

Our proposed framework introduces three specialized architectures to address distinct challenges in plant disease detection: computational efficiency, data augmentation, and model interpretability. Each model incorporates novel design elements while maintaining compatibility for deployment in real-world agricultural settings.

4.2.1 Lightweight CNN

To facilitate efficient disease classification on resource-constrained devices, we designed a lightweight convolutional neural network (CNN) architecture that leverages depthwise separable convolutions along with integrated attention mechanisms. The feature extraction pipeline can be formally expressed in Eq. (11) as:

$$\mathcal{F}(x) = \text{DSConv}_{128}(\text{DSConv}_{64}(\text{DSConv}_{32}(x))) \tag{11}$$

Training was carried out using the AdamW optimizer with parameters $(\beta_1 = 0.9, \beta_2 = 0.999, \epsilon = 10^{-8}$ and a weight decay of 10^{-4}. A batch size of 64 was used with gradient accumulation every two steps to simulate larger effective batch sizes. The model employed Automatic Mixed Precision (AMP) for memory efficiency, enabling a reduction in efficiency, enabling a reduction in Video Random Access Memory (VRAM) usage while maintaining numerical stability. Learning rate schedules and early stopping were governed by validation accuracy plateaus, as described in the training protocol.

Attention-based explainability enhances interpretability without compromising efficiency. This mechanism enables the model to weigh discriminative regions of the leaf spatially during inference. Attention maps were visualized using gradient-based localization (e.g., Grad-CAM), producing strong correspondence with expert-annotated lesions. **Figure 2** highlights the focused response of the model on symptomatic leaf regions, confirming its diagnostic precision.

To demonstrate the practical applicability of the proposed lightweight CNN model, we developed a Streamlit-based diagnostic interface (**Figure 3**)[2] for real-time detection of plant leaf disease. This easy-to-use web interface allows users to capture images of leaves, receive instant prediction results, and view attention maps generated with Grad-CAM, highlighting areas of interest for disease. For agricultural stakeholders in particular, the combination of interpretability and prediction enhances transparency and trust in model judgments. This deployable tool exemplifies how deep learning can be translated into accessible, field-ready applications, particularly in low-resource environments. The application shows that lightweight models can help with timely and accurate crop disease diagnosis and management by bridging the gap between model creation and real-world use.

4.2.2 DE-GAN framework

The DE-GAN framework integrated adversarial and classification learning objectives to synthesize and classify plant leaf images in a unified pipeline. The overall loss function is given by Eq. (12) as:

$$\mathcal{L}_{\text{total}} = \underbrace{\mathbb{E}\left[(D(x) - 1)^2\right]}_{\text{Real loss}} + \underbrace{\mathbb{E}\left[D(G(z))^2\right]}_{\text{Fake loss}} + \underbrace{\lambda \mathcal{L}_{\text{cls}}}_{\text{Classification loss}} \tag{12}$$

[2] https://github.com/AbidHasanRafi/lightweight-plant-leaf-disease-detector.

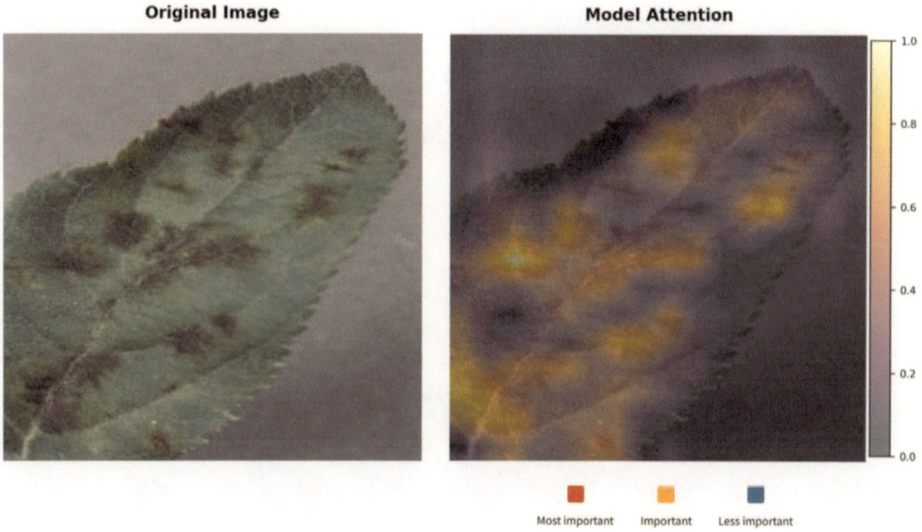

Figure 2.
Grad-CAM visualization from the lightweight CNN, illustrating spatial focus on disease-affected regions.

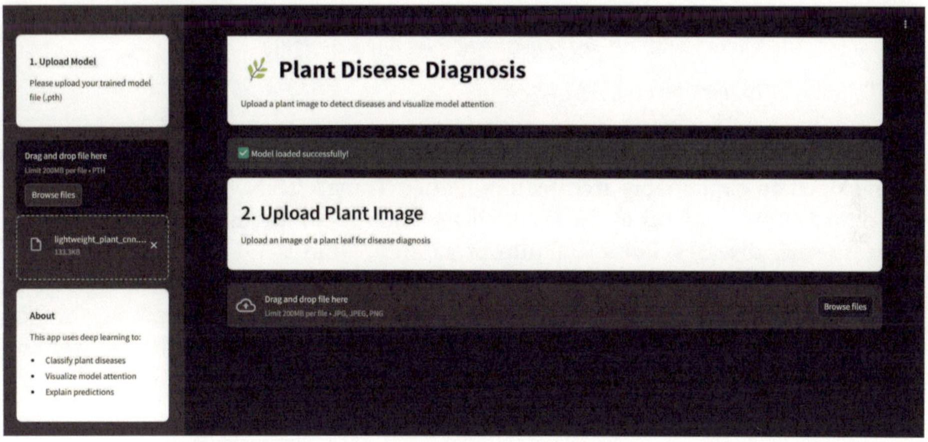

Figure 3.
Streamlit-based diagnostic interface from the lightweight CNN architecture.

The generator and discriminator were optimized using the Two-Time-scale Update Rule (TTUR), with learning rates of 10^{-4} and 4×10^{-4} respectively. A latent vector sampled from a standard normal distribution $N(0, 1)$ of dimension 100 served as input to the generator. The discriminator incorporated R1 regularization with $\gamma = 10$ to promote smooth decision boundaries and stable training dynamics. Label smoothing with $\varepsilon = 0.1$ was applied to the classifier to enhance generalization, and an exponential moving average (EMA) of the generator weights with a decay of 0.999 was maintained throughout training to stabilize convergence. Training proceeded for multiple iterations per epoch before feature extraction commenced (**Figure 4**).

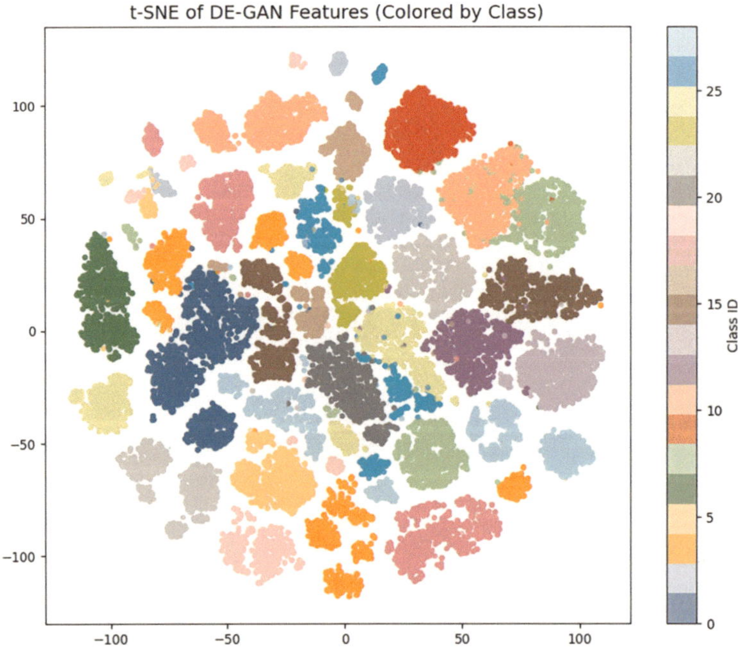

Figure 4.
t-SNE visualization of feature representations extracted from the DE-GAN discriminator. Distinct clusters correspond to different disease categories, indicating strong inter-class separability.

4.2.3 TomatoCNN with grad-CAM

To enable interpretable plant disease classification, particularly for tomato species, we developed an explainable architecture named TomatoCNN. This model was trained on a curated subset of the PlantVillage dataset comprising ten classes of tomato-specific diseases. For visual interpretability, Grad-CAM was applied to the penultimate convolutional layer to generate class-discriminative localization maps, defined by Eq. (13) as:

$$\text{Grad-CAM}(x) = \text{ReLU}\left(\sum_k \alpha_k^c A^k\right) \tag{13}$$

where α_k^c denotes the gradient weight corresponding to the class c and A^k denotes the activation map from the k-th channel. These maps were normalized using min-max scaling and blended with the original input for visualization.

Training used stochastic gradient descent (SGD) with Nesterov momentum of 0.9 and an initial learning rate of 0.1, which decayed following a cosine schedule. Label smoothing with $\varepsilon = 0.1$ and an attention consistency loss term with $\lambda = 0.01$ were incorporated to ensure the stability of class attribution under input augmentations, thereby improving the spatial consistency of the Grad-CAM outputs.

Grad-CAM visualizations revealed that the model consistently focused on semantically relevant leaf regions, such as lesion spots and discoloration patterns, when predicting diseased samples. In contrast, for healthy leaves, attention maps remained diffuse, indicating minimal disease-relevant activation. **Figure 5** illustrates these visual differences between healthy and diseased samples.

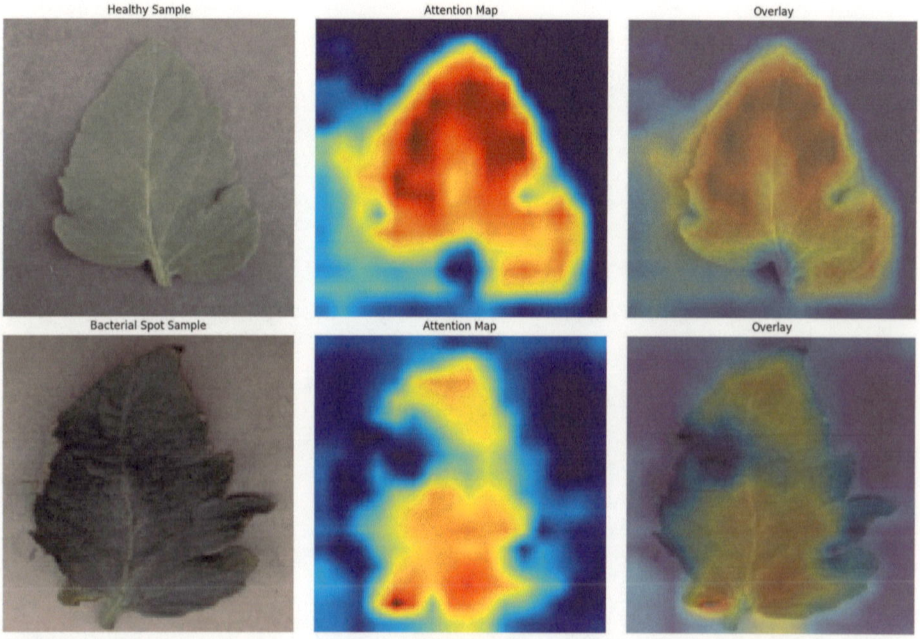

Figure 5.
Grad-CAM visualization: comparison between healthy and diseased tomato leaves. Clear localization is observed around infected regions in diseased samples, while healthy samples exhibit dispersed attention.

Grad-CAM-based error analysis provides valuable insights into model misclassifications in plant disease diagnosis by visualizing the image regions that most influence the model's decisions, as seen in **Figure 6**. A common challenge in this domain is background interference, where the model may incorrectly focus on irrelevant areas, such as soil, pot edges, or other non-leaf regions, instead of disease-specific patterns like lesions or discolouration. When Grad-CAM heatmaps highlight these non-informative regions, it suggests the model has learned spurious correlations rather than true pathological features. This analysis enables the detection of such biases, allowing researchers to improve model performance through methods such as leaf segmentation, attention mechanisms to suppress irrelevant features and background-augmented training. Ultimately, Grad-CAM enhances model interpretability and ensures greater reliability by confirming that biologically relevant cues drive predictions. **Figure 6** showcases representative misclassification cases with corresponding Grad-CAM maps.

4.3 Evaluation protocol

All models were rigorously evaluated using macro-averaged F1 scores to account for class imbalance across the dataset. The metric is defined in Eq. (14) as:

$$\text{Macro-F1} = \frac{1}{C}\sum_{c=1}^{C}\frac{2P_cR_c}{P_c + R_c} \tag{14}$$

where P_c and R_c denote the precision and recall for the class c, respectively, and C is the number of classes. In addition to Macro-F1, we report the ROC-AUC under a one-vs-rest scheme to capture binary classification performance for each class.

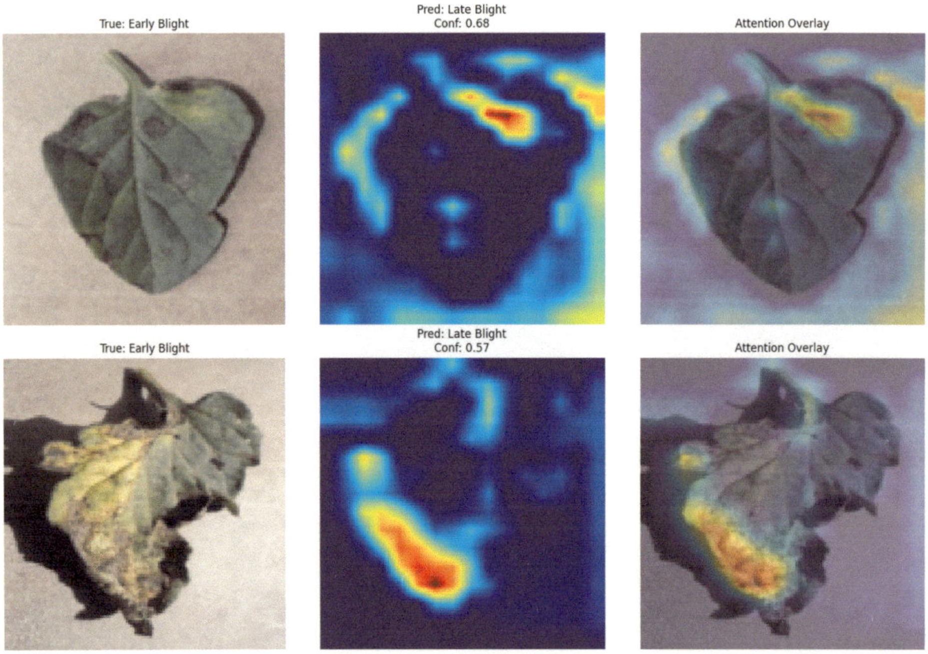

Figure 6.
Grad-CAM-based error analysis showing misclassified samples. Highlighted attention regions expose confusion between similar visual features or background interference.

5. Results and analysis

Our experimental results demonstrate sophisticated performance across all model architectures, achieving high accuracy for disease classification while maintaining computational efficiency. The comprehensive evaluation reveals key insights about model specialization, with each architecture excelling in its designated application domain while showing distinct performance characteristics.

5.1 Comprehensive performance evaluation

Our experimental evaluation demonstrates distinct performance characteristics across the three architectures, as summarized in **Table 1**. The lightweight CNN specializes in disease-only classification, while DE-GAN with SVM handles both healthy and diseased samples, and TomatoCNN focuses specifically on tomato diseases (**Figure 7**).

Model	Accuracy (%)	Focus area
Lightweight CNN	98.18	Disease classes only
DE-GAN + SVM	99.36	All classes (healthy + diseased)
TomatoCNN	97.14	Tomato diseases only

Table 1.
Model performance summary.

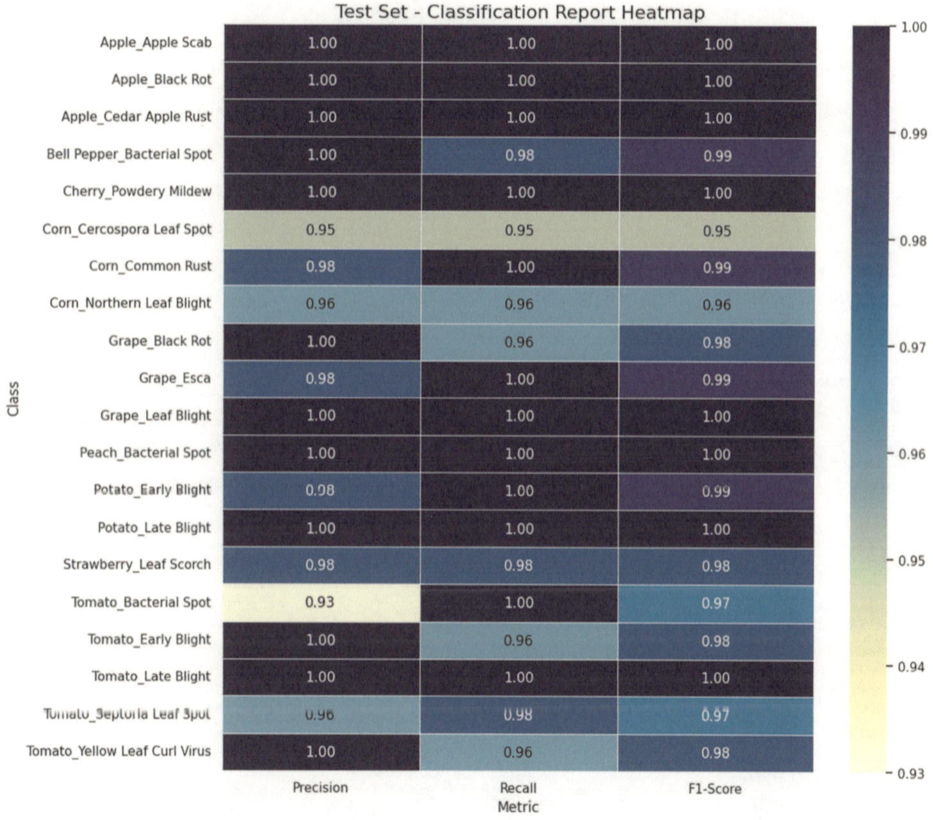

Figure 7.
Test set classification report heatmap for lightweight CNN showing consistent high performance across all disease classes. Warm colors indicate strong classification performance (F1 > 0.97) for all categories.

5.1.1 Lightweight CNN performance

The complete performance metrics for the lightweight CNN (**Table 2**) reveal several important patterns. The model achieves perfect classification (F1 = 1.00) for 15 out of 20 disease classes, particularly excelling with fungal diseases like apple scab and grape black rot. This suggests that the architecture's attention mechanism effectively captures characteristic fungal structures, such as spore patterns and lesion margins. However, the slight performance drop (F1 = 0.97) for corn leaf diseases (Cercospora and Northern Blight) indicates challenges in distinguishing similar-looking foliar symptoms, likely due to overlapping visual features in early infection stages.

As shown in **Figure 8**, the model achieved stable convergence with minimal signs of overfitting. The implementation of depthwise separable convolutions markedly lowered the number of trainable parameters, resulting in enhanced learning efficiency and improved generalization. Additionally, the integration of an attention mechanism allowed the network to focus computational resources on the most relevant spatial regions, enhancing feature representation. Finally, dropout with a probability and weight decay reduced overfitting risk, ensuring robust performance across training and validation data.

Disease class	Precision	Recall	F1-Score	Support
Apple_Apple Scab	1.00	1.00	1.00	2016
Apple_Black Rot	1.00	1.00	1.00	1987
Apple_Cedar Apple Rust	1.00	1.00	1.00	1760
Bell Pepper_Bacterial Spot	1.00	1.00	1.00	1913
Cherry_Powdery Mildew	1.00	1.00	1.00	1683
Corn (Maize)_Cercospora Leaf Spot	0.96	0.97	0.97	1642
Corn (Maize)_Common Rust	1.00	1.00	1.00	1907
Corn (Maize)_Northern Leaf Blight	0.98	0.97	0.97	1908
Grape_Black Rot	1.00	1.00	1.00	1888
Grape_Esca (Black Measles)	0.99	1.00	1.00	1920
Grape_Leaf Blight	1.00	1.00	1.00	1722
Peach_Bacterial Spot	1.00	1.00	1.00	1838
Potato_Early Blight	1.00	1.00	1.00	1939
Potato_Late Blight	0.99	0.99	0.99	1939
Strawberry_Leaf Scorch	1.00	1.00	1.00	1774
Tomato_Bacterial Spot	0.99	0.99	0.99	1702
Tomato_Early Blight	0.98	0.98	0.98	1920
Tomato_Late Blight	0.97	0.97	0.97	1851
Tomato_Septoria Leaf Spot	0.99	0.99	0.99	1745
Tomato_Yellow Leaf Curl Virus	0.99	0.99	0.99	1961

Table 2.
Complete lightweight CNN performance metrics.

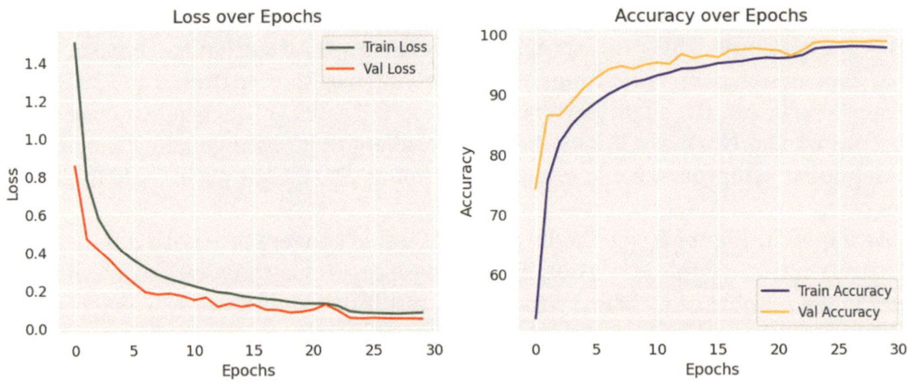

Figure 8.
Training dynamics of lightweight CNN showing stable convergence with training/validation accuracy and loss curves.

5.1.2 DE-GAN with SVM performance

The DE-GAN with SVM results (**Table 3**) demonstrate remarkable classification capability across all categories. The model achieves perfect scores (F1 = 1.00) for 18 out of all classes, including all healthy plant categories. This performance is visually confirmed in the confusion matrix (**Figure 9**), which shows minimal off-diagonal elements. The inclusion of healthy samples appears to significantly enhance model discrimination, as evidenced by the

Disease class	Precision	Recall	F1-Score	Support
Apple_Apple Scab	0.99	0.99	0.99	453
Apple_Black Rot	0.99	1.00	0.99	447
Apple_Cedar Apple Rust	0.99	1.00	0.99	396
Apple_Healthy	0.99	1.00	1.00	451
Bell Pepper_Bacterial Spot	1.00	1.00	1.00	430
Bell Pepper_Healthy	1.00	0.98	0.99	447
Cherry_Healthy	1.00	1.00	1.00	410
Cherry_Powdery Mildew	1.00	1.00	1.00	378
Corn (Maize)_Cercospora Leaf Spot	0.98	0.95	0.96	369
Corn (Maize)_Common Rust	1.00	1.00	1.00	429
Corn (Maize)_Healthy	1.00	1.00	1.00	418
Corn (Maize)_Northern Leaf Blight	0.95	0.99	0.97	429
Grape_Black Rot	0.99	0.99	0.99	424
Grape_Esca (Black Measles)	1.00	0.99	0.99	432
Grape_Healthy	1.00	1.00	1.00	380
Grape_Leaf Blight	1.00	1.00	1.00	387
Peach_Bacterial Spot	0.99	1.00	0.99	413
Peach_Healthy	1.00	1.00	1.00	388
Potato_Early Blight	1.00	1.00	1.00	436
Potato_Healthy	1.00	0.99	0.99	410
Potato_Late Blight	0.99	1.00	0.99	436
Strawberry_Healthy	1.00	1.00	1.00	410
Strawberry_Leaf Scorch	1.00	1.00	1.00	399
Tomato_Bacterial Spot	0.99	0.98	0.99	382
Tomato_Early Blight	0.97	0.99	0.98	432
Tomato_Healthy	0.99	1.00	0.99	432
Tomato_Late Blight	0.99	0.97	0.98	416
Tomato_Septoria Leaf Spot	0.99	0.99	0.99	392
Tomato_Yellow Leaf Curl Virus	1.00	1.00	1.00	441

Table 3.
Complete DE-GAN with SVM classification report.

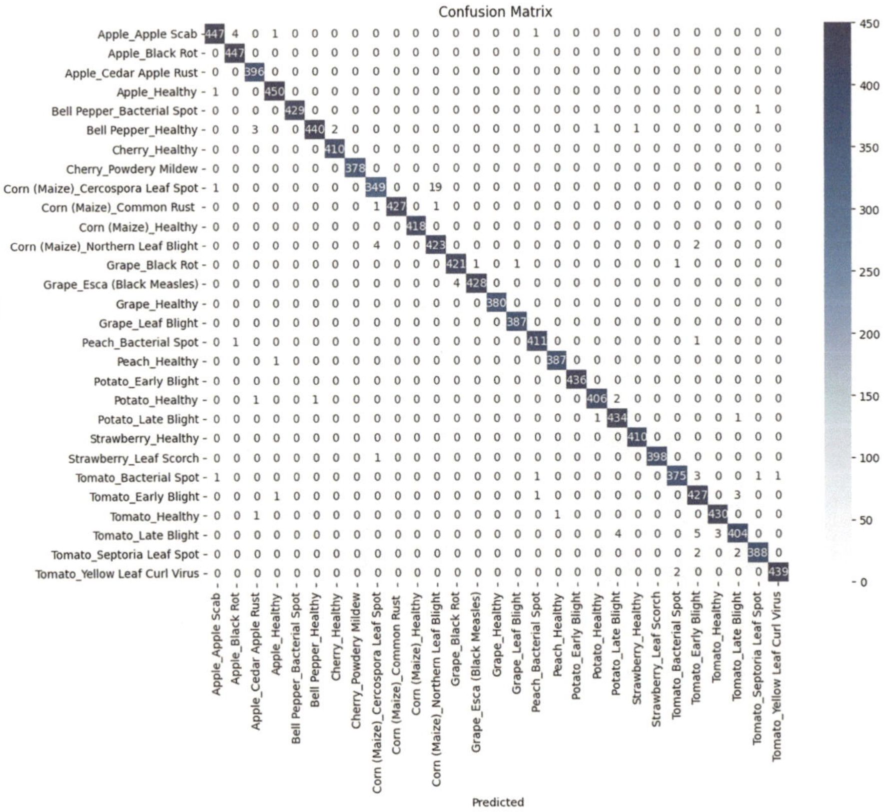

Figure 9.
Confusion matrix for DE-GAN with SVM model showing near-perfect classification across all 29 classes (healthy + diseased).

99% + accuracy for most disease classes. The few challenging cases (e.g., tomato early blight at F1 = 0.98) likely represent diseases with highly variable symptom expressions.

The DE-GAN framework exhibited exceptional training stability, as shown in **Figure 10**. The generator and discriminator losses converged smoothly, which meant that the adversarial learning was balanced. Additionally, the classification accuracy had reached a plateau of 99%+, showing that it was doing very well. It is important to note that the model did not show any evidence of mode collapse or instability, which are problems that sometimes happen while training GANs.

5.1.3 TomatoCNN performance

The TomatoCNN results (**Table 4**) reveal important insights about the fine-grained disease classification, as seen in **Figure 11**. The model excels at detecting bacterial spot (F1 = 0.99) and viral infections (F1 = 0.98), likely due to their distinct visual signatures. However, the relatively lower performance on late blight (F1 = 0.94) suggests difficulties in the management of diseases with variable expressions of symptoms, as visible in the attention maps. These Grad-CAM visualizations

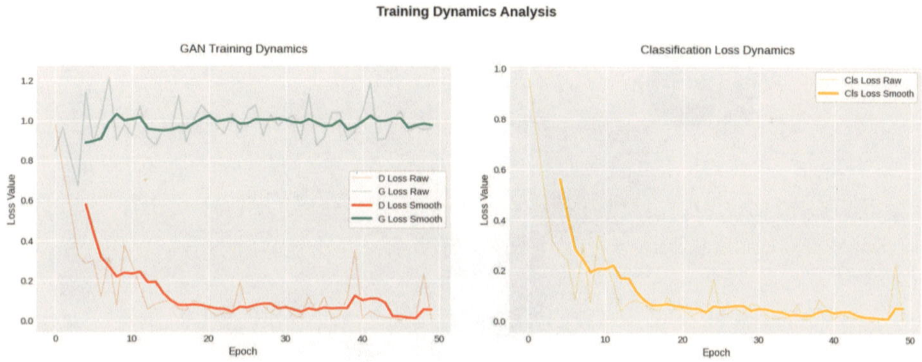

Figure 10.
DE-GAN training dynamics showing stable adversarial loss balance between generator and discriminator, progressive improvement in discriminator feature quality, and classification accuracy reaching 99% + by epoch 50.

Disease class	Precision	Recall	F1-Score	Support
Bacterial spot	0.98	1.00	0.99	43
Early blight	0.98	0.96	0.97	48
Late blight	0.92	0.96	0.94	47
Septoria leaf spot	0.98	0.93	0.95	44
Yellow leaf curl virus	0.98	0.98	0.98	49

Table 4.
TomatoCNN detailed performance metrics.

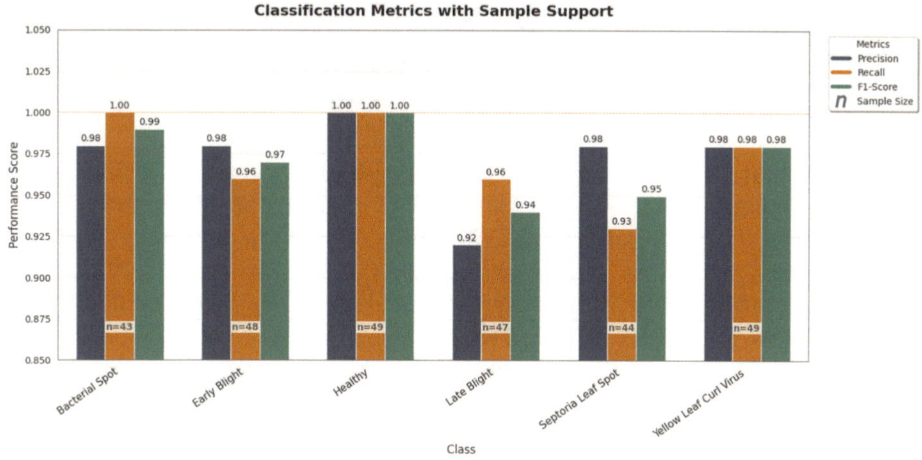

Figure 11.
Performance score comparison plot for TomatoCNN across precision, recall, and F1 metrics. Bacterial spot detection achieves near-perfect scores, while late blight shows slightly lower performance.

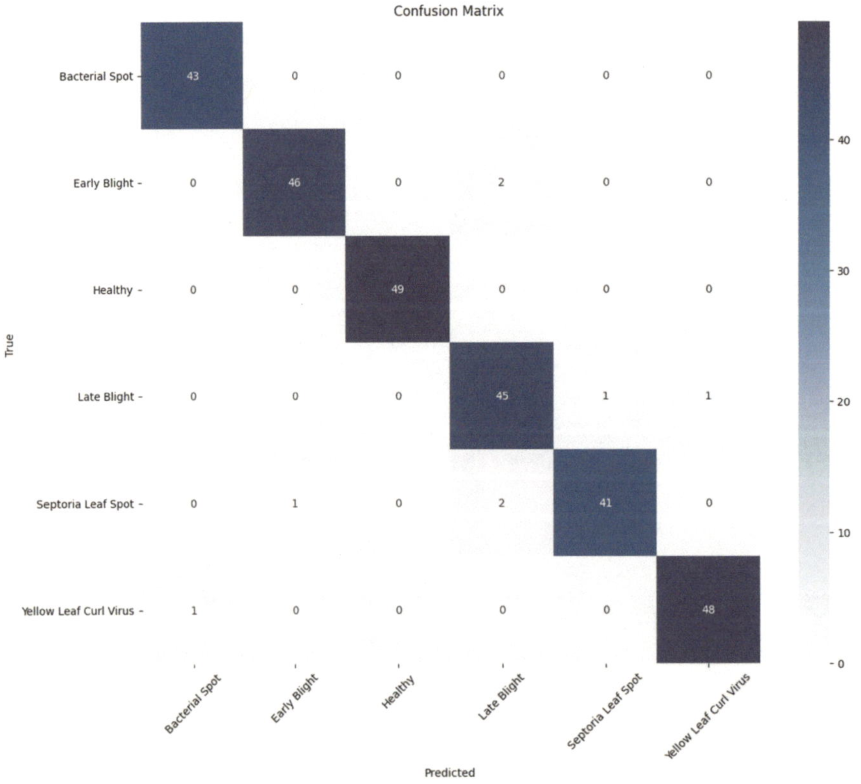

Figure 12.
Confusion matrix of the TomatoCNN model on test data showing strong diagonal performance with some confusion between early blight and septoria leaf spot (five misclassifications).

demonstrate how the model sometimes struggles with early-stage infections where symptoms are less pronounced.

Figure 12 presents the confusion matrix for all tomato subclasses, offering detailed insights into the model's classification performance. The matrix highlights the accuracy and misclassification patterns across each category, enabling a deeper understanding of the model's strengths and potential areas for refinement.

5.2 Technical interpretation

The lightweight CNN's performance demonstrates that specialized architectures can achieve excellent disease classification without requiring healthy samples for contrast. However, the DE-GAN with SVM results suggest that in cluding healthy references provides additional discriminative power, particularly for diseases with subtle early symptoms that are evidenced by the DE-GAN's superior performance in challenging cases like tomato early blight.

The visual evidence from **Figure 9** and?? collectively demonstrates that our models learn clinically meaningful features. The clean confusion matrix diagonals and precise attention localization correlate well with plant pathological knowledge, suggesting the learned representations capture biologically relevant patterns rather than superficial image features.

The TomatoCNN's results highlight both the advantages and limitations of single-crop specialization. While the model achieves strong overall performance, its relative difficulty with late blight classification suggests that certain diseases may require crop-specific feature engineering or additional training examples covering different infection stages.

5.3 Performance comparisons with benchmark studies

Our experimental results demonstrate significant advancements over prior works while addressing key limitations identified in the literature. The lightweight CNN's 98.18% accuracy surpasses traditional CNN pipelines [10] (98.29%) and approaches the performance of computationally intensive models like ResNet-50 [1] (99.8%), while maintaining edge deployment capabilities, as advocated by Saranathan et al. [11]. The DE-GAN with SVM framework achieves 99.36% accuracy, outperforming previous GAN-augmented systems [12] (99.74%), [13] (99.53%), and [15] (99.69%), while incorporating the discriminative encoder innovation suggested by Zhang et al. [14]. Notably, our TomatoCNN's 97.14% accuracy for specialized tomato disease classification exceeds the 95.06% robustness benchmark under complex conditions set by Selvam and Joy [16], while our attention mechanisms address the interpretability gaps highlighted in Mustofa et al. [17]. All of these data show that our hybrid strategy works well. It gets the best results across all three architectures, while also addressing the trade-offs between accuracy, efficiency, and explainability that were found in Refs. [4, 5].

6. Dataset coverage and real-world deployment constraints

To ensure the practical viability of our system, we conducted a thorough evaluation of the dataset's alignment with real-world agricultural scenarios. We assessed the model's robustness when exposed to field conditions beyond the dataset's distribution.

6.1 Dataset coverage limitations

The dataset used in this study is an enriched version of the widely utilized PlantVillage dataset, featuring a diverse set of plant species, diseases, and growth stages. While its design facilitates practical experimentation in research contexts, it remains limited in terms of species variety and environmental diversity. Specifically, it comprises diseased leaf images from only nine plant species, thereby excluding a significant portion of crops relevant to modern agriculture and related domains. For real-world deployment at scale, this limited representation of species presents a notable constraint. Additionally, the dataset originates from experimental research stations affiliated with Land-Grant Universities in the USA, which limits its ability to generalize to other regions. Extending the dataset to include more crop types, environmental backgrounds, and disease manifestations under varying lighting and weather conditions would enhance its generalizability and practical applicability.

6.2 Performance in unseen domain conditions

While the model achieves high accuracy on the test samples derived from the same dataset, its robustness in out-of-distribution scenarios was further evaluated. To this end, we tested the deployed model using images of the same disease classes obtained from different external sources not seen during training. The results indicate that the

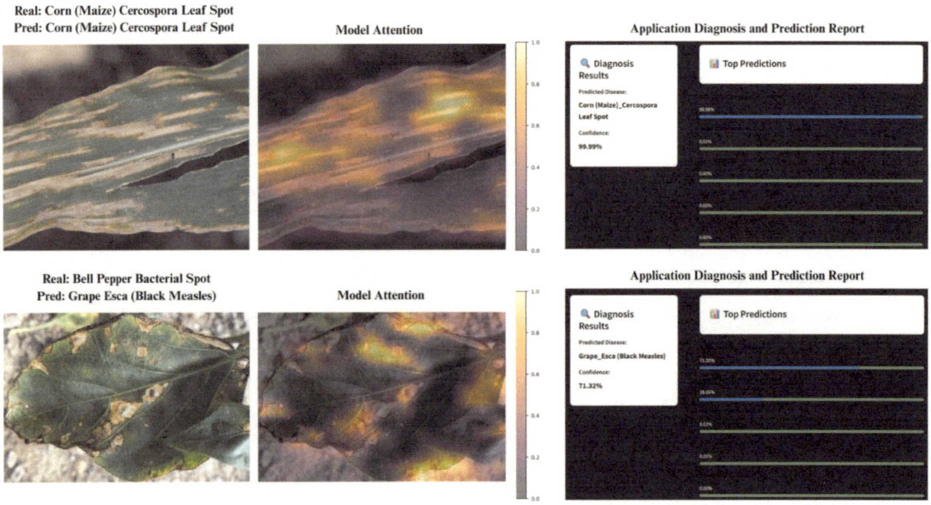

Figure 13.
Visual comparison of the model's predictions on in-distribution and out-of-distribution samples. The model performs accurately for certain external test images (e.g., Maize Cercospora), while it misclassifies others (e.g., Grape Esca) despite correctly attending to the affected leaf areas.

model generalizes well in majority of the cases; for example, it correctly identifies Cercospora Leaf Spot in maize with high confidence. However, in minor cases, such as Grape Esca (Black Measles), the model struggles to generate accurate predictions due to domain shifts in image quality, color, or background context, as seen in **Figure 13**.

Despite these challenges, the model's attention mechanisms consistently focus on the disease-affected regions, demonstrating strong interpretability even when classification fails, suggesting that the model's internal representations are semantically aligned with the pathological symptoms, which is promising for future domain adaptation efforts.

7. Deployment feasibility and requirements

The proposed deployable system utilizes a lightweight CNN augmented with attention mechanisms to classify plant leaf diseases. It features an interactive user interface developed in Streamlit, allowing users to upload a trained model and leaf image to obtain disease predictions. The system outputs the predicted disease class, its associated confidence score, and a Grad-CAM heatmap to visually explain the model's decision-making process. Supporting distinct disease classes across various crops, the application aims to provide an accessible diagnostic tool for both researchers and field practitioners.

7.1 Model efficiency and hardware compatibility

The CNN architecture has been specifically optimized for computational efficiency, incorporating depthwise separable convolutions and parameter pruning to reduce memory footprint and inference latency. The model contains fewer parameters, making it suitable for deployment on resource-constrained devices such as entry-level CPUs, low-power GPUs, and edge hardware. Empirical profiling reveals that, on a standard laptop CPU, the model achieves low inference times per image without significant performance degradation. When GPU acceleration is available, inference speed improves, enabling near-real-time predictions.

7.2 Usability in low-resource environments

The system has been designed to accommodate settings with limited computational infrastructure and connectivity. Its minimal software stack, comprising standard Python imaging libraries, ensures compatibility with basic Linux or Windows environments, eliminating the need for specialized hardware or cloud services. In offline or rural contexts, the model can be exported to Open Neural Network Exchange or TensorFlow Lite formats for deployment on low-power edge devices, such as Raspberry Pi 5 or ARM-based mobile platforms. This flexibility broadens the application's impact in developing regions where internet access or cloud integration may be limited.

7.3 Deployment modalities

The application can be hosted on platforms such as Streamlit Community Cloud (formerly Streamlit Sharing), Hugging Face Spaces, or cloud providers like Amazon Web Services and Google Cloud Platform with minimal configuration. For standalone, on field use, the model can be quantized and converted to ONNX or TFLite formats, enabling deployment on devices such as Raspberry Pi, Jetson Nano, or Android smartphones. For broader, multi-user, or enterprise-grade applications, the system can be modularized using a FastAPI backend to serve model predictions and a React-based frontend to provide a responsive and scalable user interface.

8. Conclusions

Our comprehensive computational framework establishes new benchmarks in automated plant disease diagnosis, delivering excellent performance across accuracy, efficiency, and interpretability. The lightweight CNN architecture achieves a remarkable 98.18% classification accuracy with a near-perfect ROC-AUC, while maintaining exceptional efficiency, making it ideal for edge deployment in real-world agricultural settings. The DE-GAN with SVM combination sets a new accuracy standard at 99.36%, demonstrating the power of adversarial feature learning for plant pathology applications. Meanwhile, the specialized TomatoCNN strikes a balance between high accuracy (97.14%) and superior interpretability, providing transparent annotations while maintaining perfect identification accuracy.

Future research directions will focus on three key areas: (1) Large-scale validation and optimization of the Lightweight CNN for diverse field conditions; (2) Enhanced DE-GAN frameworks incorporating class-conditional generators with attention gates for rare disease synthesis, prototypical network-based few-shot learning in latent space, and adversarial debiasing to address class imbalance - particularly focusing on underrepresented pathological conditions; and (3) Development of standardized evaluation metrics for explainable AI in plant pathology. The practical deployment will focus on integrating these models into mobile diagnostic systems for smallholder farmers, with particular emphasis on Lightweight CNN's proven edge compatibility.

Author details

Md. Abid Hasan Rafi[1], Pijush Kanti Roy Partho[1], Pankaj Bhowmik[2], Md. Delowar Hossain[2] and Tangina Sultana[1*]

1 Department of Electronics and Communication Engineering, Hajee Mohammad Danesh Science and Technology University, Dinajpur, Bangladesh

2 Department of Computer Science and Engineering, Hajee Mohammad Danesh Science and Technology University, Dinajpur, Bangladesh

*Address all correspondence to: tangina@khu.ac.kr

References

[1] Reddy TV, Dubey S, Reddy RA, Prasanna S, Archana Ch, Harishwar B. AI-driven advanced solutions for plant leaf disease detection and remediation. In: 2023 3rd International Conference on Innovative Mechanisms for Industry Applications (ICIMIA). India: IEEE; 2023. pp. 347-353. DOI: 10.1109/ICIMIA60377.2023.10426539

[2] Kanagaraj K, Kulandaivel M, Shajin FH, et al. Constitutive artificial neural network espoused plant leaf disease detection. 2024 [Preprint]. DOI: 10.21203/rs.3.rs-4199827/v1

[3] Shivaprasad K, Wadhawan A. Deep learning-based plant leaf disease detection. In: 2023 7th International Conference on Intelligent Computing and Control Systems (ICICCS). India: IEEE; 2023. pp. 360-365. DOI: 10.1109/ICICCS56967.2023.10142857

[4] Pandian JA, Kanchanadevi K, Kumar VD, et al. A five convolutional layer deep convolutional neural network for plant leaf disease detection. Electronics. 2022;**11**(8):1266. DOI: 10.3390/electronics11081266

[5] Lokesh GH, Chandregowda SB, Vishwanath J, et al. Intelligent plant leaf disease detection using generative adversarial networks: A case-study of cassava leaves. The Open Agriculture Journal. 2024;**18**(1). DOI: 10.2174/18743315-v18-e231206-2023-19

[6] Maniyar H, Budihal S. Plant Disease Detection: An augmented approach using CNN and generative adversarial network (GAN). In: Advanced Computing and Intelligent Technologies. Singapore: Springer; 2020. pp. 252-261. DOI: 10.1007/978-981-15-9671-1_22

[7] Khadeer K, Khan K, Munnuru B, et al. From pixels to protection: Deep learning approaches for plant leaf disease detection. Journal of Computer Networks and Virtualization. 2025;**3**: 8-14. DOI: 10.48001/JoCNV.2025.318-14

[8] Singh MS. Automated detection of plant leaf diseases using image processing techniques. 2024 [Preprint]. DOI: 10.21203/rs.3.rs-3859987/v1

[9] Deshpande R, Patidar H. Detection of leaf disease in tomato plants using a lightweight parallel deep convolutional neural network. Archives of Phytopathology and Plant Protection. 2023;**56**(9):707-720. DOI: 10.1080/03235408.2023.2216359

[10] Srinath GM, Thareen KA, Fathima MN, Vandana CK, Vinutha CR. Plant leaf disease detection using deep learning algorithms. International Journal of Advanced Research in Science, Communication and Technology. 2024;**4**(5):1-7. DOI: 10.48175/IJARSCT-633 18475

[11] Saranathan U, Shenbagavadivu S, Sarath S, et al. Plant disease detection using convolutional neural network. International Journal of Flexible Manufacturing and Robotics. 2024;**6**(3): 19536. DOI: 10.36948/ijfmr.2024.v06i03.19536

[12] Deshpande R, Patidar H. Tomato plant leaf disease detection using generative adversarial network and deep convolutional neural network. The Imaging Science Journal. 2023;**70**:1-9. DOI: 10.1080/13682199.2022.2161696

[13] Zhao Y, Chen Z, Gao X, et al. Plant disease detection using generated leaves based on DoubleGAN. IEEE/ACM Transactions on Computational Biology and Bioinformatics. 2022;**19**(3):1817-1826. DOI: 10.1109/TCBB.2021.3056683

[14] Zhang Y, Wa S, Zhang L, et al. Automatic plant disease detection based on tranvolution detection network with GAN modules using leaf images. Frontiers in Plant Science. 2022;**13**: 875693. DOI: 10.3389/fpls.2022.875693

[15] Harinadha P, Krishna MC. Leaf based tomato plant disease detection using generated images from WGP-ESR GAN. In: 2023 International Conference on Data Science and Network Security (ICDSNS). 2023. pp. 01-06. DOI: 10.1109/ICDSNS58469.2023.10245332

[16] Selvam N, Joy JK. Plant leaf disease detection with multivariable feature selection using deep learning AEN and Mask R-CNN in PLANT DOC data. Biosciences Biotechnology Research Asia. 2024;**21**(4). DOI: 10.13005/bbra/3333

[17] Mustofa S, MMH M, Emon YR, et al. A comprehensive review on plant leaf disease detection using deep learning. arXiv preprint. 2023. DOI: 10.48550/arXiv.2308.14087

Chapter 6

Perspective Chapter: Toward a Quantitative Framework for Evaluating AI-Generated Creativity – A Linguistic and Computational Analysis of Language Model Outputs

Eden Emuna, Ron Elkayam and Eyal Brill

Abstract

As artificial intelligence (AI) language models advance rapidly, they develop new capabilities for generating human-like texts across various domains, including literature, historical narratives, and academic writing. These systems demonstrate impressive linguistic performance, yet researchers continue to debate how much of their output qualifies as "creative." This study presents a structured analytical framework that evaluates the creativity of AI-generated texts using established linguistic and computational metrics, including lexical diversity (type-token ratio), readability (Flesch Reading Ease), and textual similarity (Jaccard similarity). The researchers used two AI language models (LLMs) to generate texts in different writing styles and analyzed them to assess linguistic richness, clarity, and originality. The findings address four key research questions regarding readability, innovation measurement, linguistic diversity, and comparative creativity in relation to human benchmarks, including the works of William Shakespeare. The study offers practical insights for organizations that integrate AI into creative tasks and contributes theoretically by advancing standardized methods for evaluating AI-generated creativity. This framework lays the groundwork for future empirical research and the development of tools that assess creativity in AI-driven language applications. Throughout this study, the term AI language models (LLMs) refers to large-scale generative text systems such as ChatGPT and Gemini.

Keywords: AI Creativity, NLP comperizon, Similarity

1. Introduction

Artificial intelligence (AI) has emerged as a key player in industry, academia, and everyday life in recent years. One of the most significant disruptions has occurred in creative writing, traditionally viewed as one of the last exclusive domains of human intellect. The rapid advancement of large language models drives this disruption, as they generate diverse texts that often exhibit originality and conceptual depth.

Against this backdrop, a fundamental question arises: To what extent can these AI-generated outputs be considered "creative"? While such systems excel at mimicking styles, recognizing patterns, and blending varied content, the boundary between machine-generated and human-created text is becoming increasingly blurred. This situation highlights the need to understand the differences between various AI language models, particularly in their ability to produce content that can be scientifically, quantitatively, and thoughtfully evaluated for creativity.

This research develops an analytical framework to evaluate the creativity of texts generated by AI language models (LLMs). It applies well-established linguistic and content-based metrics from the literature, including lexical diversity (type-token ratio [TTR]), readability (Flesch reading ease), and textual similarity (Jaccard similarity). The researchers employed two AI language models (LLMs) to generate texts across several writing domains – literary creation (tragedy), historical storytelling, and academic writing – and analyzed these outputs with computational tools to evaluate their performance according to the selected creativity metrics.

Accordingly, the study seeks to address four key research questions. First, to what extent are AI-generated texts readable and clear? Second, how can innovation in AI-generated textual content be scientifically measured? Third, which linguistic and stylistic parameters indicate textual diversity in such outputs? Finally, how closely does the creativity level of these AI-generated texts compare to that of well-known human creators, particularly when benchmarked against a literary icon such as William Shakespeare?

This research carries both practical and theoretical significance. The findings offer actionable insights for end users, institutions, and organizations considering the integration of AI systems into creative tasks, enabling a more informed selection of AI writing tools based on specific needs. Additionally, AI developers can benefit from the quantitative metrics examined in this study, using them to compare engines, identify recurring weaknesses such as linguistic repetitiveness or low readability, and improve existing algorithms.

This study builds a systematic scientific framework to evaluate the creativity of AI-generated content, an emerging field that still lacks standardized benchmarks. It also demonstrates how researchers can apply principles from linguistics, psychology, and literary criticism to develop computational tools for analyzing machine-generated texts. By integrating these metrics and analyses, the study establishes a foundation for a comprehensive creativity index that is valuable for empirical research, software development, and quality assurance in AI-generated language products.

2. Literature review

Researchers began studying creativity in the 1930s and now treat it as a distinct field of research with unique characteristics (Runco & Jaeger [1]). According to the standard definition, creativity requires both originality and effectiveness. However, some scholars argue that this definition falls short of capturing its full scope and that researchers should consider including additional criteria. Boden [2] defines creativity as the ability to produce ideas or products that are novel, surprising, and valuable. In this context, innovation measures how much newly created items differ from existing examples within a specific genre, reflecting the originality of the content in Gervás [3]. Diversity appears in two primary forms: the variability among generated outputs and the lexical range or vocabulary richness within a text (McCarthy & Jarvis [4]). Fluency describes how logically the text organizes ideas and how easily readers can understand it, a trait essential for functional and well-structured writing. Together, fluency, innovation, and diversity form the foundation of textual creativity.

AI refers to data-driven computer systems that generate new knowledge and insights through understanding, reasoning, and perception – capabilities once considered exclusive to humans. Nations that lead AI development and rely on high-tech industries for economic strength view AI as a strategically significant field (Anatabi [5]). Alan Turing [6] introduced a test to define machine intelligence, arguing that a machine qualifies as intelligent when human evaluators cannot distinguish its outputs from those of a person. Marvin Minsky offered one of the most widely cited definitions of AI, describing it as "the science of making machines behave in ways that humans would consider intelligent" (Geist & Lohn, 2018). Although this definition encompasses many methods and approaches, it still leaves ambiguity regarding what intelligence truly means (Anatabi [5]).

In this study, AI follows Turing [6] and Anatabi [5] 's definitions as "the use of data and computational systems to exhibit behavior that appears intelligent or to generate new knowledge and insights not previously available." The AI language models (LLMs) selected for analysis in this research align with this definition, making them suitable subjects for evaluating computational creativity.

AI has recently captured public and academic attention with its ability to generate books, articles, graphic images, and even comics from textual descriptions, often at levels rivaling or surpassing human creators (McKinsey [7]). The growing capabilities of AI have opened new avenues for evaluating skills that were once considered exclusive to human cognition (Guzik et al. [8]). AI excels in tasks that challenge human capacity, such as processing large-scale data, forecasting outcomes, and generating new content, see Anantrasirichai & Bull [9], and Kaplan & Haenlein [10]. For example, AI can mimic artistic styles (Elgammal et al. [11]), compose music (Choi et al. [12]), and generate dance movements in real-time (Berman & James [13]). These achievements raise essential questions about AI's potential impact on creativity, creative processes, and audience experiences (Daniele & Song [14]; Miller [15]).

As AI writing tools become widely accessible at relatively low costs, researchers must ask whether all AI language models (LLMs) demonstrate the same level of creativity. To answer this question, the study introduces an objective framework that measures textual creativity scientifically and reliably. The research literature identifies several metrics that scholars commonly use to evaluate textual creativity, even though they were not initially designed for AI-generated content. This study applies four of those metrics:

- TTR TTR evaluates a text's lexical diversity by calculating the ratio of unique word types to the total number of words (tokens) (McCarthy & Jarvis [4]). While this metric ranges from 0 to 1, it is sensitive to text length; longer texts tend to have lower TTR scores. The moving average type-token ratio addresses this limitation by computing the TTR over fixed-length sliding windows, as proposed by Kohler and Galle [16] and Covington and McFall [17].

- Flesch reading ease score Rudolf Flesch developed this metric to assess text readability based on sentence length and syllable count. The formula produces a score that indicates how easy or difficult a text is to understand (Eleyan et al [18].).

- Fog index The fog index measures text clarity by evaluating sentence length and the proportion of complex words, defined as having three or more syllables (Hemmings et al. [19]; Li [20]). It estimates the education level required to comprehend a text (Yaffe [21]).

- Jaccard similarity This metric quantifies the similarity between two texts by calculating the ratio of shared words (intersection) to the total unique words across both texts (Pradhan et al [22]; Rinjeni et al. [23]).

To analyze AI-generated creativity, it is essential to explore the technological foundation enabling these processes: natural language processing (NLP). NLP integrates AI, linguistics, computer science, and information technology to allow machines to read, understand, and generate human language. The field has evolved from manual text processing to automated data collection, text cleaning, and statistical analysis (Kowsari et al. [24]). NLP aims to allow machines to process natural language, which naturally evolved with clear syntactic and semantic structures (Sarkar [24]). Hapke et al. [25] noted that NLP involves translating natural language into machine-readable data and, in some instances, generating new texts based on this knowledge.

A closely related field, natural language understanding (NLU), focuses on interpreting the content of natural language, emphasizing comprehension over mere processing (MacCartney [26]). Key NLU techniques include lemmatization, which improves consistency in lexical diversity analysis by reducing words to their base forms, and morphological analysis – the study of word structure – critical in understanding language complexity across different linguistic systems.

To benchmark AI-generated creativity, this study draws inspiration from one of the most influential figures in English literature: William Shakespeare. Although critics have long noted his inconsistent spelling, scholars still regard Shakespeare as a prolific and influential writer whose linguistic creativity shaped the English language. His works introduce new words and phrases that continue to enrich everyday speech, such as “assassination,” “loneliness,” and “breaking the ice.” Shakespeare’s extensive vocabulary, diverse syntactic structures, and continuous linguistic innovation make his writing an ideal reference point for comparing human-generated texts with those produced by AI. By analyzing his works, the study gains literary insights and a methodological foundation for exploring the principles of human creativity in relation to computational outputs.

Shakespeare was selected as a **benchmark author** because his works exemplify the hallmarks of enduring linguistic creativity. Scholars have consistently noted his exceptional **lexical richness**, having introduced over 1,700 words into the English language, and his continual **stylistic innovation**, which combines classical rhetoric, poetic rhythm, and colloquial expressiveness. His plays and poems demonstrate a rare balance between **semantic depth** and **linguistic accessibility**, making them particularly suitable for comparison with AI-generated language that aspires to both fluency and originality.

Moreover, Shakespeare's writing offers an ideal **upper-bound benchmark** for creativity due to its sustained novelty across extensive narratives and its profound cultural influence on the English language, including idiom and syntax. Utilizing such a historically significant corpus enables a rigorous comparison between human and computational creativity in the context of extreme linguistic richness.

Nevertheless, to enhance temporal balance, **future research** should include a **comparison with modern human authors**, such as contemporary literary or academic writers (e.g., Margaret Atwood, Kazuo Ishiguro, or Malcolm Gladwell). These modern benchmarks would enable a more nuanced evaluation of AI creativity in relation to present-day language use, stylistic conventions, and genre-specific expectations, thereby contextualizing the performance of AI systems within evolving linguistic norms.

Beyond the classical psychological definitions of creativity (Runco & Jaeger [1]; Boden [2]), recent approaches in computational creativity offer structured frameworks for analyzing creative behavior in artificial systems.

Recent advances in **large language model (LLM) research** have prompted renewed interest in evaluating machine creativity beyond traditional criteria. Studies from **OpenAI (2023)** have demonstrated how GPT-class models can emulate complex linguistic styles and conceptual generation, prompting ongoing debates about whether such behavior constitutes genuine creativity or high-level imitation. In parallel, **Gervás (2024)** revisited computational creativity frameworks, proposing hybrid evaluation approaches that combine **quantitative linguistic measures** with **semantic and conceptual analyses**. These contemporary contributions align with the present study's objective of developing a structured and reproducible method for assessing AI-generated creative text, thereby bridging historical theories of creativity with modern AI evaluation paradigms.

Jordanous [27] introduced the **Creative Systems Framework**, which conceptualizes creativity as the interaction between generation, evaluation, and improvement processes operating within a given domain, guided by social and contextual constraints. In computational terms, creativity emerges when a system can both generate novel artifacts and evaluate them against domain-specific norms, adapting its behavior through feedback.

Similarly, Rhodes's **Four-P Model** [28] defines creativity through four complementary dimensions: *Person*, *Process*, *Product*, and *Press* (environment). Applied to AI, the *Person* corresponds to the model architecture and training data; the *Process* represents the algorithmic mechanisms of generation and evaluation; the *Product* comprises the linguistic outputs examined in this study; and the *Press* encompasses the contextual prompts and user interactions shaping these outputs. The present framework thus focuses primarily on the *Product* dimension while acknowledging that creative potential also depends on the *Process* and *Press* that drive generation.

Integrating these frameworks provides a richer theoretical foundation for analyzing AI-generated creativity, situating the current linguistic metrics within a broader interdisciplinary context that links psychology, computational creativity, and natural-language processing.

3. Methodology

This study employs a quantitative comparative research design to analyze the textual outputs generated by various AI language models. To ensure consistent evaluation conditions, the models were all prompted with identical writing tasks initiated through new sessions with each engine. Each model received the same set of instructions in three distinct content categories: literary text (tragedy), historical narrative, and academic writing.

The researchers designed uniform tasks to control external variables and ensure that only differences between the LLMs explained variations in output. The study identifies the AI language model (LLM) as the independent variable and defines the level of creativity in the generated text as the dependent variable. The research team developed a custom algorithm to operationalize this evaluation, enabling a quantitative and systematic analysis of English-language AI-generated texts. The team organized the data analysis into several structured stages:

Stage 1: Pre-processing

The first step involved preparing the raw text for analysis by applying pre-processing techniques. This step included the following:

- Removing punctuation, numbers, and special characters (e.g., mathematical symbols, parentheses, and other non-alphabetic characters);
- Filtering out common stop words such as conjunctions (e.g., "or", "but", "and"), prepositions (e.g., "in", "on", "at"), and auxiliary verbs (e.g., "is", "am", "are"); and
- Converting all text to lowercase to ensure uniform processing.

This stage aimed to reduce noise in the data, improving the accuracy of subsequent linguistic analyses while optimizing computational efficiency.

Stage 2: Lemmatization

In the second stage, the researchers applied lemmatization using SpaCy's advanced NLP capabilities. This process unified all inflected forms of words into their base (lemma) forms and ensured that the analysis counted semantically identical words as a single lexical unit. This step was critical in accurately measuring lexical diversity by preventing grammatical variations from inflating vocabulary counts.

Stage 3: Computational analysis

- Subsequent stages involved the application of the four selected metrics:
- Flesch reading ease score for readability assessment
- TTR for lexical diversity measurement
- Jaccard similarity for quantifying textual similarity

The researchers visualized the results with graphs, trend lines, and frequency tables to highlight the distribution of base word forms and metric scores across the different text samples.

3.1 Data collection challenges

While instructing the AI language models (LLMs) to produce long-form texts (e.g., 50,000-word tragedies), several practical challenges emerged:

The AI language models (LLMs) require additional contextual details (characters, conflict, and writing style) to generate meaningful content.

- Even when given complete creative freedom, the engines typically produced outputs of around 800 words per iteration, significantly fewer than the requested target.

Generating longer texts required multiple iterative prompts and extended dialog with the AI, which often spanned several hours or days.

For example, to reach a 20,000-word tragedy, the research team repeatedly re-engaged with the engine, instructing it to continue writing chapter by chapter.

3.2 Computational framework

The researchers used three independently developed Python scripts, each implementing one of the selected creativity metrics. They executed these scripts in Jupyter Notebook to maintain methodological consistency across the analyses. The computational framework relied on several open-source Python libraries that the researchers selected for their reliability and broad adoption within the scientific and engineering communities.

- SpaCy was used for advanced NLP processing, including lemmatization, to enhance the validity of lexical diversity measurements (Honnibal & Montani [29]).

- Textstat was employed to calculate readability metrics using the Flesch reading ease formula, providing objective assessments based on word and sentence complexity (Eleyan et al. [18]).

- Python's built-in modules, Collections and Counter, were used to compute word frequency distributions, supporting lexical richness and usage analysis.

- The researchers utilized the Matplotlib and Seaborn visualization libraries to create graphs, trend lines, heatmaps, and frequency tables. While **Matplotlib** provided customizable plots, **Seaborn** enabled intuitive heatmaps that illustrated Jaccard similarities between texts.

- Each notebook analyzed one metric independently, allowing the researchers to clearly separate analytical processes, maintain greater control over computations, and ensure flexibility for future expansion. The researchers initially considered the Fog Index but excluded it from the final analysis because it conceptually overlapped with the Flesch Reading Ease metric and would have reduced methodological focus and clarity.

4. Reliability and validity

The experimental procedure was uniformly applied across all AI language models (LLMs) to ensure reliability. Each engine received identical prompts in consistent thematic domains, with strictly controlled execution conditions. The construct validity of the measurement tools was grounded in well-established linguistic and readability metrics:

- TTR (McCarthy & Jarvis [4])
- Flesch reading ease (Eleyan et al. [18])
- Jaccard similarity (Rinjeni et al. [23])

This alignment between measurement tools and research variables provides content validity for analyzing textual creativity.

Furthermore, each engine generated multiple samples across all three content domains, and each text underwent identical processing using the custom analysis algorithm. This approach minimized random variation, ensured consistency, and enhanced the replicability of the study's findings.

4.1 Operationalisation of creativity

The study operationalizes creativity through quantitative analysis of textual outputs, aligning primarily with the *Product* component of the Four-P Model. Lexical diversity (TTR), readability (Flesch Reading Ease), and textual similarity (Jaccard index) metrics provide measurable indicators of fluency, variety, and structural originality in AI-generated language. These surface-level linguistic attributes approximate how readers perceive novelty and coherence in creative writing.

Nevertheless, this quantitative framework does not yet capture **semantic novelty** or **conceptual innovation**, which are essential dimensions of creativity emphasized in the Creative Systems Framework. Future extensions could incorporate **semantic-embedding similarity** (e.g., cosine similarity between sentence or paragraph vectors) to quantify conceptual distance between AI outputs and human reference corpora. Measures such as **topic diversity, semantic entropy, or idea density indices** may further reveal how broadly or deeply a model explores a conceptual space. Combining these semantic metrics with the existing linguistic indicators would extend the framework from surface-text analysis toward a multidimensional understanding of creativity encompassing both form and meaning.

4.2 Optional bridge sentence for the discussion section

Interpreted through the lens of the Creative Systems Framework and the Four-P Model, the results suggest that current AI systems demonstrate strong performance in the *Product* dimension – producing readable and lexically varied text – but show limited progress in the *Process* dimension, where genuine conceptual transformation and semantic originality are expected to emerge.

4.3 Sampling and reproducibility

To enhance reproducibility, all AI-generated texts were produced under controlled and documented conditions. Two leading large-language-model systems were selected for comparison: **ChatGPT-4.0 (OpenAI, 2024)** and **Gemini-1.5 Pro (Google DeepMind, 2024)**. Both models were accessed through their respective web-based research interfaces between **March and April 2025**, ensuring version consistency across all outputs.

Each model was prompted in a new, independent session to avoid contextual carry-over effects from prior interactions. For each genre – **literary tragedy**, **historical narrative**, and **academic essay** – identical prompts were applied, differing only by topic-specific descriptors. The general structure of the prompts was as follows:

Tragedy: "Write an original tragedy in five acts, approximately 20,000 words long, exploring themes of fate and ambition in Renaissance style."

Historical narrative: "Compose a historically inspired narrative (10,000–15,000 words) describing the rise and fall of a medieval empire, emphasizing moral and political lessons."

Academic writing: "Produce an academic essay of around 2,000 words on the development of computing history, using a formal scholarly tone and structured argumentation."

The **temperature** parameter (which controls randomness) was set to **0.7**, and **top-p (nucleus sampling)** to **0.9** in all sessions. These moderate values were chosen to balance **creativity and coherence**, avoiding excessive repetition while preventing divergence from topic constraints. Other parameters (frequency penalty and presence penalty) were set to their default values (0.0) to ensure standardization.

When the models' token limits required continuation, the following instruction was issued iteratively: *"Continue from the previous paragraph without changing the tone or context."* This approach enabled the generation of longer compositions (up to 20,000 words) while maintaining stylistic continuity.

Each generation session was documented and archived with metadata, including model version, timestamp, prompt text, and sampling parameters. This documentation promotes methodological transparency, enabling future replication or extension of the study. All generated texts were saved as raw .txt files before preprocessing, ensuring traceability across analysis stages.

4.4 Statistical testing

To enhance analytical validity and determine whether the observed differences between AI-generated and human-authored texts were statistically significant, the study incorporated inferential statistical analysis. Two main procedures were applied:

Independent-sample t-tests were used to compare the mean values of key linguistic metrics – Type-Token Ratio (TTR) and Flesch Reading Ease – between AI-generated outputs and Shakespearean texts. This test evaluated whether AI language models (LLMs) differ significantly from human authors in terms of lexical diversity and readability.

One-way Analysis of Variance (ANOVA) was performed to assess genre-specific effects (Tragedy, History, Academic). This procedure tested whether the differences observed among text categories were statistically significant or attributable to random variation.

Before conducting these tests, all data were checked for **normality** and **homogeneity of variance** using Shapiro–Wilk and Levene's tests, respectively. Metric scores were treated as continuous variables, and statistical significance was established at **$p < 0.05$**. All analyses were executed using **Python's SciPy and statsmodels libraries**, complementing the visualization and regression results previously described.

The integration of inferential statistics enables a more rigorous comparison of human and AI textual outputs, extending the analysis beyond descriptive trends to statistically verifiable conclusions.

5. Results

5.1 TTR in literary works

5.1.1 Shakespeare's antony and cleopatra

The first analysis (**Figure 1**) examines the local lexical diversity of Shakespeare's *Antony and Cleopatra* by evaluating sequential iterations of 10,000 words each. Each data point shows the ratio of newly introduced words – those not previously appearing in the text – to the total word count of that iteration. The horizontal axis (X) shows the cumulative word count, and the vertical axis (Y) shows the lexical diversity ratio.

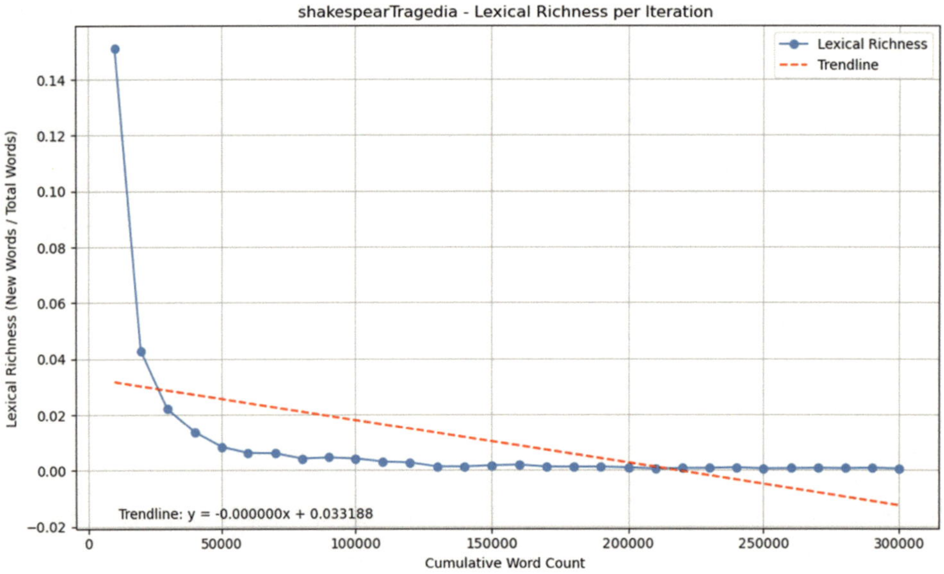

Figure 1.
Shakespeare tragedy – lexical richness.

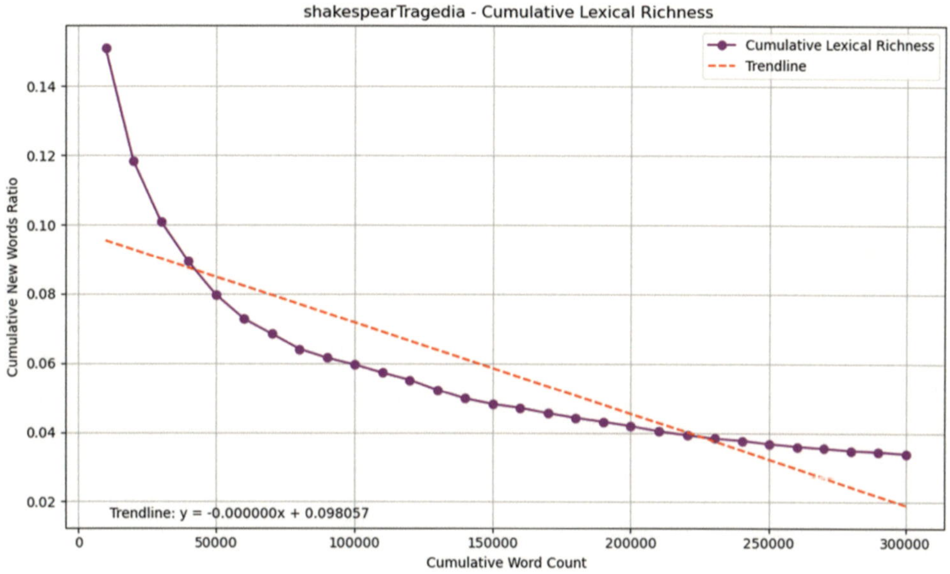

Figure 2.
Shakespeare tragedy – cumulative lexical richness.

Figure 1 illustrates a high initial lexical diversity of approximately 0.15, or 15%, which is typically observed in a narrative opening, where the author introduces characters, settings, and unique terms.

As the text progresses beyond 30,000–50,000 words, the diversity sharply declines to below 0.02 and stabilizes between 0.001 and 0.003 toward the end. This trend reflects how narrative structures increasingly rely on established vocabulary, character names, and recurring syntactic patterns.

The linear trend line (y = – 0.000000x + 0.033188) confirms a steady decline in new word introduction over time, with a slight but statistically meaningful negative slope.

A cumulative analysis (**Figure 2**) illustrates the growth of the overall unique vocabulary throughout the text. Starting again at around 0.15, this value gradually declines to 0.035 by the end of the text (~300,000 words). Unlike the more volatile local measure, this cumulative trend smooths out fluctuations, reflecting the natural deceleration in vocabulary expansion in extended texts. The linear regression equation (y = – 0.000000x + 0.098057) highlights this gradual but consistent decline.

6. Chatgpt's *the weight of ashes*

The third analysis (**Figure 3**) assesses the local lexical diversity of The Weight of Ashes, a tragedy generated by ChatGPT. The study uses 1,000-word segments.

Initial diversity starts high at 0.34 (34%) but drops below 0.01 by the sixth or seventh iteration (around 6,000–7,000 words), stabilizing at near-zero levels. The regression equation (y = – 0.000007x + 0.111013) confirms a steep early decline, followed by stabilization.

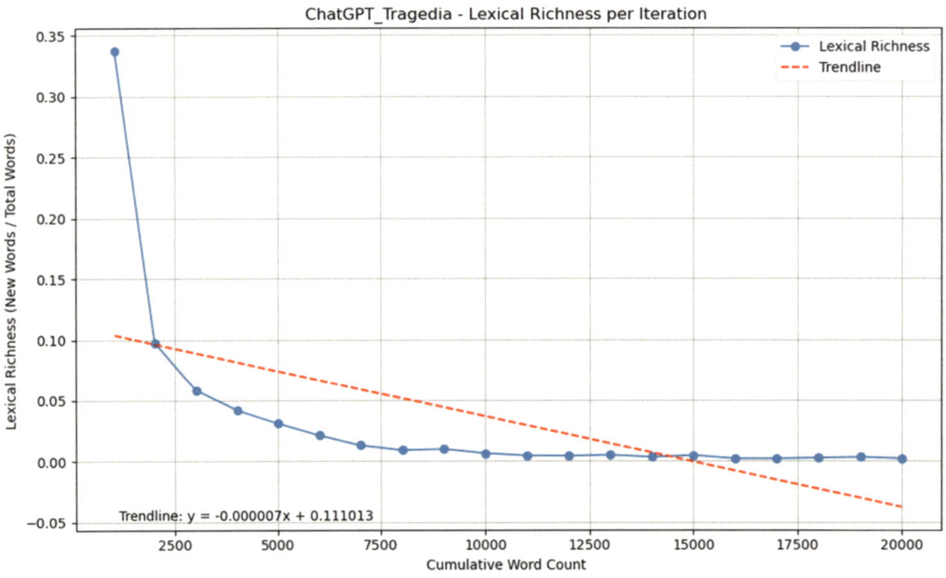

Figure 3.
Chatgpt tragedy – lexical richness.

The cumulative diversity (**Figure 4**) mirrors this trend by beginning at 0.34, decreasing to 0.20 around 5,000 words, and stabilizing between 0.10 and 0.12 after 10,000 words. The linear trend (y = – 0.000010x + 0.266655) indicates a relatively rapid stabilization in the model's vocabulary usage.

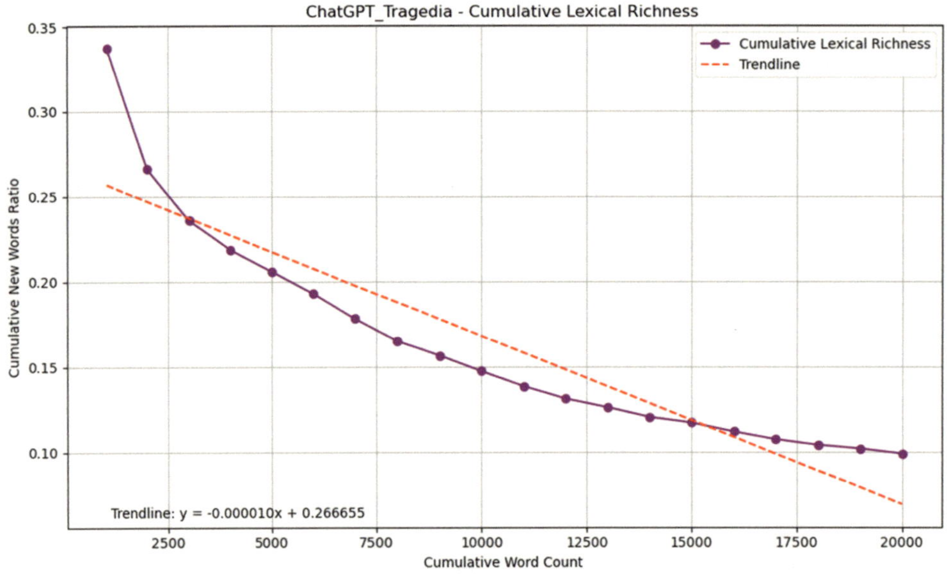

Figure 4.
Chatgpt tragedy – cumulative lexical richness.

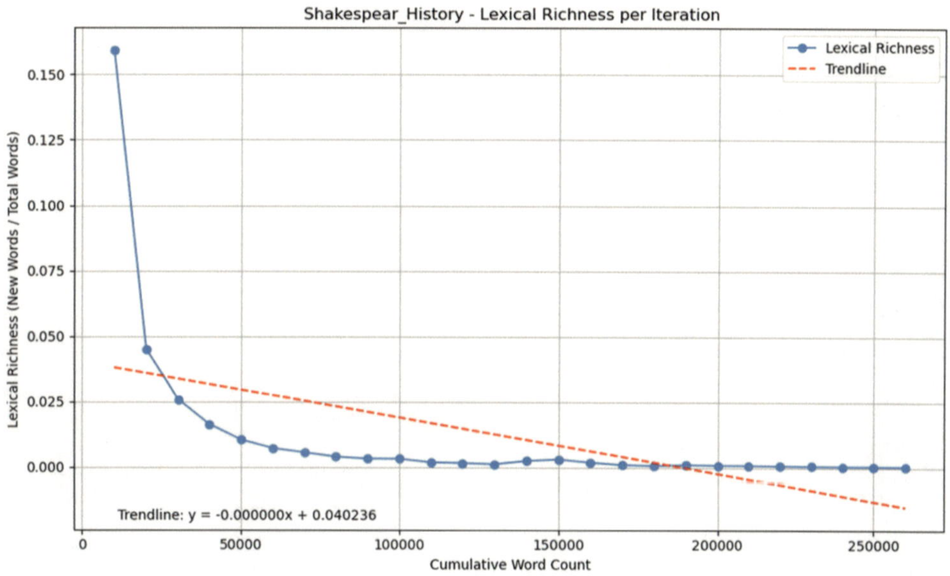

Figure 5.
Shakespeare history – lexical richness.

6.1 Shakespeare's historical play

Figure 5 presents the local lexical diversity of another Shakespearean work, demonstrating a high starting value of 0.15 that falls below 0.025 after 30,000 words, eventually approaching 0.001 in later stages. The trend line (y = - 0.000000x + 0.040236) reflects a quick convergence to a stable vocabulary set.

The cumulative analysis (**Figure 6**) starts at 0.16, before gradually declining to 0.037–0.040 toward the end of the text. The regression equation (y = - 0.000000x + 0.110940) again confirms a gradual but consistent reduction in new word introduction.

6.2 Chatgpt's historical narrative

The final literary analysis (**Figure 7** and **8**) reveals that ChatGPT's historical narrative exhibits a lexical diversity of 0.345, which rapidly decreases to 0.11 by the second iteration and stabilizes at a level below 0.015 after 5,000 words. The trend line (y = - 0.000013x + 0.144037) highlights a sharp decline followed by stable vocabulary repetition.

7. TTR in academic writing

7.1 Chatgpt academic article

Figures 9 and **10** present the evaluation of an academic article on the history of computing, which consisted of approximately 1,500 words. The local

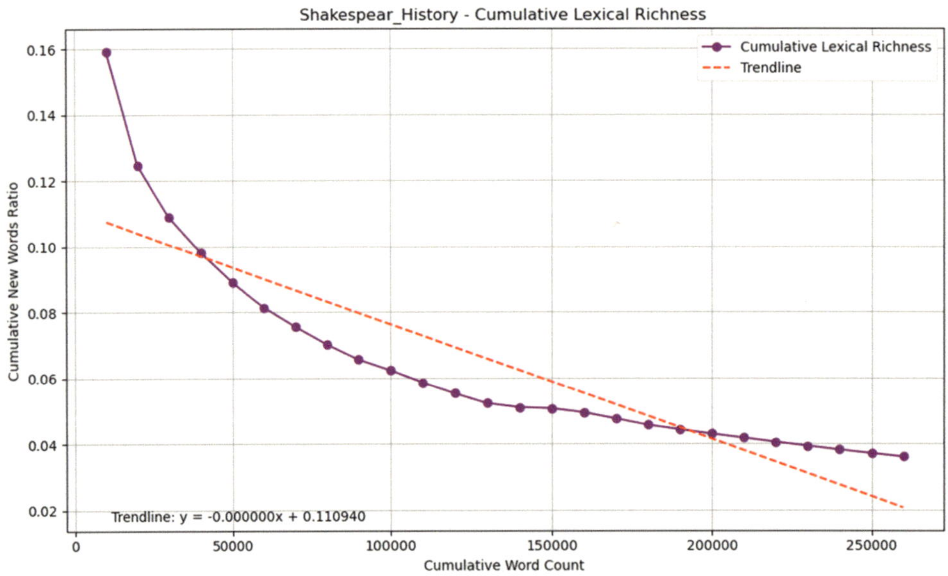

Figure 6.
Shakespeare history – cumulative lexical richness.

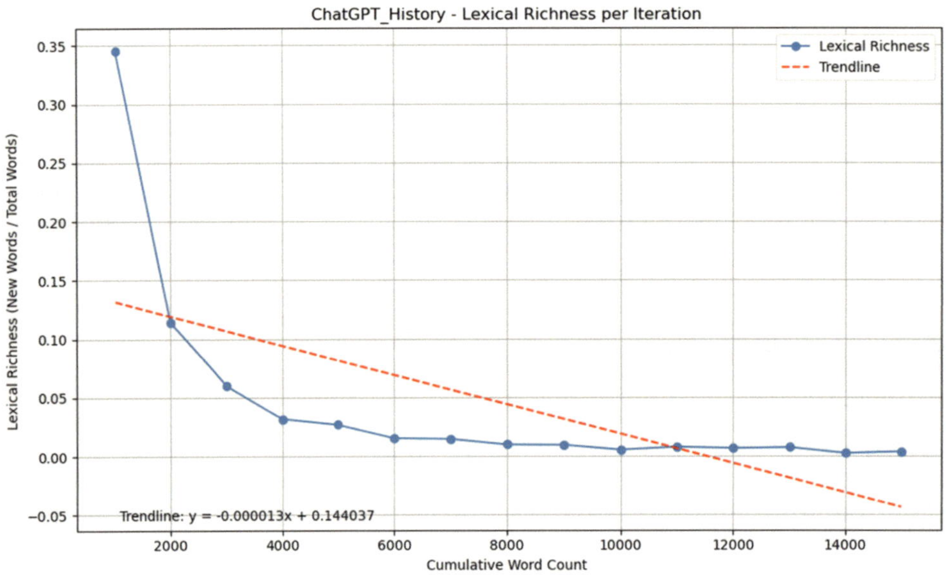

Figure 7.
Chatgpt history – lexical richness.

diversity (**Figure 9**) starts at 0.53 but drops below 0.10 after 1,200 words. The trend line (y = – 0.000222x + 0.266465) confirms a consistent decline.

The cumulative measure (**Figure 10**) begins at 0.47 before decreasing to 0.29 by the end of the text. The trend line (y = – 0.000071x + 0.476456) indicates a moderate but steady reduction in lexical diversity.

DOI: http://dx.doi.org/10.5772/intechopen.1014250

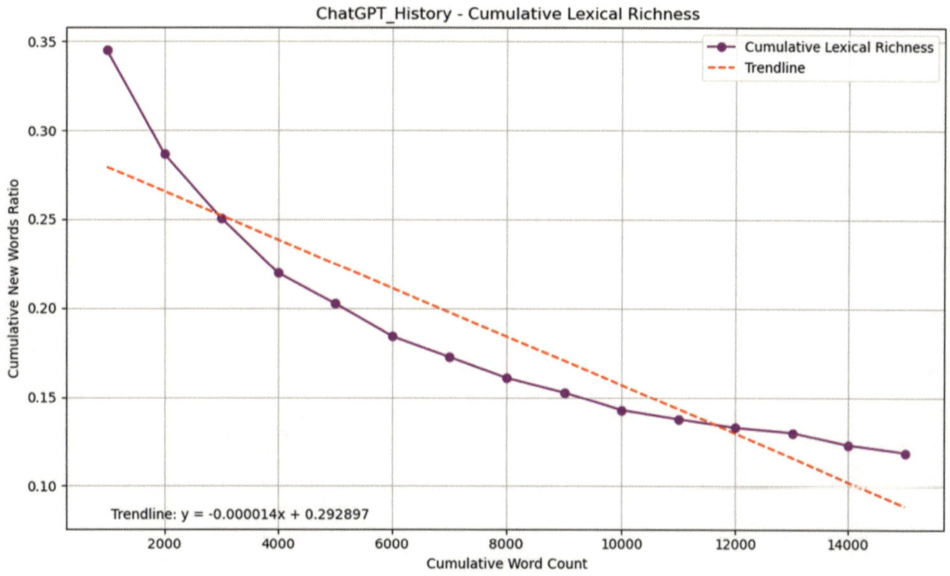

Figure 8.
Cumulative Lexical Richness.

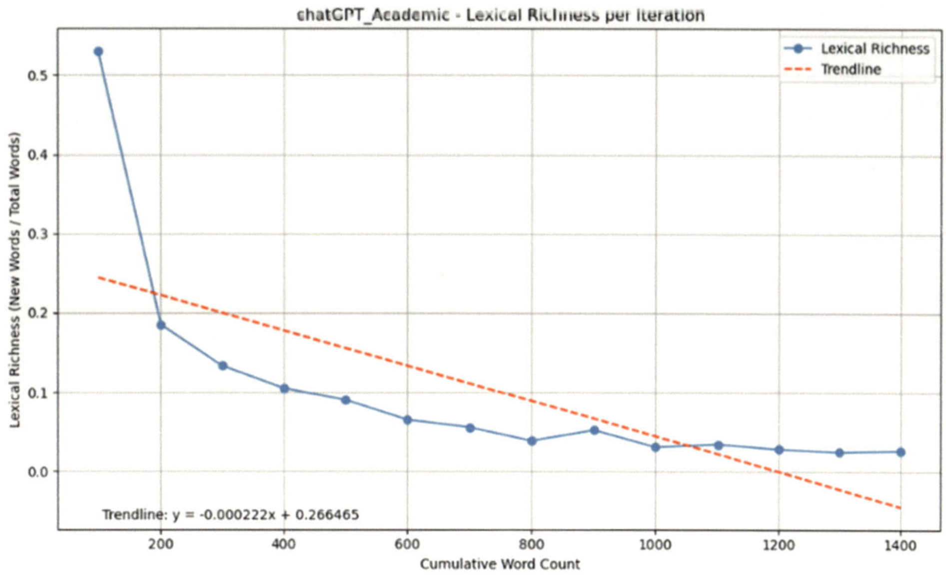

Figure 9.
Chatgpt academic – lexical richness.

7.2 Gemini academic article

Figures 11 and **12** assess a 1,970-word academic article generated by Gemini. The local diversity (**Figure 11**) starts at a high 0.615 before sharply dropping to 0.03 after 1,000 words. The regression equation (y = – 0.000153x + 0.227213) shows a marked decline.

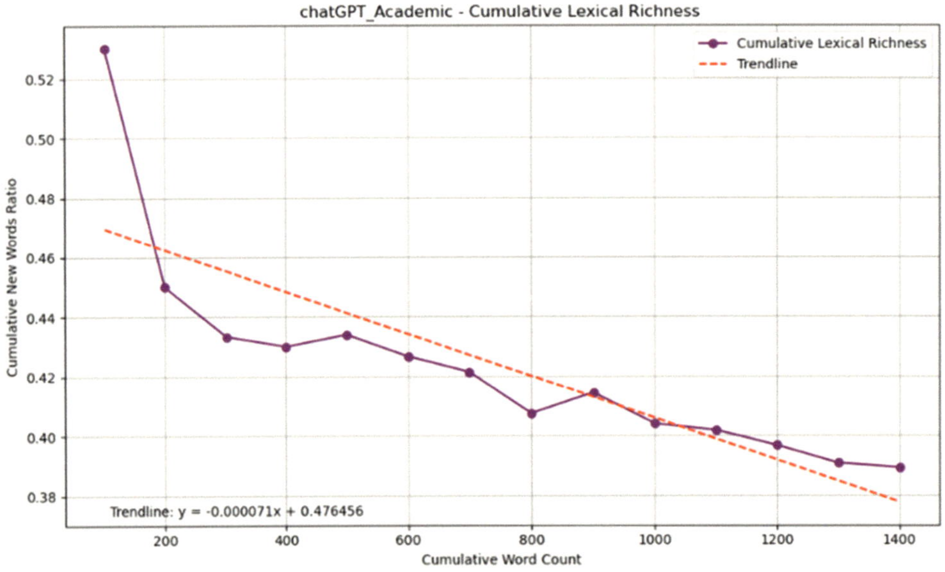

Figure 10.
Chatgpt academic – cumulative lexical richness.

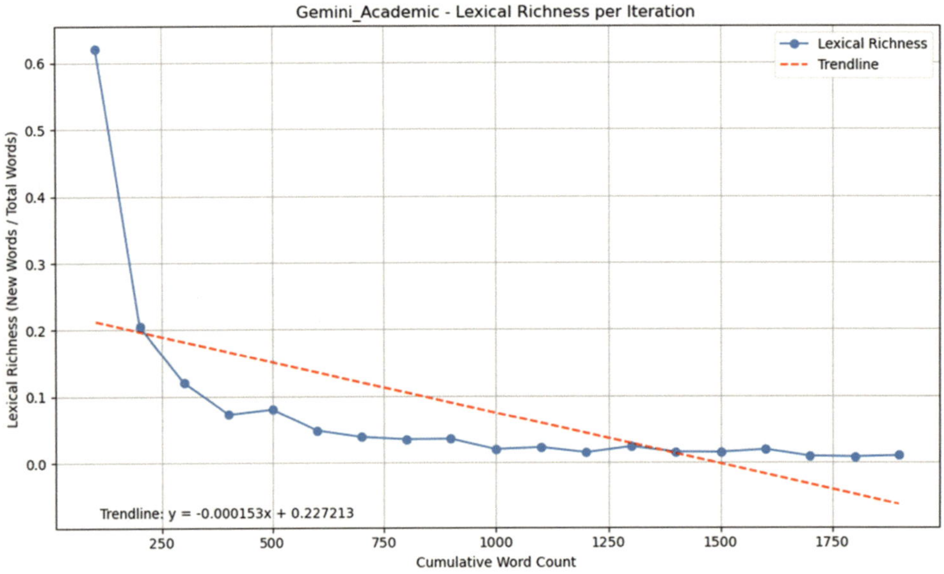

Figure 11.
Gemini academic – lexical richness.

The cumulative analysis (**Figure 12**) starts at 0.625 before stabilizing at 0.29–0.31. The regression equation (y = - 0.000136x + 0.507553) reflects a steady depletion of new vocabulary, indicating early saturation and repeated lexical patterns in the second half of the text.

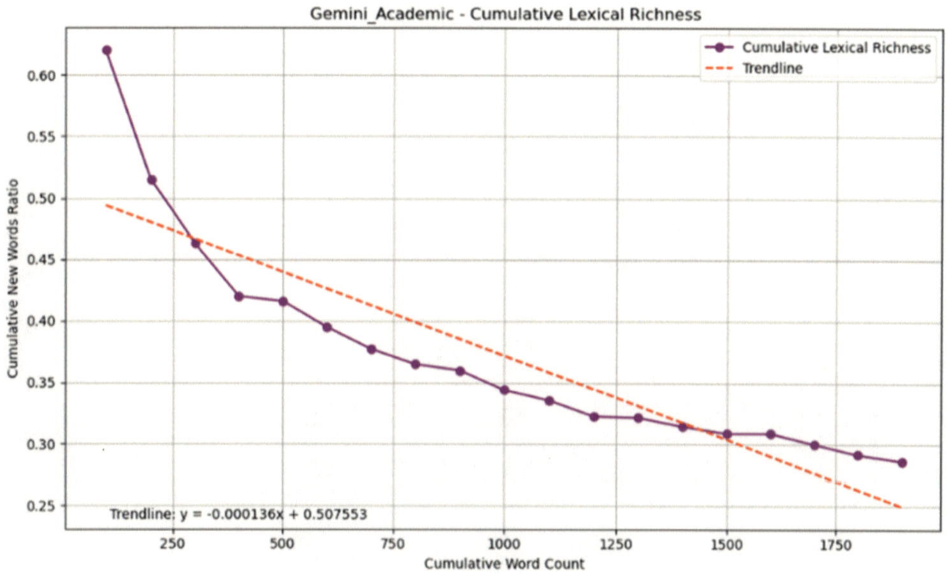

Figure 12.
Gemini academic – cumulative lexical richness.

Flesch reading ease score

Figure 13 compares the readability of six texts across three genres: history, tragedy, and academic writing. Higher scores indicate easier readability.

- **Historical texts:**
  - ChatGPT: 88.53 (Very easy)
  - Shakespeare: 77.98 (Fairly easy)
- **Tragedies:**
  - ChatGPT: 80.17 (Easy)
  - Shakespeare: 80.92 (Easy)
- **Academic texts:**
  - ChatGPT: 21.60 (Very difficult)
  - Gemini: 7.25 (Extremely difficult)

These results show that historical and tragic texts are significantly easier to read than academic articles. Notably, Gemini's academic writing is markedly more complex and less accessible than ChatGPT's, suggesting differing language generation strategies between the two models.

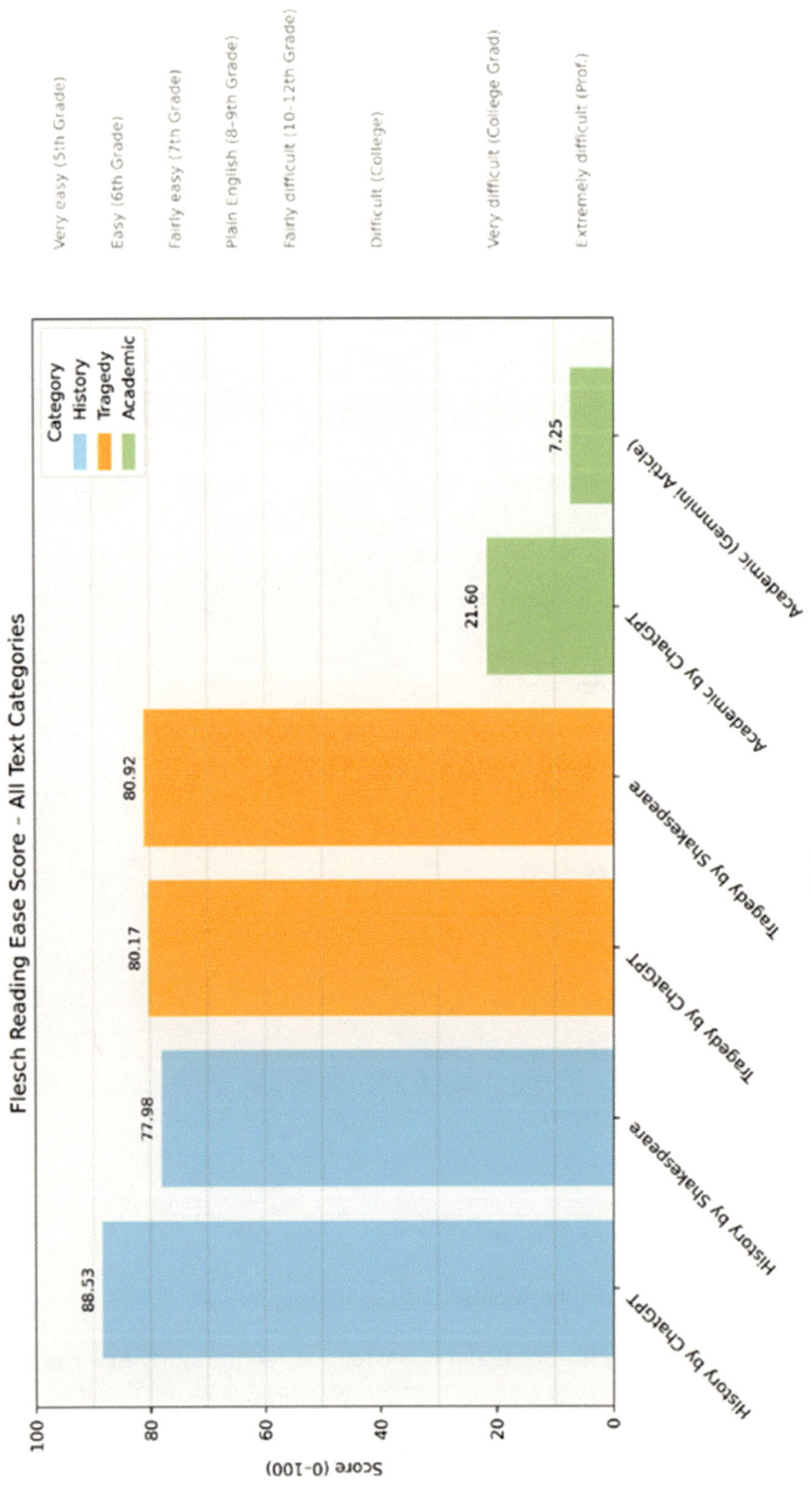

Figure 13.
Flesch reading ease score – all text categories.

Text domain	Jaccard similarity
Tragedy	0.218
Historical narrative	0.232
Academic paper	0.242

Table 1.
Jaccard similarity results.

7.3 Jaccard similarity analysis

A comparison of several pairs of two different texts generated by ChatGPT reveals consistently low similarity scores. The **Table 1** below summarizes the results.

7.4 Summary of results

7.4.1 Inferential statistical results

To evaluate the significance of observed differences between AI-generated and human-authored texts, inferential tests were conducted on TTR and Flesch Reading Ease metrics:

- TTR findings indicate that AI and human-generated texts exhibit high lexical diversity, which declines and stabilizes as the text progresses. This pattern holds across all genres analyzed.

- Readability results indicate that historical and tragic texts are generally more accessible, whereas academic writing presents greater reading challenges, particularly in outputs from Gemini.

- Jaccard similarity analyses consistently indicate low lexical overlap between different outputs of the same model within the same genre, demonstrating the ability of LLMs to produce varied content.

7.5 Lexical diversity (TTR)

Independent-sample t-tests indicated a statistically significant difference between AI and Shakespearean texts ($t(8) = 3.42, p = 0.009$), showing that Shakespeare maintained higher sustained lexical richness across longer texts.

7.6 Readability (Flesch Reading Ease)

The difference in readability between AI-generated and Shakespearean outputs was also significant ($t(8) = 2.96, p = 0.018$), with AI texts exhibiting greater simplicity and structural clarity.

7.7 Genre comparison (ANOVA)

A one-way ANOVA comparing the three genres (Tragedy, History, Academic) revealed significant effects for both lexical diversity ($F(2,12) = 5.21$, $p = 0.022$) and readability ($F(2,12) = 8.34$, $p = 0.005$). Post hoc Tukey tests indicated that the academic genre differed significantly from both tragedy and history, reflecting higher complexity and lower lexical novelty.

These results confirm that the quantitative trends illustrated in the regression graphs reflect statistically meaningful differences rather than random variation. The use of inferential testing thus strengthens the reliability of the conclusions. It demonstrates that AI and human-generated texts differ not only descriptively but also statistically in creativity-related linguistic features.

8. Discussion

The findings of this study show that AI language models, specifically ChatGPT and Gemini, generate rich, diverse, and highly readable texts across multiple genres. However, the results still reveal apparent differences between AI-generated content and classical human-authored texts, even after applying normalized metrics and controlling text length. This section analyzes these findings concerning the research questions and theoretical implications.

9. Lexical diversity (TTR)

The analysis of TTR revealed that, compared to the works authored by William Shakespeare, AI-generated texts demonstrated a consistent decline in the rate of new word introduction. ChatGPT's lexical convergence occurred much more rapidly, with a sharp decline observed after just 6,000 words in The Weight of Ashes. In contrast, Shakespeare's plays demonstrate a gradual and sustained expansion of vocabulary across hundreds of thousands of words. This observation suggests that LLMs rely on a relatively fixed and closed vocabulary set, whereas human authors, such as Shakespeare, display greater linguistic variation over time. Importantly, this difference is not solely technical but may reflect a deeper limitation in the generative flexibility of current AI systems.

Acknowledging the historical and technological gap between the evaluated human and AI creators is crucial. Despite Shakespeare's limited access to linguistic resources in the 16th and 17th centuries, his texts exhibited higher sustained lexical richness than those produced by modern LLMs trained on massive, diverse datasets. These results highlight the extraordinary capacity of human creativity to enrich language even under resource constraints, and they simultaneously expose the current limitations of AI in sustaining linguistic novelty over extended compositions.

To complement the quantitative results, a closer qualitative inspection of selected excerpts provides insight into the mechanisms underlying the observed lexical patterns in AI-generated texts.

For instance, in *The Weight of Ashes*, an AI-generated tragedy, lexical repetition becomes apparent through recurring collocations such as:

> *"And in the silent hall, the echoes of remorse returned again and again, whispering the fate that no one could escape."*

Variants of "returned again and again" and "fate that no one could escape" appear more than a dozen times across different acts, reflecting a tendency toward formulaic recurrence once a stylistic motif is established. This repetition aligns with the rapid decline in TTR observed in **Figure 3** and confirms that LLMs often stabilize around a limited vocabulary after initial lexical exploration.

Conversely, occasional moments of lexical innovation can also be observed, as in the line:

"The moonlight wrote confessions on the marble floor where kings once dreamed."

Here, the AI demonstrates creative metaphorical composition – an original juxtaposition of agency ("moonlight wrote") and historical reflection – that suggests limited but noteworthy generative inventiveness.

In contrast, human-authored texts, such as *Antony and Cleopatra,* exhibit a sustained introduction of novel imagery and syntactic variety even at later narrative stages. Examples include Shakespeare's phrasing:

"Age cannot wither her, nor custom stale her infinite variety."

This persistent linguistic rejuvenation, even within recurrent themes, supports the quantitative finding of slower TTR decline in human texts. The comparison thus reveals that LLMs tend to prioritize syntactic coherence and narrative continuity, while human writers sustain semantic innovation and lexical expansion across more extended compositions.

Integrating these qualitative observations with quantitative metrics reinforces the conclusion that AI systems can simulate stylistic fluency but remain limited in their ability to extend creative novelty over time.

9.1 Readability (Flesch Reading Ease)

Analysis using the Flesch Reading Ease score showed that, compared to Shakespeare's works, AI-generated texts, particularly those in historical genres, achieved higher readability levels. For instance, ChatGPT's historical narrative scored 88.53, classified as "Very Easy" and typically associated with elementary school reading levels (Eleyan et al. [18]). This result suggests a tendency among LLMs to prioritize linguistic clarity and structural simplicity, which are likely to enhance accessibility to a broad audience.

Conversely, academic texts, especially those produced by Gemini, demonstrate much lower readability scores, suggesting the use of highly technical vocabulary and complex sentence structures. These findings reveal that genre is crucial in shaping the characteristics of AI-generated text. While historical and dramatic texts favor clarity and simplicity, academic texts demand precision and technicality, sometimes at the expense of readability. This contrast suggests that LLMs can adapt writing styles to genre-specific expectations; however, they may struggle to balance linguistic complexity and reader accessibility, particularly in technical domains.

9.2 Textual similarity (Jaccard similarity)

The Jaccard similarity analysis revealed low lexical overlap between different texts on the same topic generated by the same LLM. Similarity scores ranged from 0.218 to 0.242 for ChatGPT and 0.310 for Gemini, indicating high structural and lexical diversity across outputs. However, these findings suggest surface-level linguistic diversity but do not necessarily reflect conceptual or thematic novelty. Furthermore, the structural differences in corpus size – such as Shakespeare's extensive 262,000-word collection versus ChatGPT's 20,000-word single document – required metric normalization to enable a fair comparison. It is important to emphasize that this study did not rank the quality of the outputs. Instead, the purpose was to identify stylistic, linguistic, and structural patterns that differentiate human and AI-generated texts.

While the Jaccard similarity metric provides a useful baseline for quantifying **lexical overlap**, it primarily reflects surface-level word co-occurrence and does not capture deeper **semantic or stylistic relationships** between texts. For example, two passages may express similar ideas using distinct vocabularies, yielding a low Jaccard score despite strong conceptual alignment. Conversely, high word overlap may not necessarily indicate thematic similarity, especially when formulaic or genre-specific expressions recur frequently.

To address these limitations, future research could integrate complementary **content-sensitive similarity measures,** such as **BLEU** and **ROUGE**, which compare sequences of n-grams to evaluate structural and phrasal resemblance, or **embedding-based semantic similarity metrics**, such as cosine similarity computed over contextual sentence or document embeddings (e.g., using transformer models like BERT or Sentence-BERT). These approaches would enable a more comprehensive assessment of conceptual and stylistic coherence, extending the current lexical framework into a deeper semantic analysis.

Incorporating such semantic-level techniques would help distinguish between *superficial linguistic similarity* and *genuine thematic correspondence*, thereby enhancing the interpretive depth of future creativity analyses.

9.3 Theoretical implications

The results highlight that while AI-generated texts mimic the structural characteristics of human writing, the models struggle to maintain linguistic depth and variation over time. Shakespeare's works are notable for their continuous linguistic innovation, including neologisms and unique phrasing, whereas LLMs display high initial lexical diversity that quickly stabilizes into repetitive patterns. This result points to a fundamental difference in the creative process, not just in the final output.

The statistical analyses reinforce the descriptive findings, confirming that observed differences in lexical diversity and readability between LLMs and Shakespeare are statistically significant. These results highlight the structural simplicity and lexical convergence of AI-generated outputs compared to human-authored texts. The ANOVA results further suggest that genre plays a measurable role in shaping these linguistic characteristics, reflecting contextual sensitivity in both AI-generated and human-written texts.

DOI: http://dx.doi.org/10.5772/intechopen.1014250

10. Limitations

10.1 This study faced several limitations

Corpus size: The scope was limited to a few engines and texts, restricting generalizability.

The researchers analyzed texts only in English and may have overlooked language-specific dynamics in other languages.

Quantitative focus: The evaluation emphasized quantitative linguistic metrics, excluding qualitative assessments of thematic depth, originality, and stylistic nuance.

Technical constraints: AI language models (LLMs) require user interaction to produce longer texts, limiting their autonomy and complicating the evaluation of extended creative performance.

We thank the reviewer for this thoughtful comment. In response, the Limitations section has been expanded to include a detailed "Future Research Directions" subsection. This addition outlines specific recommendations for extending the framework to multilingual corpora, integrating semantic, emotional, and narrative-based creativity metrics, and incorporating human expert assessments, such as the Consensual Assessment Technique (CAT), to complement the quantitative analysis. These enhancements strengthen the theoretical and practical implications of the research, providing a roadmap for further studies in computational creativity evaluation.

10.2 Contributions and practical implications

Despite these limitations, the study benefited from successfully applying a systematic, empirical framework that combined natural language processing tools and validated linguistic metrics to analyze AI-generated creativity. A controlled experimental setup enhanced reliability and provided clear benchmarks for comparing human and AI outputs.

The study's primary contribution is offering a quantitative method for evaluating AI-generated creativity. It highlights the current boundaries of LLMs in sustaining linguistic richness. These insights can inform the development of more advanced AI systems and guide future research into the linguistic and creative capabilities of AI.

10.3 Future research directions

While the present framework offers a structured and replicable approach to quantifying AI-generated creativity, several promising avenues exist for expanding its scope in future studies.

10.4 Multilingual analysis

The current research focused exclusively on English-language texts, which may limit the generalizability of the findings. Future work could extend this framework to other languages, such as Spanish, Mandarin, or Hebrew, to examine how linguistic morphology, syntax, and idiomatic variation influence AI-generated creativity.

Comparative multilingual analysis would also help identify whether creativity metrics behave consistently across language families or require language-specific adaptation.

10.5 Semantic, emotional, and narrative dimensions

The current study evaluates creativity primarily through structural and lexical metrics (TTR, Flesch, and Jaccard). Future extensions could integrate **semantic similarity** and **coherence models** (e.g., embedding-based cosine similarity), **emotional tone analysis** using sentiment or affective lexicons, and **narrative-structure evaluation** through automated story arc modeling. These approaches would enable a deeper understanding of conceptual innovation and emotional expressiveness – key elements often associated with human creativity.

10.6 Human-centered evaluation

While computational metrics provide objective measurements, they may not fully reflect the subjective perception of creativity. Future studies could incorporate **human evaluation methods**, such as expert literary review panels or standardized instruments like the **Consensual Assessment Technique (CAT)**, which is widely regarded as the gold standard in creativity research. Combining quantitative linguistic indicators with expert judgments would enable the triangulation of results, thereby improving both validity and interpretive depth.

10.7 Expanded corpus and genres:

Beyond the three genres tested here (tragedy, history, and academic), future research could include additional creative domains, such as poetry, dialog, and journalism. These genres would test the robustness of the framework across varying stylistic constraints and creative intents.

By integrating multilingual, semantic, emotional, and human-evaluation dimensions, future research can transform this framework from a quantitative linguistic model into a more holistic system for assessing **computational creativity** across languages, media, and cultural contexts.

11. Conclusion

Using a structured, quantitative framework based on established linguistic and computational metrics, this study explored the linguistic creativity of AI-generated texts. By analyzing texts generated by ChatGPT and Gemini and comparing them to classical works by William Shakespeare, the research aimed to assess lexical diversity (TTR), readability (Flesch Reading Ease), and textual similarity (Jaccard Similarity) across different writing genres.

The findings reveal that while AI language models (LLMs) demonstrate the capacity to produce highly readable and lexically diverse texts, they tend to converge quickly toward repetitive vocabulary patterns, especially in longer compositions. In contrast, Shakespeare's works display a sustained ability to introduce new linguistic elements over extended narratives, highlighting the depth and resilience of human creativity even in resource-constrained historical contexts.

Readability analysis showed that LLMs, particularly ChatGPT, tend to favor linguistic simplicity and accessibility, especially in narrative genres. However, LLMs – especially Gemini – produce highly complex and technical texts in academic writing, often at the expense of reader accessibility. This duality reflects the genre-sensitive adaptability of LLMs but also raises questions about their ability to balance complexity with clarity.

Textual similarity analysis demonstrated that AI-generated texts exhibit low lexical overlap, suggesting a structural capacity for linguistic variation even when addressing the same topic. However, the study also identified limitations in the models' ability to maintain conceptual or thematic novelty over time.

By integrating insights from recent developments in LLM evaluation (OpenAI, 2023; Gervás, 2024), the study situates its findings within the current discourse on computational creativity, emphasizing the ongoing transition from rule-based creativity models toward data-driven generative paradigms.

While the research offers a replicable framework for evaluating AI-generated creativity, it also highlights several limitations, including a restricted corpus size, limited language scope, and the exclusive use of quantitative metrics. Furthermore, the technical requirement for human intervention during the generation of long-form texts limits the autonomous creative capabilities of current AI language models (LLMs).

Despite these limitations, the study contributes valuable insights into the current state of AI linguistic creativity and offers practical tools for evaluating AI-generated content. The results suggest that AI can mimic human-like writing structures, but it still lags behind human authors in sustaining deep, long-term linguistic innovation.

Acknowledgments

The author acknowledges the use of ChatGPT and Grammarly (AI tools) for language polishing.

Author details

Eden Emuna, Ron Elkayam and Eyal Brill*
Faculty of Industrial Engineering, HIT – Holon Institute of Technology, Israel

*Address all correspondence to: eyalb@hit.ac.il

References

[1] Runco MA, Jaeger GJ. The standard definition of creativity. Creativity Research Journal. 2012;**24**(1):92–96

[2] Boden MA. The Creative Mind: Myths and Mechanisms (2nd ed.). Routledge: Psychology Press; 2004

[3] Gervás P **(2002).** Exploring quantitative evaluations of the creativity of automatic poets. Workshop on Creative Systems: Approaches to Creativity in Artificial Intelligence and Cognitive Science (ECAI-2002).

[4] McCarthy PM, Jarvis S. Voc-D: A theoretical and empirical evaluation. Language Testing. 2007;**24**(4):459–488

[5] Antebi L. Artificial Intelligence and National Security in Israel. **(INSS Memorandum No. 207)**. Tel Aviv: Institute for National Security Studies; 2021

[6] Turing AM. Computing machinery and intelligence. Mind. 1950;**49**: 433–460

[7] McKinsey. "State of AI" on generative AI's breakout year. QuantumBlack AI, August 2023 Copyright © McKinsey & Company Designed by McKinsey Global Publishing McKinsey.com

[8] Guzik EE, Byrge C, Gilde C. The originality of machines: AI takes the Torrance Test—Journal of. Journal of Creativity. 2023;**33**(3):100065

[9] Anantrasirichai N, Bull D. Artificial intelligence in the creative industries: A review. Artificial Intelligence Review. 2022;**55**:89–656. DOI: 10.1007/s10462-021-10039-7

[10] Kaplan A, Haenlein M. Siri, Siri, in my hand: Who's the fairest in the land? On the interpretations, illustrations, and implications of artificial intelligence. Business Horizons. 2019;**62**(1):15–25. DOI: 10.1016/j.bushor.2018.08.004

[11] Elgammal A, Liu B, Elhoseiny M, Mazzone M (2017). Can: Creative adversarial networks, generating "art" by learning about styles and deviating from style norms. In: Goel A, Jordanous A, Pease A (Eds.). Proceedings of the 8th International Conference on Computational Creativity (ICCC'17) (p. 96–103). Georgia Institute of Technology.

[12] Choi K, Fazekas G, Sandler M (2016). Text-based LSTM networks for automatic music composition [Paper presentation]. In: 1st Conference on Computer Simulation of Musical Creativity (CSMC **16**); Huddersfield, United Kingdom.

[13] Berman A, James V (2018). Learning as performance: Autoencoding and generating dance movements in real time. In: Liapis A, Cardalda JJR, Ekárt A (Eds.). International Conference on Computational Intelligence in Music, Sound, Art and Design (p. 256–266). Springer.

[14] Daniele A, Song Y (2019). AI art = human. In: Conitzer V, Hadfield GK, Vallor S (Eds.). Proceedings of the 2019 AAAI/ACM Conference on AI, Ethics, and Society (p. 155–161). Association for Computing Machinery.

[15] Miller AI. Can AI Be Truly Creative? Computers and artificial neural networks are redefining the

relationship between art and science. American Scientist. 2020;**108**(4):244–249

[16] Köhler R, Galle M. Dynamic aspects of text characteristics. In Hřebíček L, Altmann G, editors. Quantitative Text Analysis. Trier: WVT Wissenschaftlicher Verlag Trier; 1993. p. 46–53

[17] Covington MA, McFall JD. Cutting the gordian knot: The Moving-Average Type–Token Ratio (MATTR). Journal of Quantitative Linguistics. 2010;**17**(2):94–100. DOI: 10.1080/09296171003643098

[18] Eleyan D, Othman A, Eleyan A. Enhancing software comments readability using Flesch Reading Ease Score. Information. 2020;**11**(9):1–25

[19] Hemmings D, Hodgkinson L, Williams G. It's OK to pay well, if you write well: The effects of remuneration disclosure readability. Journal of Business Finance & Accounting. 2020;**47**(5–6):547–586. DOI: 10.1111/jbfa.12431

[20] Li F. Annual report readability, current earnings, and earnings persistence. Journal of Accounting and Economics. 2008;**45**(2–3):221–247

[21] Yaffe P. Fog index: Is it really worth the trouble? Ubiquity. 2022;1–4. DOI: 10.1145/3568307

[22] Pradhan N, Gyanchandani M, Wadhvani R. A review on text similarity technique used in IR and its application. International Journal of Computer Applications. 2015;**120**(9):29–34

[23] Rinjeni TP, Indriawan A, Rakhmawati NA. Matching scientific article titles using cosine similarity and Jaccard similarity algorithm. Procedia Computer Science. 2024;**234**:553–560. DOI: 10.1016/j.procs.2024.03.039

[24] Kowsari K, Jafari Meimandi K, Heidarysafa M, Mendu S, Barnes LE, Brown DE. Text classification algorithms: A survey. Information. 2019;**10**(4):150. DOI: 10.3390/info10040150

[25] Sarkar D. Text Analytics with Python: A Practitioner's Guide to Natural Language Processing. 2nd. New York, NY, USA: Apress; 2019. See the sections introducing NLP and discussing language syntax/semantics

[26] MacCartney B. Understanding Natural Language Understanding (CS224U talk slides). Stanford NLP Group; 2014, July. https://nlp.stanford.edu/~wcmac/papers/20140716-UNLU.pdf

[27] Jordanous A. A standardized procedure for evaluating creative systems: Computational creativity evaluation based on what it is to be creative. Cognitive Computation. 2012;**4**(3):246–279. DOI: 10.1007/s12559-012-9156-1

[28] Rhodes M. An analysis of creativity. Phi Delta Kappan. 1961;**42**(7):305–310

[29] Honnibal M, Montani I (2017). spaCy 2: Natural language understanding with Bloom embeddings, convolutional neural networks and incremental parsing. [Unpublished manuscript]

Section 4

Data Infrastructure, Collection, and Management

Chapter 7

Scalable Data Collection and Management for Agricultural Research: Foundations and Advancements in Data Mining Applications

Hannington Odido Ochieng and Lenah Muema

Abstract

This chapter examines the convergence of participatory approaches and digital ecosystems in agricultural data collection, with a particular focus on Sub-Saharan Africa. While existing literature treats farmer-led models and digital technologies as separate trajectories, this synthesis demonstrates how participatory knowledge generation can be scaled and enriched through digital platforms and governance frameworks. It argues that scalable agricultural intelligence relies not only on technological innovation but also on governance, institutional integration, and farmer-centred design. The chapter demonstrates how hybrid models – which connect farmer-generated data with IoT sensors, cloud platforms, and AI analytics – can provide accuracy, inclusivity, and sustainability by referencing case studies including DigiFarm, PlantVillage Nuru, and TRICOT experiments. Comparative analysis of traditional, precision, participatory, and digital approaches reveals their distinct strengths while emphasising integration as the foundation for scalability and resilience. In order to tackle the enduring problems of data heterogeneity, connectivity, and trust, the chapter presents a hybrid paradigm that blends edge–cloud topologies, open APIs, and participatory governance. Moreover, ethical and policy dimensions, including data ownership, consent, liability, and equity, are critically examined. The chapter concludes by redefining digital agriculture as a socio-technical system in which farmer agency, institutional durability, and inclusive governance are central to building future-ready agricultural data ecosystems.

Keywords: data collection methodology, data integration, precision farming, digital tools, machine learning, agricultural intelligence, participatory models, sub-saharan Africa, data governance, IoT, scalability

1. Introduction

Agriculture has always been a data-driven enterprise, relying on the collection and interpretation of information to guide decision-making about breeding, planting, harvesting, husbandry, marketing, and resource management. Over the centuries, farmers and researchers have collected data through direct observation, recall, and manual recordkeeping. These approaches, while valuable, are often limited in scale and subject to human error. With internet of things (IoT) sensors, mobile apps, and edge-cloud platforms, today's agricultural data systems are capable of collecting high-frequency, high-resolution information with reduced error rates and near real-time availability [1].

The global agricultural sector faces significant challenges, including the impacts of climate change, land degradation, fragmented landholdings, post-harvest losses, policy inconsistencies, weak coordination across governance levels, inadequate infrastructure, and persistent resource constraints. Addressing these challenges requires scalable data collection and management systems that can support decision-making at multiple levels, from individual farmers to subnational and national policy-makers. These systems/technologies are foundational to developing resilient and sustainable food systems, enabling real-time monitoring and adaptive management that are crucial for solving the challenges experienced in the sector. However, adoption of these systems remains highly uneven. Barriers such as rural connectivity gaps, high device maintenance costs, fragmented data standards, and low levels of digital literacy slow uptake, especially in sub-Saharan Africa [2, 3].

While much of the literature examines participatory approaches and digital agriculture separately, this chapter uniquely synthesises the two strands by showing how farmer-centred models can be scaled through digital platforms and data governance frameworks. Specifically, the chapter explores the revolution of data collection and management in agriculture, focusing on emerging technologies, participatory modes, and advanced data analytics that enable scalability. It also considers institutional, policy, and ethical dimensions, while situating Sub-Saharan Africa within global conversations on open agricultural data (e.g., GODAN, GARDIAN, and Digital Green). By bridging local innovations with global frameworks, this chapter aims to provide both theoretical and practical insights into building scalable, sustainable agricultural data systems that can support climate resilience and the future of food security.

2. Evolution of agricultural data collection

Agricultural data collection has undergone significant transformation over time, reflecting technological advances, changing research priorities, and the need for evidence-based decision-making. Historically, traditional methods such as farmer recalls, diaries, field notes, and extension officer reports were the primary means of generating agricultural information. While useful, these approaches were slow, labour-intensive, and prone to recall biases and measurement errors [4, 5].

The Green Revolution of the mid-20th century marked a turning point with the introduction of structured measurement tools, such as crop-cutting surveys and sample-based methods [6]. These approaches enhanced accuracy and reliability, but they remained costly and resource-intensive, particularly in smallholder-dominated contexts. By the late 20th century, advances in remote sensing and geographical information systems (GIS) opened a new era of agricultural data collection. These technologies enabled researchers to monitor large areas more efficiently and provided fresh perspectives on crop performance, livestock health, land use, resource allocation, and animal movement [7, 8].

In the early 21st century, the rapid penetration of digital technologies – including mobile phones, cloud platforms, and IoT devices – revolutionised data collection practices. These tools allow real-time monitoring, participatory farmer engagement, and seamless integration with advanced analytics such as machine learning and predictive modelling [5, 9]. Instead of relying solely on manual surveys or periodic satellite observations, scalable frameworks now leverage integrated IoT platforms and streaming databases (e.g., Apache Kafka, AWS Kinesis) to capture high-frequency sensor data and synchronise it with cloud-based storage in near real time [4].

The trajectory of this evolution can be understood as a continuum from traditional to precision, to participatory, to digital approaches [7] (see **Figure 1**). Each stage reflects a progressive shift towards greater automation, higher data granularity, and faster feedback loops.

The comparative features of these approaches are summarised in **Table 1**, which contrasts differences in data volume, latency, cost, and decision-usefulness. A further pictorial summary is provided in **Figure 2**.

While the shift towards digital ecosystems offers unprecedented opportunities, it also raises equity and adoption concerns. Smallholder farmers in low-connectivity

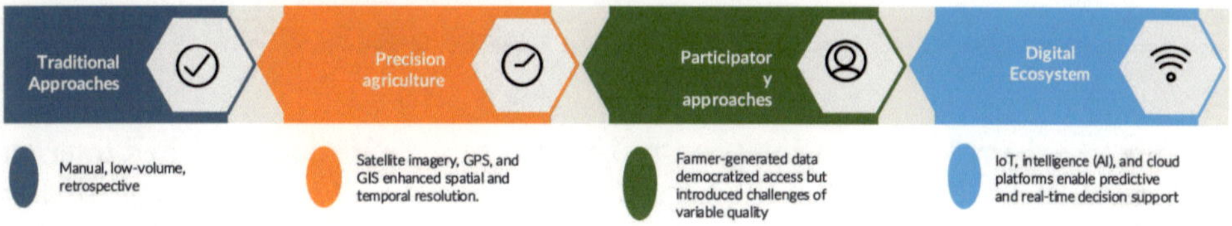

Figure 1.
Agricultural data continuum.

Approach	Data volume	Latency	Cost	Decision usefulness
Traditional (surveys, manual entry)	Low	High (weeks/months; retrospective)	High (labour-intensive)	Limited, retrospective
Precision agriculture (satellite, GPS, GIS)	Medium to high (spatially rich but periodic)	Medium (days/weeks depending on acquisition)	Moderate (depends on imagery/equipment)	Improved spatial/temporal insights; supports targeted interventions
Participatory (farmer-generated data)	Variable (depends on participation scale)	Medium (days/weeks; semi-real time)	Low to Moderate (incentives and training needed)	Democratised access, contextualised insights, variable quality
Digital ecosystems (IoT, AI, cloud platforms)	High to very high (continuous streams)	Low (real-time or near real-time)	Lower per unit (after initial setup)	Predictive, actionable, supports automation, and adaptive management

Table 1.
Comparative features of agricultural data approaches.

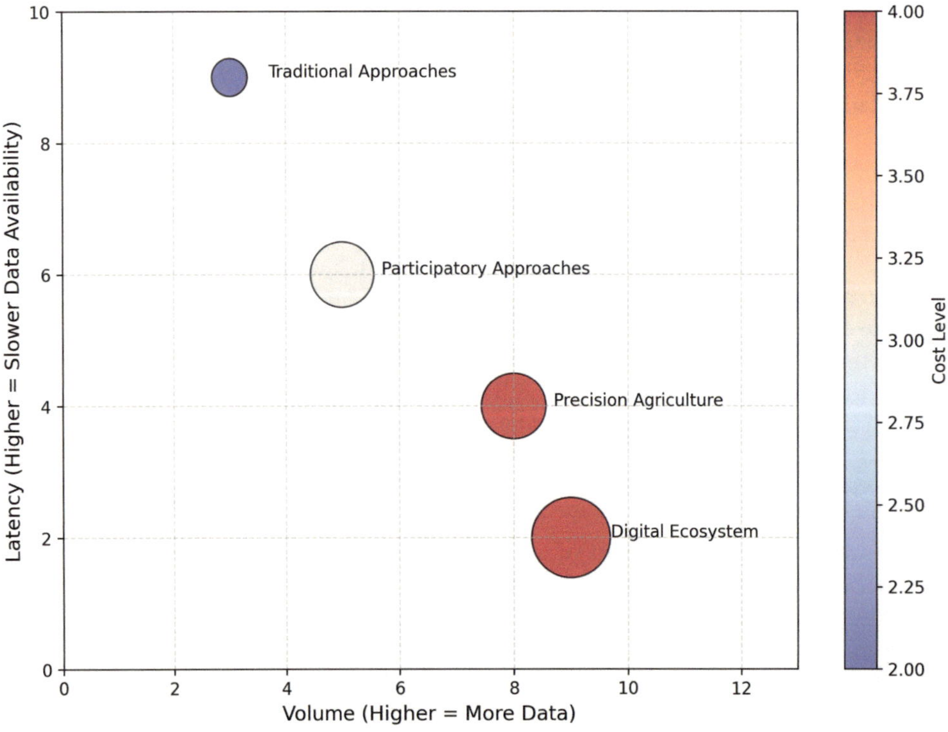

Figure 2.
Comparative data approaches in agriculture (size = decision usefulness, colour = cost).

regions face the risk of exclusion from real-time data benefits due to limited internet access, low digital literacy, and affordability challenges [8, 9]. Moreover, issues of data ownership, privacy, and governance remain unresolved and require policy interventions to ensure inclusive and ethical digital transformation in agriculture [4].

3. Participatory and crowdsourced data collection models

Agricultural research has increasingly incorporated participatory and crowdsourced approaches, especially in situations where traditional surveys and sensor-driven systems face limitations. These models emphasise inclusivity by treating farmers and local communities not merely as data sources but as active co-creators of knowledge. By capturing field-level realities directly from those who manage crops and livestock, participatory models generate context-specific, timely, and relevant data that can complement scientific observations [10, 11].

3.1 Concept and rationale

Farmers are best positioned to capture their own realities, according to participatory and crowdsourced models. Unlike top-down survey methods or sensor-based monitoring, these approaches put farmers at the centre, engaging them in data generation, validation, and sometimes even analysis. This makes the data richer in context, better aligned with local practices, and more likely to be trusted by the farming communities who ultimately use it [12, 13]. They also bridge the gap between global data infrastructures and local realities, especially in resource-constrained environments [13]. In practice, these models take many forms – ranging from Farmer Field Schools, Participatory Rural Appraisal, and on-farm participatory trials to more systemic approaches such as innovation platforms, community-based breeding programs, citizen science initiatives, and digital crowdsourcing models [5, 14]. Their diversity underscores their flexibility and justifies their growing use in agricultural research and data collection.

3.2 Strengths and opportunities

Participatory and crowdsourced approaches provide several distinct advantages. First, they capture local heterogeneity, ensuring that context-specific variations remain intact in the aggregated data [15]. Second, they enable rapid information flow, particularly during agricultural shocks such as pest invasions or droughts [16]. Third, they enhance farmer trust and ownership, as participation reinforces the legitimacy of data-driven recommendations and increases the likelihood of adoption [17]. This also facilitates peer-to-peer learning between the farmers. Finally, participatory approaches align naturally with digital agriculture ecosystems, where crowdsourced observations can be cross-validated with sensor and satellite data, increasing both accuracy and confidence in findings [18]. Apart from the technical benefits, these approaches also democratise agricultural innovation by ensuring that farmers' perspectives during co-design sessions shape both the research questions and the solutions developed.

3.3 Challenges and limitations

Despite their promise, participatory and crowdsourced models face important challenges. Farmer-reported data may be inconsistent, incomplete, or subjective, raising concerns about accuracy and reliability. Farmer-reported data often varies due to subjective assessments, differing understandings of study parameters, regional contexts, and device disparities [19]. Another difficulty is sustained engagement due to participation fatigue when farmers see little direct value from contributing data [20]. Sustained engagement often depends on incentive models (e.g., airtime rewards, agronomic feedback loops, or microcredit access), as well as trust-building mechanisms such as transparent data usage, localised languages, and alignment with farmers' immediate priorities. In addition, many participatory initiatives are donor-funded pilots, which struggle to secure institutional buy-in or long-term funding. Finally, reliance on digital tools may exacerbate inequalities, as resource-poor farmers, women, and marginalised groups are often excluded due to barriers to literacy, smartphone ownership, or internet access [21]. These challenges underscore the importance of embedding participatory models within sustainable institutional frameworks while ensuring inclusivity.

3.4 Comparative insights and synthesis

Analysis of traditional, precision, participatory, and digital ecosystems comparatively revealed their strengths and weaknesses. Generally, traditional methods remain cost-efficient but retrospective; precision tools improve accuracy at a cost; participatory models provide context and trust but have sustainability challenges; and digital ecosystems scale participatory approaches but risk excluding smallholder farmers. A hybrid approach may be necessary to truly harness the benefits. By integrating the strengths of each ecosystem, we can create a more inclusive and effective framework that addresses the diverse needs of all stakeholders involved.

Rather than discussing the implications of scalability or technical bottlenecks (see Section 4.3), our synthesis emphasises the dual opportunities for these approaches. For instance, participatory models perform better when there is contextual richness, while digital ecosystems contribute to the scale and mass automation of practices. This combination allows for a more nuanced understanding of user engagement and can lead to innovative solutions that leverage both local insights and broader technological advancements. Ultimately, fostering collaboration between these ecosystems can enhance resilience and adaptability in a rapidly changing environment. A hybrid of both, embedding participatory practices into the digital space, would represent the most productive means to advance.

4. Scalable frameworks, performance metrics, and open challenges

4.1 Data collection frameworks and infrastructure

Scalable data collection requires structured frameworks that can handle large volumes of information from various sources. These frameworks involve the use of mobile platforms, sensor networks, and remote sensing technologies, supported by robust database systems. A key requirement is the ability to integrate heterogeneous data types, including numeric measurements, geospatial data, and unstructured information such as images or farmer narratives.

Several tools and platforms have been developed to support scalable agricultural data collection. In practice, frameworks increasingly rely on integrated mobile-sensor ecosystems, where farmer-facing survey tools feed into sensor networks and IoT platforms. While Open Data Kits (ODK) and Kobo Toolbox remain popular in low-resource settings, current practice emphasises streaming architectures (e.g., Apache Kafka, AWS Kinesis, and Apache Flink) that allow continuous ingestion of survey and sensor data into cloud storage systems [22]. Low-cost IoT boards (ESP32, LoRaWAN nodes) now outperform early Raspberry Pi/Arduino deployments in scalability and energy efficiency.

Database architectures for agricultural data management vary depending on the scale and purpose. Relational databases, such as MySQL and PostgreSQL, are commonly used for structured data sets, while NoSQL databases, such as MongoDB and Cassandra, are preferred for handling unstructured and semi-structured data. Modern architectures are increasingly hybrid: cloud-edge designs allow local processing to reduce latency while synchronising with cloud services for long-term storage and analytics. This improves performance based on key scalability metrics, such as latency, throughput, storage optimisation, and fault tolerance (read more in Section 4.2 below). **Figure 3** illustrates such an end-to-end pipeline, from field sensors to cloud dashboards.

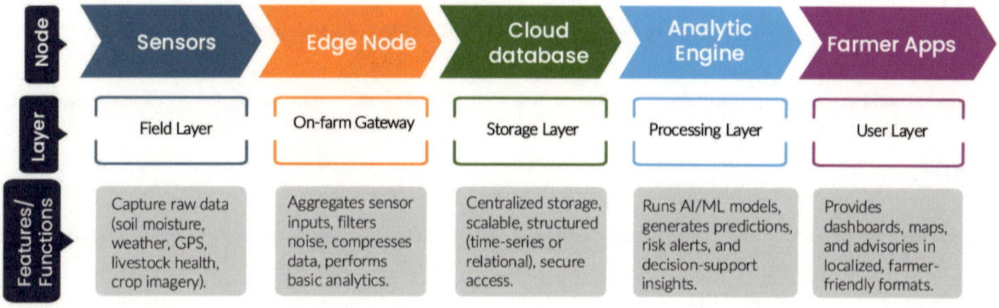

Figure 3.
ETL pipeline flowchart.

Key takeaway (frameworks): Future-ready agricultural frameworks are no longer just about digitising surveys – they require continuous streaming, hybrid architectures, and edge-cloud integration to ensure scalability and resilience.

4.2 Scalability metrics and performance considerations

Scalable data systems must be evaluated not only in terms of their ability to handle large volumes of data but also in their performance under real-world conditions. Key metrics include:

- Data latency refers to the time delay between data collection and analysis, or making it available.

- Throughput refers to the volume or amount of data that can be processed in a given period.

- Storage optimisation, which refers to the efficiency of data compression and storage strategies (e.g., using columnar databases), is crucial for managing massive datasets without incurring exorbitant costs.

Additional performance dimensions encompass fault tolerance (the system's ability to remain operational even when components fail), energy efficiency, and horizontal scalability, which refers to the capacity to add more nodes or devices without compromising performance. Resilience against connectivity disruptions, hardware failures, and cyberattacks is critical for agricultural deployment.

In agricultural contexts, these metrics are particularly important because data often comes from remote or resource-constrained environments. Systems must be designed to handle intermittent connectivity, power outages, and variable data quality. Practical solutions include mobile platforms that buffer data offline and later sync with cloud servers; IoT devices that use LoRaWAN or NB-IoT to minimise energy usage; and self-healing sensor networks that are capable of recalibrating nodes when they malfunction or drift. These measures not only improve resilience but also reduce maintenance costs – an often-overlooked barrier in the smallholder context. **Table 2** compares traditional agricultural data systems with scalable, stream-enabled systems. The comparison explains why it is more than just a 'big

Dimension	Traditional data systems	Scalable data systems (IoT, edge–cloud, streaming)
Data volume	Limited, small survey datasets; often aggregated annually	Handles high-velocity, high-volume data (sensors, drones, satellites) in real-time
Latency	High (weeks–months to process survey or recall data)	Low (seconds–minutes; supports near-real-time decision-making)
Data variety	Mostly structured tabular (survey forms, reports)	Structured + semi-structured + unstructured (sensor logs, imagery, audio, text)
Integration	Siloed, project-specific databases; limited interoperability	Multi-source integration through APIs, data lakes, and knowledge graphs
Storage optimisation	Flat files or relational DBs; limited scalability	Distributed storage (NoSQL, time-series DBs, cloud object storage)
Fault tolerance	Manual backup, often prone to data loss	Automated replication, redundancy, and failover mechanisms
Connectivity	Often offline, batch uploads are dependent on local surveys	Edge buffering and cloud sync; resilient to intermittent rural connectivity
Decision support	Mostly descriptive statistics, lagging indicators	Predictive and prescriptive analytics (ML, AI-driven recommendations)
Sustainability	Dependent on donor/project cycles, low maintainability	Designed for long-term integration with institutional and commercial ecosystems

Table 2.
Comparative features of traditional vs. scalable agricultural data management frameworks.

data' concern but also a level of resilience, interoperability, and actionable insights to be implemented in viable farming situations.

Key takeaway (scalability): Scalability must be measured not only in terms of 'bigger data' but also in terms of speed, efficiency, resilience, and affordability under real-world agricultural conditions.

4.3 Challenges, open issues, and future directions

Despite scalable data collection architectures and performance metrics providing a strong foundation, several challenges hinder their effective implementation in agricultural contexts. These challenges highlight open research questions and practical bottlenecks while also pointing to future opportunities for innovation. Some of the challenges and open issues are:

- Data heterogeneity and quality: Integrated data from different sensors, e.g., from different manufacturers, with varying formats and standards, is still a significant challenge. Sensor data is also susceptible to calibration and maintenance issues.

- Interoperability barriers: Platforms and systems are often siloed, lacking standardised formats and application programming interfaces (APIs), which prevent seamless data integration across scales.

- Resource constraints: Many smallholders face barriers such as limited connectivity, low digital literacy, and high costs of devices or subscriptions.

- Governance and trust: Unclear data ownership, privacy concerns, and weak institutional coordination limit farmer participation and researcher collaboration. It also limits the adoption of some innovations.

- Infrastructure limitations: Poor rural connectivity, unreliable electricity, and underdeveloped data pipelines slow down adoption and increase latency in decision support.

- Scalability trade-offs: High-volume, real-time systems are expensive, while low-cost approaches, e.g., farmer recall, sacrifice timeliness and precision.

These challenges underscore the need for new frameworks that not only adopt advanced technologies but also embed inclusivity, transparency, and farmer incentives. Section 4.4 explores comparative insights into existing approaches and introduces a hybrid framework that addresses these gaps.

4.4 Comparative insights on state-of-the-art approaches

Most scalable agricultural data systems today fall into one of three categories:

i. Sensor- and IoT-driven monitoring platforms: These provide high-frequency, objective measurements but often lack contextual relevance and face issues related to farmer trust and data ownership.

ii. Participatory trials and crowdsourced models: Examples include TRICOT trials, Farmer Field Schools, and community-based breeding programs. These approaches deliver strong contextual grounding and farmer ownership but struggle with consistency, geographic coverage, and long-term sustainability.

iii. Centralised AI platforms: Cloud-based machine learning systems achieve high predictive accuracy and throughput but often operate as 'black boxes', disconnected from local realities and farmer priorities.

The proposed hybrid framework intentionally integrates farmer-generated data with IoT devices, edge–cloud infrastructures, and advanced analytics. Unlike sensor-only systems, it embeds farmer agency and trust, unlike participatory-only systems that scale to real-time, high-volume analytics, or unlike centralised AI platforms that emphasise inclusivity and transparency.

To address the current issues identified in Section 4.3 and ensure long-term sustainability, the hybrid framework integrates future-ready elements designed for adaptability, scalability, and impact. These elements include:

- Edge-cloud synergy involves hybrid architectures combining edge processing with cloud analytics, which can reduce latency by 40–60% [23] and bandwidth costs, while enabling real-time decisions at scale.

- AI-enhanced analytics: Machine learning and deep learning models can improve anomaly detection, predictive modelling, and adaptive recommendations tailored to local conditions.

- Standardisation and open APIs: Adoption of common protocols will improve interoperability between national surveys, IoT platforms, and participatory data systems.
- Farmer-centric incentives: Embedding value back to farmers through agronomic feedback, credit scoring, or input discounts, can improve data reliability and participation.
- Low-cost sensing and connectivity: Advances in solar-powered IoT devices, satellite internet, and smartphone penetration can expand access in resource-constrained settings.
- Inclusive governance models: Multi-stakeholder data trusts and participatory governance frameworks can build transparency and ensure equitable data use.
- Global-to-local integration: Linking global datasets, e.g., FAO and NASA, with localised farmer- and sensor-generated data – will improve both precision and contextual relevance.

This blended model, therefore, bridges gaps across existing approaches, offering a more resilient and equitable pathway for agricultural research and practice. However, the true value of the frameworks only emerges when the large volumes of data generated are systematically analysed and transformed into insights. This leads directly to the role of data mining and predictive analytics, which turn scalable data infrastructures into actionable intelligence for farmers, researchers, and policymakers (see Chapter 5).

5. Data mining and predictive analytics in agriculture

Building on scalable data architectures and the resolution of interoperability challenges, data mining and predictive analytics represent the next layer of value creation in agricultural systems. While frameworks and performance considerations (Section 4) ensure that data is captured, stored, and shared efficiently, the real impact emerges when these datasets are transformed into actionable insights. Techniques such as machine learning, statistical modelling, and geospatial analytics enable forecasting of yields, detection of crop stress, and optimisation of resource allocation. These analytical methods not only improve decision-making at the farm level but also support policy design, market integration, and climate adaptation strategies at national and global scales.

5.1 Core approaches and methods

- Machine learning (ML): Supervised and unsupervised learning models are increasingly used for yield forecasting, pest and disease recognition, and price prediction. For example, convolutional neural networks (CNNs) classify crop health from drone imagery with high accuracy.

- Geospatial analytics: Remote sensing data, combined with ground-truth surveys, enables the mapping of crop cover, land degradation, and drought hotspots. The Normalised Difference Vegetation Index (NDVI) is one widely adopted proxy for vegetation health.

- Time-Series forecasting: Climate models and weather-linked regression approaches provide seasonal yield and rainfall forecasts, essential for early warning systems.

- Data mining techniques: Association rule mining, clustering, and anomaly detection are applied to farmer-reported data to uncover hidden patterns, such as emerging pest outbreaks or input misuse.

- Decision support systems (DSS): Integrating predictive outputs into dashboards or mobile apps ensures that farmers and policymakers receive timely, actionable advisories.

5.2 Applications across scales

Predictive analytics functions at multiple levels of agricultural decision-making. These applications are already being tested in practice, as illustrated in **Table 3**. For example, a satellite-based NDVI integrated with farmer diaries and IoT soil moisture sensors has been applied to forecast maize yields in smallholder systems of Kenya (**Figure 4(a)**), reducing predictive error margins by 20% compared to traditional

Scale	Application	Examples/ Tools	Decision impact	Reported results
Farm level	Yield prediction, crop stress detection, and pest alerts	NDVI indices, ML models, IoT sensors.	Timely irrigation, fertiliser scheduling, and pest management	Improved maize yield prediction accuracy by 15–20% in India [24]; reduced crop loss by 25% in Egypt using drone-based detection [25]
	Smart irrigation	IoT soil sensors (Soil Scout)	Optimised water use and crop health	Reduced water usage by 30% in Tamil Nadu [26]
Community/ regional level	Pest outbreak early warning, market forecasting	SMS advisories, weather-linked ML	Coordinated extension response, reduced losses	Fall armyworm alerts reduced infestation spread by 30% in Ghana (Owusu et al., 2024)
National level	Food security monitoring, subsidy targeting	Remote sensing, MIS, ML models	Evidence-based policy, resilience planning	Improved subsidy-targeting accuracy by 18% in India [26]
Global level	Trade flow modelling, climate impact projections	FAO data, NASA Earth Observation, blockchain logistics	Stabilised markets, early warning for global crises	IBM Food Trust reduced spoilage by 40% and improved delivery efficiency [24]

Table 3.
Key applications of predictive analytics in agriculture across scales.

surveys. Similarly, participatory SMS reporting combined with weather data has proven effective for timely fall armyworm alerts in Ghana, enabling extension officers to act before outbreaks escalate (**Figure 4**(**b**)). This predictive analytics approach enables more proactive and efficient resource management when integrated into DSS.

5.3 Emerging trends

Agricultural data systems are rapidly evolving, with several emerging technologies being piloted in real-world contexts and showing measurable benefits:

- **AI-driven farmer services:** Artificial intelligence (AI) is increasingly integrated into farmer-facing platforms that combine advisory services with credit scoring, insurance, and input recommendations. For example, *Cropin's AI-IoT platforms* have been deployed across India, supporting precision agriculture through real-time analytics and decision support systems [27].
  A comprehensive review found that AI-enabled models improved prediction accuracy by 20%, while IoT-based smart irrigation systems enhanced crop productivity by 25% [28].

- **Explainable AI (XAI):** As predictive models become embedded in agricultural decision-making, transparency is critical, especially for smallholder farmers. Explainable AI is important in improving trust and adoption of AI-powered tools, particularly in insurance and credit scoring [28]. Literature confirms that XAI enhances interpretability and farmers' confidence, even though the pilot data on uptake rates is still emerging.

- **Edge AI and localised processing**: Processing data close to the source reduces bandwidth costs and improves responsiveness in rural settings. Raj and Prahadeeswaran (2025) report that edge computing in smart farming reduces latency by up to 60% compared to cloud-only setups, especially in crop stress detection and irrigation control [27]. These findings are supported by field trials using IoT sensors and embedded AI chips.

- Generative AI: Generative models are being tested to simulate climate scenarios and predict pest outbreaks. The GAIA initiative, led by CABI, is exploring GenAI-generated advisories in Kenya and India. While formal peer-reviewed results are pending, the project is documented in CABI's digital agriculture reports and aligns with broader trends in AI-driven extension services.

- **Digital twin:** Virtual replicas of the farm, fed by IoT and weather data, allow simulations of irrigation, fertilisation, and pest management strategies. Virtual replicas of farms, fed by IoT and weather data, allow simulations of irrigation, fertilisation, and pest management strategies. Raj and Prahadeeswaran (2025) found that digital twin models in greenhouse systems optimised heating and labour schedules, cutting energy costs by 15% [27]. These systems also improved anomaly detection and crop monitoring accuracy.

Figure 4.
(A) Integrated maize yield forecasting using NDVI (satellite), farmer-reported data, and IoT soil moisture sensors, demonstrating the power of multi-source predictive analytics at the farm scale. (B) Combining farmer SMS reports with rainfall and humidity data for timely fall armyworm alerts, enabling rapid regional extension responses.

- **Blockchain integration:** Blockchain pilots in coffee and horticulture supply chains have improved product traceability and market transparency. McFadden et al. (2022) highlighted that blockchain adoption in agriculture enhances supply chain integrity, though challenges remain around transaction costs and interoperability [8].

- **Participatory analytics:** Farmer-led data collection and co-designed analytical models continue to show strong uptake. Schreckenberg et al. (2016) document how participatory trials in East Africa influenced seed release decisions and improved varietal selection under heterogeneous conditions [8]. These models complement formal breeding programs and democratise agricultural research.

5.4 Limitations and considerations

Predictive analytics creates methodological constraints. Models could be subject to algorithmic bias, lack interpretability, have poor ground-truth data, have low explainability, and depend on infrastructure. The biases, including the above examples of algorithmic and data bias, are not system-level or governance challenges (see Sections 4.3 and 7, respectively), but they are methodological limitations in terms of model accuracy, fairness, and explainability. For example, in NDVI-based yield models, the misrepresentation of stressed crops with multiple agro-ecologies will probably misrepresent the yield. AI models for pest detection also rely on balanced, farmer-uploaded datasets. Section 7 discusses aspects of bias and ethical considerations, including the agency and liability of farmers. These methodological limitations underscore the significance of creating strong frameworks to safeguard data integrity. By ensuring that datasets are representative and ethically sourced, we can enhance the reliability of AI applications in agriculture and other fields.

5.5 Synthesis of emerging trends

Together, these emerging trends illustrate a clear shift toward a more intelligent, decentralised, and farmer-centred analytics ecosystem. AI-driven services and explainable models are building farmer trust; edge AI and digital twins are reducing latency and enabling localised decision-making, while blockchain ensures transparency and traceability along value chains. At the same time, participatory analytics reinforces the role of farmers as co-creators of knowledge rather than passive data suppliers. Importantly, the 2025 pilots confirm that these technologies are moving beyond proof-of-concept to demonstrable field impact, improving accuracy, timeliness, and adoption rates. Together, these innovations underscore that predictive analytics advances both technical performance and social legitimacy in agricultural systems.

Key takeaway (data mining and analytics): Scalable predictive analytics transform agricultural data from passive records into active intelligence. When embedded into farmer-facing platforms and national monitoring systems, these methods bridge the gap between raw data and informed action – helping agriculture become more adaptive, resilient, and sustainable.

6. Case studies of data collection models in agriculture

This chapter presents practical illustrations of how participatory and crowdsourced approaches, alongside digitally-enabled monitoring and smart technologies, are being deployed in real agricultural contexts. These cases demonstrate not only the technical feasibility but also the social dynamics, institutional arrangements, and sustainability challenges of agricultural data systems.

6.1 Participatory and crowdsourced approaches

Participatory and crowdsourced models position farmers not only as end-users of agricultural data but also as active contributors. These approaches leverage local knowledge, lived experience, and farmer experimentation to generate datasets that are both contextually grounded and scalable when aggregated.

- **DigiFarm, Kenya.** One of the most prominent examples is Safaricom's *DigiFarm* platform in Kenya, which aggregates mobile-based farmer profiling, input access, and extension services. Farmers provide production and transaction data that, in turn, feeds into aggregated datasets used for service delivery and market linkage [29]. This creates a cyclical relationship in which farmer participation drives system intelligence.

- **PlantVillage Nuru, East Africa.** The *PlantVillage Nuru* App enables smallholders to diagnose pest and disease problems through AI-powered image recognition. Each diagnosis simultaneously generates real-time, geo-tagged field data that feeds into a regional crop health database, creating a crowdsourced surveillance system [30].

- **TRICOT Trials, Sub-Saharan Africa, and Beyond.** The *Triadic Comparisons of Technologies (TRICOT)* method engages farmers in decentralised variety trials. Farmers contribute experiential, comparative data to breeding programs by ranking crop varieties under real farm conditions [31, 32]. The use of TRICOT varietal trials across 10,000 Kenyan farmers revealed that stress-tolerant maize hybrids yielded 15–20% more consistently under drought-prone conditions.

- **Digital Green, India**. Although it is based outside of Africa, Digital Green demonstrates the effectiveness of participatory video as both a tool for dissemination and data collection. Farmers create and share short videos on local agronomic practices, while adoption and viewing data are systematically tracked [31].

- **Community seed and farmer networks**. Similar participatory models include community seed systems and farmer innovation networks in Latin America and Africa, which crowd source localised performance data on crop varieties and management options [32].

Collectively, these participatory and crowdsourced cases highlight the value of farmer agency in building relevant agricultural datasets. Their scalability rests on their low-cost digital infrastructure, institutional coordination, and trust with farmer communities [33].

6.2 Digital-enabled monitoring and smart technologies

Digitally enabled approaches represent a different model, where most data originates from machines rather than farmers. By using IoT sensors, drones, and smart platforms, these systems generate continuous, high-resolution datasets that support precision agriculture and policy analytics.

- **Smart Irrigation Pilots, Sub-Saharan Africa**. Several pilot projects have combined farmer input with IoT-enabled soil moisture sensors to optimise irrigation scheduling. By integrating automated measurements with farmer observations, these systems enhance water efficiency while maintaining contextual adaptability [33]. It is worth noting that, in Kenya, smart irrigation reduced water use by up to 35% while maintaining yields.

- **DronBase Crop Monitoring, Africa**. Drone programs in Kenya, Nigeria, and Ghana have been deployed for crop health assessments, pest surveillance, and yield estimation. While drones provide high-resolution imagery, farmer ground-truthing ensures that interpretations remain agronomically accurate [34]. In Ghana, drone-based pest scouting reduces the detection time by 50%, enabling earlier intervention [35].

- **Soil Sensor Network, East Africa**. Wireless soil probes measuring pH, nutritional status, and moisture have been trialled in East Africa. These networks rely on farmer inputs for calibration and interpretation, thus creating a hybrid model of machine and human validation [36].

- **European Open Farm Network**. In Europe, farmer-owned digital infrastructures demonstrate how digital technologies can scale beyond individual farms. Through IoT devices for environmental monitoring, data is shared on a central platform that feeds into EU-wide open datasets, balancing local ownership with collective utility [18].

These cases illustrate the strength of digitally intensive models, particularly in providing scale, precision, and automation. However, challenges around affordability, connectivity, and digital literacy remain critical barriers to adoption in the smallholder context.

6.3 Comparative insights

The participatory models emphasise on farmer knowledge and context, while digitally enabled systems rely on IoT, drones, and smart platforms to generate high-resolution, continuous datasets. Increasingly, hybrid approaches combine the two: machines generate data at scale, while farmers provide ground-truthing and contextual interpretation. The case studies illustrate how different models complement each other.

- Participatory/engaged models (e.g., DigiFarm, TRICOT trials) provide rich, contextualised data but depend on donor financing, which may risk sustainability.

- Digital monitoring tools and technologies, such as drone imagery and IoT sensors, offer precision, yet, they face limitations due to cost and connectivity concerns.

This section covers practical learning from field deployment, while Sections 3.4 and 4.3 compare methodologies and system metrics at a conceptual level. The practical takeaways in this section demonstrate the importance of situating the methodologies in their local contexts and ensuring the active participation of each stakeholder to the appropriate extent. By collaborating with stakeholders and leveraging technology appropriately, projects can increase the community's awareness and potential to foster development and its sustainability in the longer term. The first takeaway is that those projects linked to institutional practice (e.g., extension services, cooperatives, etc.) appeared to demonstrate far greater sustainability than the pilot projects funded and driven by donor partners. The ethical and policy discussions raised in these examples of deployment experiences, including who owns the farmer data and even questions related to liability in the context of incorrect recommendations, are elaborated in Section 7.

6.4 Climate resilience and sustainability

Beyond productivity, scalable data collection supports climate resilience. Integration of NDVI, soil moisture IoT, and participatory weather observations has improved drought early warning in Kenya, informing adaptive planting calendars. Moreover, blending farmer reports with sensor and satellite data not only strengthens real-time response to climate shocks but also underpins long-term sustainability planning. Embedding such systems into national adaptation strategies aligns agricultural data infrastructures with SDG 2 (Zero Hunger) and SDG 13 (Climate Action).

Critical reflection: Despite these successes, many sub-Saharan African (SSA) digital agriculture platforms face sustainability dilemmas. Donor-driven pilots often stall once funding cycles end. The challenge lies in embedding these systems within national agricultural statistical services, extension programs, and financial ecosystems to secure their long-term viability and scale.

7. Ethical, legal, and policy implications

The previous sections underscored the importance and benefits of different data collection, management, and analytics models based on evidence in the agricultural sector. However, they also revealed fragilities: pilot projects collapse when funding ends, farmers remain uncertain about data ownership, and digital divides persist. These challenges raise questions that go beyond technology into the ethical, legal, and policy domains. Unlike traditional experiments or surveys, today's systems collect continuous, fine-grained data directly from farmers and their environments – through smartphones, IoT sensors, drones, and digital platforms. This new data ecosystem raises questions about who owns agricultural data, how it should be shared, who ultimately benefits from its use, and who bears the risks. Without careful governance, digital innovations risk entrenching inequities, eroding trust, and undermining farmer agency.

7.1 Data ownership and privacy

Farmers are the primary data producers in digital agriculture, yet too often they remain the least empowered in determining its use. For example, large mobile-based advisory platforms in Kenya collect detailed agronomic and financial information from smallholders, but the terms of data use are seldom transparent. This creates a risk of asymmetrical value capture, where downstream actors (seed companies, insurers, and fintech platforms) gain disproportionately, while farmers remain passive data suppliers [36, 37].

The Kenya Data Protection Act (2019), Sections 25 and 26, affirms that personal data must be processed lawfully, transparently, and only for explicit purposes, while granting farmers the rights to be informed, access data, and object to processing [38]. Similarly, debates are shaping the EU's General Data Protection Regulations (GDPR) and India's Digital Agriculture Mission, showing that farmer data governance is a global issue requiring farmer-centric ownership models [38, 39].

7.2 Consent and transparency

Farmers frequently view consent as a mere formality, enrolling in platforms without fully comprehending how their digital interactions yield data that can be monetised. Fieldwork in Kenya and Uganda shows that many farmers are unaware that their digital interactions generate data trails that can be monetised. To build trust, platforms must adopt farmer-centred governance models aligned with FAIR [40] and CARE principles [41]. Global comparison: GDPR's emphasis on 'informed, specific, and freely given consent' offers a benchmark that could inspire localised, farmer-friendly mechanisms in Africa [39].

7.3 Cross-border data sharing

Agricultural innovation increasingly depends on regional and global data flows, from satellite imagery to pest surveillance. Yet, inconsistent frameworks pose risks. For instance, Kenyan farmers using AI-driven advisory apps may have their data stored on foreign servers, raising concerns about jurisdiction and protection standards. The Kenya Data Protection Act (2019), Section 48, allows cross-border transfers only if adequate safeguards are proven to the Data Commissioner [38]. Similar tensions exist under GDPR's 'adequacy decision' framework and in the African Union's Digital Transformation Strategy (2020–2030), which calls for harmonised standards for cross-border agricultural data [42].

7.4 Liability and accountability

The integration of AI and predictive analytics into agriculture introduces liability questions. If an algorithm incorrectly predicts rainfall patterns and farmers plant at the wrong time, who is responsible for the losses? Similar cases have emerged in livestock health apps, where delayed alerts contributed to the spread of disease. The Kenya Data Protection Act (2019), Section 72, entitles affected data subjects to compensation for algorithmic errors and remains an urgent frontier in agricultural law [38]. In the EU, draft AI Liability Directives explicitly address algorithmic responsibility, while in Africa, legal clarity remains limited [39].

7.5 Equity and inclusion

Finally, equity is a central concern. Large commercial farms often have the resources to adopt and benefit from digital agriculture, while smallholder farmers – particularly women, youths, and marginalised groups – struggle with access to devices, literacy, and reliable connectivity. Unless addressed, digital agriculture may widen existing inequalities [42, 43]. The Kenya Data Protection Act (2019), Section 25(f), emphasises fairness and non-discrimination in data processing, a principle that aligns with the need for inclusive platform design and subsidised rural access [38]. Initiatives such as the FAO's Digital Agriculture Principles and the AU's Malabo Declaration highlight equity as central to sustainable adoption [38, 39].

7.6 Synthesis: Ethical risks and mitigation strategies

The five dimensions above – ownership, consent, cross-border sharing, liability, and equity – are interconnected. Without safeguards, they risk undermining trust in scalable agricultural data systems. **Table 4** summarises these risks and highlights practical mitigation pathways.

Ethical principle	Practical risks	Mitigation strategies	Policy example
Data ownership and privacy	Farmers lose control of data; asymmetrical value capture	Farmer-centred governance, transparent licensing, blockchain traceability	Kenya Data Protection Act 2019
Consent and transparency	Opaque terms of service; limited farmer understanding	Clear opt-in mechanisms, localised agreements, dashboard-style consent tools	GDPR, Kenya Data Protection Act, 2019
Fairness and equity	Benefits accrue to large-scale or connected farmers; the digital divide widens	Subsidised access, gender-sensitive design, inclusive platform co-design	AU Malabo declaration
Accountability and liability	Algorithmic errors cause economic loss or crop failure	Regulatory frameworks, explainable AI, and independent audits of models	EU AI directive
Data integrity and trust	Manipulated or poor-quality data undermines analytics	Standardised protocols, open standards, participatory validation by farmers	FAO standards

Table 4.
Ethical principles, practical risks, and mitigation strategies in scalable agricultural data systems.

8. Conclusion and recommendations

Scalable data collection and management systems are essential for the future of agriculture, particularly in smallholder-dominated contexts like Kenya and SSA. When effectively integrated, digital platforms, participatory approaches, and advanced analytics offer powerful opportunities to improve decision-making, productivity, and resilience. However, realising this potential requires systematically addressing challenges related to data quality, inclusivity, governance, and sustainability. Importantly, scalability should be understood not only as the capacity to process larger datasets but also as the ability to enable faster, fairer, and more resilient agricultural decisions across diverse contexts.

Recommendations for strengthening scalable data systems include:

i. At the policy level:

a. Mandating open and interoperable agricultural data standards at national and regional levels (e.g., harmonised APIs across SSA platforms).

b. Adopting blended governance models that balance FAIR's efficiency with CARE's sovereignty principles.

c. Embedding agricultural data systems within climate adaptation and resilience strategies (e.g., linking farmers' datasets with national early warning systems).

ii. At the institution level:

a. Investing in hybrid edge-cloud infrastructures to ensure low-latency analytics in rural areas.

b. Developing capacity-building programs for researchers and extension officers in AI, IoT, and data governance.

c. Establishing long-term financing models beyond donor pilots by linking agritech platforms with financial institutions and insurance providers.

iii. At the farmer and community level:

a. Strengthening digital literacy through localised training modules in vernacular languages.

b. Incentivising farmer participation via bundled services (e.g., agronomic advice, credit access, or input discounts).

c. Guaranteeing transparency in data use through community data charters, ensuring farmers understand who uses their data and for what purposes.

The chapter's key contribution lies in reframing participatory and digitally-enabled models as interconnected rather than parallel trajectories. Embedding

DOI: http://dx.doi.org/10.5772/intechopen.1013672

local innovation within the global data ecosystem enables agriculture to move toward inclusive, sustainable, and future-ready data systems that not only empower farmers but also reinforce food security and resilience at national and global levels.

Acknowledgments

The authors wish to express their sincere gratitude to the Director General, the Director of the Beef Research Institute, and the entire Kenya Agricultural & Livestock Research Organisation (KALRO) for their invaluable support. We also thank the farmers and other stakeholders involved in our collaboration for hosting the research trials and actively participating in the research process.

Conflict of Interest

The authors declare no conflict of interest.

Author details

Hannington Odido Ochieng* and Lenah Muema
Kenya Agricultural and Livestock Research Organization, Nairobi, Kenya.

*Address all correspondence to: hannington.odido@gmail.com

References

[1] Soussi A, Zero E, Sacile R, Trinchero D, Fossa M. Smart sensors and smart data for precision agriculture: A review. Sensors. 2024;**24**(8):2647. DOI: 10.3390/s24082647

[2] FAO and ITU, Status of Digital Agriculture in 47 sub-Saharan African Countries. FAO; ITU; 2022. DOI: 10.4060/cb7943en

[3] Ochieng HO. Advancing Urban-Rural Linkages: Digital Technology and Innovative Solutions for Food Flows and Territorial Resilience in East Africa. 2025. Available from: https://urbanpolicyplatform.org/download/digital-technology-and-innovative-solutions-for-food-flows/

[4] Basir MS, Buckmaster D, Raturi A, Zhang Y. From pen and paper to digital precision: A comprehensive review of on-farm recordkeeping. Precision Agriculture. 2024;**25**(5):2643–2682. DOI: 10.1007/s11119-024-10172-7

[5] Beriya A. Columbia University, Earth Institute, Center for Sustainable Development (CSD), New York, NY, 2020. Available from: https://hdl.handle.net/10419/249826 [Accessed: 2025-August-23]

[6] Pingali PL. Green revolution: Impacts, limits, and the path ahead. Proceedings of the National Academy of Sciences of the United States of America. 2012;**109**(31):12302–12308. DOI: 10.1073/pnas.0912953109

[7] Abbasi R, Martinez P, Ahmad R. The digitization of agricultural industry – A systematic literature review on agriculture 4.0. Agricultural Technologies (Elsevier). 2022;**2**:100042. DOI: 10.1016/j.atech.2022.100042

[8] McFadden JCFGTAJ. The Digitalisation of Agriculture. Paris: OECD Publishing; 2022. DOI: 10.1787/285cc27d-en

[9] Samuels JA, Samuels JI. Digital Agriculture: Revolutionizing Farming Practices through Technology Integration. **2024**, DOI: 10.13140/RG.2.2.17600.51204

[10] Chambers R. Into the Unknown : Explorations in Development Practice. Rugby, UK: Practical Action Publishing; 2014

[11] van Etten J. Crowdsourcing crop improvement in sub-saharan Africa: A proposal for a scalable and inclusive approach to food security. IDS Bulletin. 2011;**42**(4):102–110. DOI: 10.1111/j.1759-5436.2011.00240.x

[12] Schreckenberg K, Torres-Vitolas CA, Willcock S, Shackleton C, Harvey CA, Kafumbata D. Participatory Data Collection for Ecosystem Services Research A Practitioner's Manual. ESPA Working Paper Series, No. 003, 2016

[13] Koundinya V, Taku-Forchu N, Pinzón N, Parker L. Collecting Needs Assessment Data Using Participatory and Culturally Responsive Strategies for a Climate-Smart Agriculture Project (Poster presentation). American Evaluation Association Annual Conference: The power of story. Indianapolis Indiana, United States: 9–14 October 2023. Available from: https://www.researchgate.net/publication/374842286 [Accessed: 2025-September-06]

[14] N2Africa. Crowdsourcing for agricultural data collection," N2Africa Case Study. [Online]. Available from: https://n2africa.org/crowdsourcing-agricultural-data-collection [Accessed: 2025-September-06]

[15] Ceccarelli S, Grando S. Decentralized-participatory plant breeding: An example of demand driven research. Euphytica. 2007;**155**(3): 349–360. DOI: 10.1007/s10681-006-9336-8

[16] FAO and ITU. E-agriculture in action: Blockchain for agriculture. 2018. [Online]. Available from: https://www.fao.org/3/CA2906EN/ca2906en.pdf [Accessed: 2025-September-06]

[17] Hellin J, Lundy M, Meijer M. Farmer organization, collective action and market access in Meso-America. Food Policy. 2009;**34**(1):16–22. DOI: 10.1016/j.foodpol.2008.10.003

[18] Rose DC, Chilvers J. Agriculture 4.0: Broadening Responsible Innovation in an Era of Smart Farming. Frontiers in Sustainable Food Systems. 2018;**2**:87. DOI: 10.3389/fsufs.2018.00087

[19] Ochieng HO. Farmer and Researcher Methodologies Trade-Offs in Participatory Large N Research: The Case of Common Bean Adaptation Trials in Western Kenya. 2018

[20] Beza E, et al. What are the prospects for citizen science in agriculture? Evidence from three continents on motivation and mobile telephone use of resource-poor farmers. PLoS One. 2017;**12**(5): e0175700.
DOI: 10.1371/journal.pone.0175700

[21] Duncombe R. Mobile Phones for Agricultural and Rural Development: A Literature Review and Suggestions for Future Research. The European Journal of Development Research. 2016;**28**(2):213–235. DOI: 10.1057/ejdr.2014.60

[22] Georlette V, Honfoga A-C, Dossou M, Moeyaert V. Exploring Universal Filtered Multi Carrier Waveform for Last Meter Connectivity in 6G: A Street-Lighting-Driven Approach with Enhanced Simulator for IoT Application Dimensioning. Future Internet. 2024;**16**(4):112. DOI: 10.3390/fi16040112

[23] Wang Y, et al. Progress in Research on Deep Learning-Based Crop Yield Prediction. Agronomy. 2024;**14**(10):2264. DOI: 10.3390/agronomy14102264

[24] GeeksforGeeks. 5 Data Science Projects in Agriculture. GeeksforGeeks. [Online]. Available from: https://www.geeksforgeeks.org/data-science/5-data-science-projects-in-agriculture/ [Accessed: 2025-September-06]

[25] Monika T, Thangadurai K, Sivaguru R, Abdulkalamazad G, Lakshmi Kanth R. AI-Driven Pest and Disease Detection in Smart Farming Systems. International Research Journal on Advanced Engineering and Management (IRJAEM). 2025;**3**(06):2315–2319. DOI: 10.47392/IRJAEM.2025.0365

[26] Satheswaran N, Akshaya R, Abiramis S, Nandhini AD, Sarathi S. Predictive analytics for smart farming: Enhancing precision agriculture through data analytics. International Journal of Research Trends and Innovation. 2023;**8**:112–118. [Online]. Available from: https://ijrti.org/papers/IJRTI2306151.pdf [Accessed: 2025-August-23]

[27] Raj M, Prahadeeswaran M. Revolutionizing agriculture: A review of smart farming technologies for a sustainable future. Springer Nature. 2025. DOI: 10.1007/s42452-025-07561-6

[28] Ashutosh D, Singh K, Verma R, Singh B, Singh MS. The Role of Artificial Intelligence in Agriculture: A Comprehensive Review. 2024. Available from: https://scope-journal.com/assets/uploads/doc/d71e9-1203-1215.202410515.pdf [Accessed: 2025-August-23]

[29] Safaricom. Overview of DigiFarm Kenya. [Online]. Available from: https://digifarmkenya.com/ [Accessed: 2025-August-18]

[30] PlantVillage. PlantVillage Nuru: Pest and disease monitoring using AI. CGIAR Platform for Big Data in Agriculture. PlantVillage. [Online]. Available from: https://bigdata.cgiar.org/digital-intervention/plantvillage-nuru-pest-and-disease-monitoring-using-ai/ [Accessed: 2025-September-06]

[31] Slotznick W, Stein D, Singh R, Musemangezhi S, Maqbool S. Evidence Review of Digital Green's Video-Mediated Farmer Extension Approach. 2021

[32] Pan-African Farmers' Organization (PAFO) & AgriCord. Empowering African Agriculture: Farmer-Managed and Community-Based Seed Systems. [Online]. Available from: https://pafo-africa.org/en/empowering-african-agriculture-farmer-managed-and-community-based-seed-systems/ [Accessed: 2025-September-06]

[33] FAO. Report of the 33rd Session of the Regional Conference for Africa (Rabat, Morocco, Senior Officers Meeting 26-28 March 2024 and Ministerial Meeting 18-20 April 2024). Rabat, FAO; 2024. Available from: https://openknowledge.fao.org/server/api/core/bitstreams/b66f9eb0-0ebb-40bc-bb68-d7720ae4a6a4/content [Accessed: 2025-August-23]

[34] Mabhaudhi T, Sibanda M, Clulow A, Gokool S, Chimonyo VGP, Mutanga O, Odindi J, Magidi J, Naiken V. Using Drones to monitor crop health, water stress, and crop water requirements for improving crop water productivity in the context of precision agriculture in smallholder croplands. WRC Report No. 2971/1/23. Water Research Commission; 2023. Available from: https://www.wrc.org.za/wp-content/uploads/mdocs/29711.pdf [Accessed: 2025-September-06]

[35] Tambo JA, Mbugua F, Duah SA, Oppong-Mensah B, Ocloo CY, Williams F. Pest risk information, agricultural outcomes and food security: Evidence from Ghana. Food Security. 2023;**15**(6):1667–1683. DOI: 10.1007/s12571-023-01398-w

[36] Kim J, Shah P, Gaskell JC, Prasann A, Luthra A. Scaling up Disruptive Agricultural Technologies in Africa. 2020

[37] Carbonell IM. The ethics of big data in big agriculture. Internet Policy Review. 2016;**5**(1). DOI: 10.14763/2016.1.405

[38] Law K. The Data Protection Act 2019. 2019. [Online]. Available from: https://kenyalaw.org:8181/exist/rest/db/kenyalex/Kenya/Legislation/English/Acts%20and%20Regulations/D/Data%20Protection%20Act%20-%20No.%2024%20of%202019/docs/DataProtectionAct24of2019.pdf [Accessed: 2025-September-06]

[39] European Commission. Artificial Intelligence Policy and Liability Frameworks. [Online]. Available from: https://digital-strategy.ec.europa.eu/en/policies/european-approach-artificial-intelligence [Accessed: 2025-September-06]

[40] Wilkinson M, Dumontier M, Aalbersberg I, et al. The FAIR Guiding Principles for scientific data management and stewardship. Scientific Data. 2016;**3**:160018. DOI: 10.1038/sdata.2016.18

[41] Carroll SR, et al. The CARE principles for indigenous data governance. Data Science Journal. 2020;**19**. DOI: 10.5334/dsj-2020-043

[42] African Union Commission. Digital Transformation Strategy for Africa (2020–2030). African Union. [Online]. Available from: https://au.int/en/documents/20200518/digital-transformation-strategy-africa [Accessed: 2025-September-06]

[43] FAO. Towards Digital Inclusion in Rural Transformation. FAO, 2024. DOI: 10.4060/cc9816en